MW01601481

VISUAL BEHAVIOR

BEVERLY JONES

with additional material
by Karen Wolff Klaine

LOCKWOOD
PRESS
Cincinnati

other books by author
WHERE'S HANNAH? with Jane Hart
LET'S GET ORGANIZED

Cover and logo design by Judith O. Baird
Graphics by Vic Halpin & Lauren Koller

Publisher's Note:
Grateful acknowledgment is made for permission to reprint excerpts from the following copyrighted works:

Excerpt from "Nature as Measure" from *What Are People For?* by Wendell Berry. Copyright © 1990 by Wendell Berry. Reprinted by permission of North Point Press, a division of Farrar, Straus & Giroux, Inc.

Excerpt from *Visual Thinking* by Rudolf Arnheim. Copyright © 1969 The Regents of the University of California. Reprinted by permission of University of California Press.

Excerpts from *Liberation Management* by Tom Peters. Copyright © 1992 by Tom Peters. Reprinted by permission of Alfred A. Knopf, Inc.

Excerpts from *A Feeling for the Organism* by Evelyn Fox Keller. Copyright © 1983 by W.H. Freeman and Company. Used with permission.

Library of Congress Catalog Card Number 95-75986

ISBN 0-9627939-1-4

Printed in the United States of America

Bruce and Elaine

1919-1989   1920-1985

TABLE OF CONTENTS

PREFACE

The seeds for this book were planted by the people through the years who have asked, "Where can I read about this?"; "this" meaning the unfamiliar connections between vision, learning and behavior they found as they became acquainted with the clinical work of Bruce R. Wolff, O.D. (1918-1989).

Visual Behavior is a seedling, a sprout in a creative scientific evolution that's growing away from our traditional ways of thinking about human behavior toward new sources, unfamiliar models and structures. *Visual Behavior* is a summary of one of these new models which germinated in the 50's and 60's from sources that reach back before 1940. Bruce Wolff's career as a clinician-philosopher-scientist bridges these two scientific eras, the traditional and the new, post-traditional. His model of visual behavior turns us beyond his discipline of behavioral optometry toward innovative paths of inquiry and clinical practice in education and the healing therapies, including medicine.

Anytime we have a bridging experience there's an awareness of where we've been, of what we're leaving, as well as the anticipation of where we might be headed. In *Visual Behavior* I have tried to make plain this unsettling disparity between old and new which eventually touches us all.

While preparing for this book I met a seventeenth century, middle European, philosopher-teacher, Comenius. His story became for me a talisman and a prod. The illnesses, wars, fires and family dissolutions in his life would make a wonderful TV docudrama; but, it was the fate of his life's work that kept dogging me. According to the tale I read, on his death bed in 1670 Comenius, who had traveled and taught throughout Europe, asked his son to oversee the publication of his unfinished manuscripts. For whatever reason, the son had other goals and it was not until 1966 that a Russian scholar found the original manuscripts in an orphanage in Germany and they were finally published, almost three hundred years later. It seemed to me that was just too long to wait for the drop of an individual's contribution to enter the river of our collective knowledge. Consequently many of us have collaborated on *Visual Behavior* so that its ideas may feed the contemporary streams of behavioral science.

Foremost among collaborators are two: Carolyn Reisinger who has initiated, supported and sustained the project as well as faithfully proofread. The other is Karen Wolff Klaine, Bruce Wolff's daughter and professional colleague, and author of chapter 7, who has provided not only enthusiasm but a reality check to see that no major deviations from her father's model crept in. We have relied on Conni Berns to get the manuscript in printable shape and to create the index. Jean Reisinger, marketing consultant, is helping to see that this project does not fulfill the prophecy of poor Comenius' manuscript. A grant from Vera Jones has been a contributing funding source for the project.

In many ways *Visual Behavior* is contradictory. It is intended to present principles more than practices; it is not a cook-book of techniques for improving human potential or for self-improvement, even though the clinical application of these principles can bring about both. It is not a description of specific applications of this new knowledge, although the examples included may serve as models. Many have asked for the "how to". The parenting, educational practices and specific therapeutic applications of this visual model require other books; they will rest on this foundation.

In part because his science was clinical, in part because he saw his work as fluid and changing, Wolff did not get much of it on paper. What we have is in Appendix A. Through the years he was badgered by people who urged, cajoled, and criticized him so he would write what he knew. It was always overwhelming, once comprehension dawned, to think that no permanent record existed so that others could learn.

In the later years of his life he became quite serious about teaching and writing what he knew. But those more solitary endeavors always had to compete with his huge enjoyment of life in other areas. And to those of us who knew him well, it would not have been uncharacteristic of him to smile knowingly at the way it has turned out: He did find a way to take it with him.

But, which rarely happened when he was alive, we're not letting him have this last word. *Visual Behavior* is my attempt to record as faithfully as I can and in accessible form, what I experienced of his work. It is Bruce Wolff's work in visual behavior seen through my lens.

This book is not the objective, all-inclusive description of Bruce Wolff's life work, but a continuation of the apprentice tradition. I stayed to learn. I did not become a secondhand Bruce Wolff, nor did I want to be. I could only do what anyone does, what Wolff had done before: incorporate what I learned from him with my own experience, test out my new understanding in the real world of the clinic, add to what I learned from him all that I learned from my students, from my reading, from my life. And, through professional collaboration, I offered him opportunities for observation, connections with people, books and ideas that were outside his personal experience and knowledge. In this way I think our discussions contributed to some of the directions of his later work.

I wanted, also, to capture the flavor of the man, to give you a glimpse of a special person, rare in his completeness and his influence on those who knew him. The hopes which prodded our collaborative efforts have been to present Bruce Wolff's ideas so that others could be stimulated to continue in the direction of his insights and to make easier the work of those in the helping professions. The realization of these hopes lies in the future, in our imaginations - sight unseen.

Editorial Method: For emphasis I have used italics within quotations from other sources; they did not appear in the original text.

All references in the book to particular persons' visual status and responses to training were created from *composites* of actual case histories. They are intended as examples and any similarity to actual persons, living or dead, is coincidental.

Author's Professional Note:

The discussion of visual therapy consists of two parts: a general description in Chapter 7, and detailed descriptions of selected visual behavior training procedures in Appendix B. These are included in the book *for information only;* neither the general nor specific descriptions are intended as instructions for personal experimentation. If you are interested in the benefits of this kind of training and experience, take this book to your own eyecare professionals and discuss with them the alternatives for your particular situation. Specific visual behavior training is the province of licensed professionals. However, the *principles* of *Visual Behavior* are accessible for everyone and can be generally applied as indicated in Part III: Implications.

CHAPTER 1 INTRODUCTION

"Oh, I see!" - three little words, a spontaneous phrase we all say.

"*Oh, I see,*" you mutter when you discover how piece A fits into slot B and the new shelves take shape.

"*Oh, I see,*" you say when you predict who-done-it in the murder mystery on TV.

"*Oh, I see,*" lets your child know you appreciate why she and her friend are no longer playing together.

We seem, in our colloquial wisdom, to equate "I see" with situations that may mean: "I understand", "I know something new", "I appreciate another point of view"; yet none of these contexts has a direct connection with our eyesight. Isn't this curious? Why do we connect seeing with thinking and knowing? How does our sight help us to understand another person?

That we see we have no doubt, provided we are physically capable of sight. We know the ball is red, we recognize chairs, tables, cars. We smile when we see a friend coming down the street; we respond compassionately to TV pictures of starving children. And, just as we know we see, we're also aware that we act. We have no choice but to "behave"; we do things, we react to our world, we think. There is a growing body of knowledge that says *what we see actually may be what we know*; that how we see may explain a lot of what we do.

Since the 30's, a discipline has developed around these issues of sight, knowing and behavior. It began with a need to understand why people need glasses to see clearly, to explain the dynamics of visual acuity.

> Some laymen and a few professionals were concerned about a continuous loss of acuity that frequently occurred, as well as why it happened at all. To consider these changes due to heredity, a favorite explanation, did not make sense. They did not follow the laws of heredity, especially since they occur variously at any time of life, and no specific cause was evident. Another oddity was that some people were more comfortable and performed better with a pair of glasses even though they could "see" very well without them. Since the solution was so simple, a pair of glasses (or another pair), and this loss of acuity never resulted in blindness, not much progress was made to find definitive answers to these questions until early in this century. [1]

Some answers to these and other questions were proposed by one contributor, Bruce R. Wolff, 1921-1989. His work has enlarged the the emerging field of behavioral vision. Its roots tapped a variety of disciplines: Arnold Gesell, M.D., Yale researcher in child development; A. M. Skeffington, optometrist from St. Louis; Darell Boyd Harmon, Texas engineer and physiologist; Sam Renshaw, experimental psychologist at Ohio State University. They began, in the 30's, 40's and 50's, to create a collaborative elephant of vision from the feet, tail and ears of their individual investigations. Each had an idea of how we see, how seeing and moving work together, what's involved in visual acuity and what its influence could be in human behavior. Their work stimulated a generation of professionals, including Bruce Wolff, to pursue answers to these questions in their clinical work. A description of his model of vision and its implications in human learning and behavior follows.

Most of us are aware and know a lot about our own sight, our own experience of visual acuity. We know when the signs on the freeway seem blurry, when the features on TV faces are indistinct, when our arms are too short to hold the telephone book where we can read the numbers. Eventually we're all aware that we don't see as clearly as we used to. We even have language for these changes, nearsighted if we have trouble with clarity in the distance; farsighted when the words on the page blur and we need to move the book out to see clearly. But it's rare that we connect these experiences of acuity with the "Oh, I see" of understanding. Sometimes we substitute the word *vision* for seeing, as in our boast, "My vision is perfect, it's 20/20." Most often we mean we see clearly in the distance, we are neither nearsighted nor farsighted, but we use vision in other contexts:

"The only kind of leadership worth following is based on vision."[2]

"Where there is no vision, the people perish," (Proverbs 29:18 King James Bible).

Here vision means something other than the literal clarity of our sight; it implies human qualities we want in leaders; problem solvers who *see* solutions we cannot.

Although we may not have a precise definition for vision, we probably would find a high degree of agreement that people with vision have leadership potential, are likely to be problem solvers. They know what to do. Bruce Wolff and others found a direct connection between the processes that determine our sight (near-sightedness and far-sightedness) and the kind of vision we want in our leaders and would be thrilled to have for ourselves. Understood in this way, the links between what we see, know and do make sense and the phrase "Oh, I see" exactly expresses this connection.

We use other sight words to describe these mental processes of understanding consequences, predicting, planning, problem-solving which allow us to live independently in our universe. These qualities are often attached to the word "vision"; but, we say we had the "fore-sight" to invest in X stock; or we gained "in-sight" from that movie; or the coach's "hindsight is 20/20". This mental, cognitive vision, according to Bruce Wolff, depends upon the quality of our actual visual/seeing process. He uniquely defined and illuminated this connection in human behavior, and with lenses and training helped people develop and enhance it. His work demonstrated that the quality of *what we do and how we do it depends on what and how we see.*

Because this connection between sight and behavior is learned, it is changeable. If our behavior is intimately linked to what we see, then changes in our sight, our vision, mean changes in our behavior. Conversely, changes in behavior can be detected as changes in our visual status. Understood from this new perspective, *seeing and knowing*, as well as *seeing and doing* are not what common knowledge has taught us. Encountering this new perspective requires a different set of mental assumptions. The traditional cause-and-effect, stimulus-response mold into which our assumptions have been poured cannot match the observations and relationships of sight/vision/behavior. This contradiction of assumptions and relationships is discussed more fully in Chapter 2.

Evaluating this model of vision and behavior allows parents, educators, therapists to see human behavior from another perspective, one that can give their own work new dimensions. This discussion is not all we will ever know about the role of vision in human behavior; it is only a fresh direction. Although the ideas presented here are in their theoretical form, the clinical data from which the theories grew and were tested exist, some are included here as examples. In addition to existing clinical data, a start has been made in the direction of controlled research. The full development and extension of these ideas is the work of the future. A new world first must be discovered before its total form takes shape and it can be explored. In our era of instantaneous communication, this sequence is often ignored. Some will always clamor for the application of new scientific breakthroughs at the first hint of discovery and be disappointed and disparaging when the developmental phase takes longer than an instant.

Many who read the manuscript in process commented that this seems like two books: one, the treatment of the science of behavioral vision, and the other, the personal and professional characteristics of Bruce Wolff, the person. For those who want only the facts, the hard data, you will find that in Chapters 4 through 7 where the theory is presented in detail. The chapters before and after are softer in content; they provide context so that the details may come to life. Knowing something about the personhood of thinkers like Madame Curie, Buckminster Fuller, Margaret Mead, Barbara McClintock and familiarity with their ways of thinking, their goals, and pursuits helps to answer the why, how, when and where as well as the what. But, if that is not your interest, or time does not allow you a broader look, please skip Chapters 2, 3, 8-10.

POST-TRADITIONAL SCIENCE

Traditional viewpoints and institutions creak and totter during this time of profound change in our culture. Many of us on this shifting ground bemoan the lack of security we feel about what we've known so we hang on even more tightly to the safety of our ideas; what we thought was certain, *our assumptions*. If you have already shifted into a new world-view, you may find this discussion and Chapters 2 & 3 superfluous. Get on with it, you'll say. If that's your feeling, please skip around. But, many of us will struggle against the ideas presented here. Seen from the traditional viewpoint, the ideas aren't "exact", they don't explain "how to", there is little "hard" data, no "cause-and-effect" when looked at with the assumption of tradition. The new viewpoint and its implications are often dismissed before they are actually encountered.

The 90's are difficult times; overt clashes of ethnic groups, political, economic, educational, and intellectual forces that push and pull. Even if we are not directly affected by such skirmishes, we are involved by default. This whirlwind of change blows into our lives through the windows of our TV screens and print media; social interchange. These are windows we cannot close. It is hoped that *Visual Behavior* helps to ease us through these upheavals by offering a dynamic view of our situation. The information and observations presented here can point us toward new directions for gathering up the ashes of our defunct systems in parenting and education. It can show us how to design new systems which will better fit our actual human needs and behavior. That Bruce Wolff was one among many coming to similar conclusions about how humans actually work shows that, culturally, we may be reaching a critical mass. Even this idea is an example of the shift in our basic assumptions about how things work, how change occurs. Since we cannot get back to the good old days, we can only move ahead using new knowledge and trusting our powers of reason, its logic and effects. Knowledge about vision and behavior added to what we already know of human behavior will push us a little farther toward a time when our institutions and cultural practices match and support more closely the lives we actually live instead of providing structures and forces that set up obstacles to maximum growth and development.

WHENCE VISION?

In the din of our cultural clashes, we have not heard much from the voice of behavioral vision, even though many have been thinking and talking about it for decades. Yet, it blends well with other strains emerging in our culture. Such as the idea that, in part, we can create ourselves. Wendell Berry, in *A Continuous Harmony*, says that life used to be a fact, not something we considered. Now we jog, diet, and meditate so our bodies and our lives will match our mental ideas. We are self-aware in ways unknown to our parents, but as we rearrange our lives in the present so we can design our futures, we carry with us assumptions that, aware or not, direct our journeys and influence the quality of the trip. What we think about sight, seeing and vision are among those influences.

Most of us are aware that our sight is apt to get worse as we get older, and we dread the time when we'll need those tell-tale bifocals. We know we would be devastated by blindness and can't even imagine it for ourselves. We go for our annual eye check-up, change our prescription or frames, or decide to get contact lenses without much soul searching. We want to be able to see - clearly, if possible - and we do what we must to get what we want.

One assumption that lurks behind our awareness is: *the eye works like a camera*. That idea we owe to our grade school science classes. Because of it we understand that when things get blurry we need glasses to adjust our "camera's" focus. So common is this idea that we rarely think about why it is that the majority of us need to wear glasses in order to correct our focus.

If we do think about it, we eventually run into the *short/long eyeball* explanation. Do we wonder why it is that so many of us should have defective eyeballs when our other parts come in good shape? Dr. Wolff's work answers these and other questions about how we see; these are questions that have no answers for most of us; we may not even have had the question.

To look at anything from a fresh point of view lights up the shadows surrounding our assumptions. From this discussion of sight and vision, we will look anew at our ideas of how people function, how we learn and how we can best help ourselves and others. What a perfect place for the cliché, "There is more here than meets the eye."

FROM THERE TO HERE

I discovered the shadows of my own assumptions of how children learn and communicate when, as a newly-minted speech-language pathologist, I met a group of children who were called brain-injured children - today's learning disabled and children with ADD or ADHD- attention deficit disorder or attention deficit with hyper-activity.

When one six year old thanked me for "putting the school back" one Monday morning, I knew then that what I knew could not be enough. This youngster's logic was impeccable: On Friday I had said there would be no school on Saturday and Sunday. We had marked it on the calendar; I had assured them they would be at home with their families, and I would see them on Monday. Could he possibly think the school had vanished and re-appeared? What was he doing? Why did two and two make six to him? So, he and his classmates began to teach me that all I had learned in school was not enough to explain why individual children developed their own patterns of learning and deficits. As that first year went on I found that I could not teach I.Q.'s or diagnostic labels; that I needed to know more about what these atypical kids actually were trying to do. At that time I did not realize that by understanding them, I would also come to know a great deal more about what makes *normal* normal.

My fresh degree and certificates said I knew how to help kids listen, talk and use words for thinking. What I found first was that they couldn't use what I wanted to teach unless they learned to sit down; that walking without bumping into things, hopping, skipping, throwing, catching were obstacles in their development just as much as talking in sentences.

Such was the case for Hannah, one of the six year olds in the group. Her needs and my curiosity to understand them sparked a quest; this book is a record of a major part of that professional journey. Hannah's own developmental travels were documented in *Where's Hannah?*, written by her mother, Jane Hart, and myself. Why could Hannah, and others with similar problems, not be contained in normal spatial restrictions (sitting at a table, her room, her yard)? If I could know the learning patterns behind their diagnostic labels of brain-injury, cerebral-palsy, mental-retardation, perceptual handicap,* then I could figure out a way to help them move out of their developmental rut. I could teach them what they didn't know.

I looked at Hannah and her classmates and saw "regular kids" trying to get out. To me their developmental glass was half-full, not half-empty, and I was naive enough to think there was a way, somehow, to help them fill it.

So in 1963, two years before I met Bruce Wolff, Hannah's needs took her parents and me by the hand and together we found Ray Barsch, a psychologist from Wisconsin, an outstanding clinician who explained spatial perception and Hannah's ignorance and distortion of it. Because of Dr. Barsch's work with Newell Kephart and Gerald Getman, we next traveled to Minnesota where Hannah got her first pair of glasses from Dr. Getman and I, skeptical, wary and intrigued became acquainted with behavioral optometry.

During a summer at the University of Wisconsin with Drs. Barsch and Getman, I met Darell Boyd Harmon - an influential, early contributor to behavioral optometry. His knowledge of humanbehavior - the physiology and perceptual processes of vision and movement and the effects of environmental correlates opened a world I had never heard of: postural warps related to light distribution, language as the descriptor of an individual's visual space, movement as the pre-cursor of seeing and doing. Chapter 4 explains these postural-light-vision connections *a la* Harmon.

Dr. Harmon pointed me to Bruce Wolff in Cincinnati, just 80 miles from my home in Lexington, Kentucky. In Dr. Wolff's office I met A.M. Skeffington, the optometrist who was a seminal thinker

---

* These were the preferred labels of the 60's and correspond to the contemporary categories of: developmentally-disabled, learning-disabled, hyperactive and attention-deficit-disorder.

in the discipline of behavioral optometry. Dr. Skeffington sat in on my own examination and discussion with Dr. Wolff. I was there because of my skepticism. What could an optometrist tell me about learning and language? What could vision have to do with the learning and language problems I saw in my students? How could I explain the changes I had seen in Hannah to other than her new glasses, since my teaching was basically the same? If there was something of benefit here, and it certainly seemed so, then I couldn't refer students unless I learned, first-hand, how these new ideas actually worked. I became a patient. I still would recommend this as the fastest and most illuminating way to understand the visual-behavior connection; however, there are few behavioral optometrists and even fewer who follow the Wolff model. From this first meeting with Bruce Wolff - in 1966 - until his death in 1989, I came to understand his work, to incorporate it with my own perspective and clinical experience with people who wanted to improve their learning and communication.

An advantage of a long career is the luxury of a broad view. My era has allowed me to witness the expansion and development of the field of behavioral vision as well as public special education. I studied with Darell Boyd Harmon, met A. M. Skeffington. I've known students before and since the growth of Special Education in the public sector. I've watched generations of professionals change their diagnostic labels more frequently than the kids' problems have been resolved - minimally brain-damaged became perceptually-handicapped became learning-disabled and attention deficit disorder. I have felt the cold front of our cultural atmosphere which confuses teaching kids how to compensate with helping them change their learning patterns. Too often tape recorders supplant reading, calculators replace computation, tutoring enables assignments to get done while the learning-deficits remain. These sometimes necessary adjustments can be temporary if students are offered the opportunity to learn the visual-movement-language skills which underlie school performance. *Without help that actually helps, these temporary adjustments become permanent, and another prophecy is self-fulfilled.*

I have not lost my original naiveté; teaching, to me, still means helping people start wherever they are and learn whatever they need to learn in order to do whatever task they've selected. Success means starting on the sequence of steps necessary so they can complete that task as independently as possible, and learn skills that will help them make up their developmental lags. For example, reading fluently may mean beginning with form recognition (the parts and their relationships), with spatial relationships of form (left-right, visual pattern recognition) as the raw material of sound-symbol matching necessary for decoding the graphic symbols on the page (end goal). Granted that decoding is not reading ideas, but it is a vital part of the sequence necessary to tap into the ideas hiding in print. It is too often neglected. Compensation for decoding problems underlies much of the work in special education, because *many students' needs are at a developmental level that precedes the reading curriculum.*

Because Bruce Wolff's work offers a way to help people tap into the foundation of their learning needs, I have been able to resist contemporary trends toward early compensation. Acceptance and celebration of differences can be too much of a good thing if they are offered at the expense of helping people *actually solve* their learning, academic and communication problems.

THE FUTURE NOW

Enough time has passed so that Bruce Wolff's work now can be seen as part of the new scientific endeavor that springs from a root developed within the previous generation. Chapter 2 speaks to this new science; so new it has yet to have a name and is best described by what it is not: not linear, not traditional cause-and-effect, not confined only to quantifiable data. Epochal changes in other disciplines have been described as post: post-Christian, (Harold Bloom); post-capitalism, (Peter Drucker), post-modern. Perhaps we are entering, or some would say are in, the era of post-scientific method, where all that we know of traditional, linear science blends with new ways of knowing (chaos theory, quantum physics) and old ways rediscovered (human reason and logic). Bruce Wolff, philosopher as well as optometrist, bridged these two worlds of science. He was always available to those who were interested in what he knew and led many of us into the new science. Never was a teacher more patient with those who were sincerely puzzled by what he was saying; and few could be more scathingly impatient with those who preferred intellectual gamesmanship to stretching their cognitive muscles.

THE RIVER OF AUTHORITY

All of us are left, finally, with only the opportunity to pass on what we've learned. As in any apprentice system, Wolff learned from Harmon, Skeffington, Renshaw and others, incorporated their knowledge with his background in philosophy, his astute observational skills, and 40 years of clinical work. Just as we cannot see and isolate the contribution of all the springs, streams and creeks flowing into a river, we cannot at any point in history, whether cultural or personal, identify all the sources of information that created the knowledge. It flows. Perhaps in these pages you will recognize ideas whose sources you can identify. Whatever they are, they blend into the river of knowledge organized by Bruce Wolff. He was very conscious of acknowledging authors of original work; but, I cannot know all of them. For example, Dr. A. M. Skeffington had this to say in 1950 about Sam Renshaw, an experimental psychologist at Ohio State University.

> Many years ago Professor Samuel Renshaw made two assertions: that seeing is learned and that seeing is motor.[3]

These ideas are fundamental to what you will read here, it's the base from which Bruce Wolff started; but, Skeffington goes on to say,

> ...Considerable lip service was given the ideas. On the whole, however, the investigations continued largely to hinge around the different phases of the visual process that traveled inward from the retina.[4]

Meaning, I think, that researchers were more interested in the physiology of vision from retina through cortex than they were prepared to observe the learned and motor components involved - two concepts heavily weighted in human *behavior*. Bruce Wolff took Renshaw seriously; his observations and clinical therapies directly linked the observed visual process to human learning and movement in ways that had not been done before. When introduced to these ideas are you meeting Renshaw, or Renshaw through Wolff? Either way you see a freeze-frame, a stage in development, only the present piece of sequential knowledge. What came before is embedded in the present, and this current knowledge seeds future developments. But, what we know now of vision and behavior, we know. This reality becomes the base camp from which explorations and discoveries of the future can embark.

It is virtually impossible to approach understanding the work of Wolff and other new-scientists, without giving up some pre-conceived ideas acquired through exposure to our mechanistically oriented culture and educational process. Many of us prefer to reject the message, and certainly the messenger, when faced with this kind of choice. If a snapshot of an idea is not included in our album of reality, we think it's not real, that it doesn't exist, is wrong, subversive, quackery or just a marketing ploy. The intellectual dissonance created by such an encounter has to be resolved: reject it or try to understand, evaluate and incorporate it. Such is the history of all unorthodox ideas.

I hope you encounter in these pages a scientific process and viewpoint that adds some balance to the traditional cause-and-effect, stimulus-response, linear science of our tradition. I hope it becomes apparent, particularly in our dealings with children, that there are alternatives to many situations we now label hopeless, where we feel there is nothing we can do, where we feel we've tried everything and are tempted to blame the child. I hope the conversation continues so we keep the river of knowledge flowing; talk back, mumble or wonder - just keep paddling.

Chapter 2 NEW SCIENCE

The world we live in is not the place where we grew up. Technology - our car phones, e-mail, VCRs, computers, fax machines and the Internet have seen to that. We're confronted with issues never discussed by our parents: ozone depletion, disintegration of our educational system, medically assisted suicide and on and on. Are you in touch with virtual space? Have you put on a helmet for a trip in virtual reality? Glimpses of our future world described by scientists continually flash through our culture. Change has chiseled away at what we thought was certain and true, from quantum physics to theology. We are in the midst of not only political but scientific and philosophical revolutions and evolutions as well.

Change has brought us new ways to consider how we think and solve problems. Bruce Wolff's work in vision can be understood most easily by placing it in the context of these rapidly changing intellectual and philosophical ideas. These ideas offer as profound an effect on the ways we think and order our lives as technology's influence has had. Explorers of the 16th and 17th centuries traced out our physical world; the scientists introduced here trace the unexplored areas of human behavior. They are changing the maps we've known, creating exciting, undeveloped trails in our knowledge of who we are as human beings and how we actually work. They can take us to places filled with treasures that could enrich our lives and help us live more effectively in these now foreign lands of our adulthood. What follows is a glimpse of the new cloth being woven by some of these contemporary explorers. The multi-colored pattern they make rests on warp threads spun from the wool of tradition.

Bruce Wolff explored the land of vision as a clinician, an optometrist in private practice. That he and other individual explorers, unknown to one another, should describe similar landscapes points to the validity of their experience and conclusions. Geography and professional disciplines do not seem to be barriers to the discovery of truth. What is there to be found, will be found.

To decide intelligently whether or not a viewpoint that differs from our own actually may be *true*, we need to understand it; otherwise we respond from prejudice rather than scientific inquiry and genuine skepticism. Since new knowledge emerges from assumptions that are not apparent, this discussion tries to bridge some of these new assumptions with our traditional viewpoints. Bruce Wolff and his colleagues' revolutionary ideas are logical, *when seen as extensions of new assumptions*. What follows is an attempt to compare and contrast these two points of view (Bruce Wolff/et al and traditional science), in what I hope is an accurate summary and accessible language.

TRADITIONAL REALITY

When we think about reality we tend to think of it as an accumulation of parts. Whatever we consider, we often think about it as pieces of a puzzle. Taste an interesting dish and we want to know what's in it, what is the *specific* ingredient that gives it a distinctive taste. We want to know what was the *best* part of your vacation. We think we must know about each part in order to understand the whole. That's one way to do it, and it's the way we all learned about the world. Our school curricula were constructed from this pattern of parts. Textbooks reflect the separateness of traditional thinking - chapters in the health books on: digestion, respiration, muscular-skeletal system. We've even come to equate "knowledge" with the quantity of specific data that can be amassed.

We tend to look for the parts of those parts and seek to know how they work together - separate pieces - making up machines. This mechanical model of the world accurately describes much of our physical experience. But, it has come to be our primary viewpoint for all of our experience; it is still the model of choice for our scientific times. It has been considered good science; when in fact, it is only *one kind* of science. Linear, cause and effect thinking is *one way* to organize our experience, *one way* to connect to "reality".

Ken Wilber, philosopher-psychologist-scientist, is an explorer who tells us there are ways other than the mechanical parts way to organize our experience. In *Eye to Eye, A Quest for a New Paradigm*, he gives an historical perspective on how it happened that we developed the assumptions that serve as the infra-structure of our thought about the world. He highlights how traditional science has been done, the way we all recognize:

> Science, in fact, began as an anti rationalism, as a direct revolt against the rational systems of the scholastic age. As Whitehead put it: "Galileo keeps harping on how things happen, whereas his (rationally minded) adversaries had a complete theory as to why things happen. Galileo insists upon "irreducible and stubborn facts;," and Simplicius, his opponent, brings forward *reasons*.

> Notice that the clash between Galileo, with his "irreduc-
> ible and stubborn facts" and Simplicius, with his "satis-
> factory reasons" is precisely a clash between the eye of
> flesh and the eye of reason - between empiricism and
> rationalism.[1]

Wilber uses St. Bonaventure's "Three Eyes of the Soul" as a vehicle to understand the development of scientific thought. Here is a paraphrased description of the use of these "three eyes" of knowledge in human structures of thought.

Eye of the Flesh: Sensory information, the means by which we perceive the external world of space, time and objects - empiricism. It's the information we get through touching, hearing, seeing; what we usually term "reality".

Eye of Reason: Thought, the means by which we know philosophy, logic and the mind itself.

> The truth of ideas cannot be seen by the senses. For
> example, mathematics is a nonempirical knowledge. It is
> discovered, illuminated and implemented by the eye of
> reason...it is statements of logical relationships...no one
> has ever seen, with the eye of flesh, the square root of a
> negative one. But that doesn't make it untrue. It can be
> seen, but with the mind's eye.[2]

Eye of Contemplation: This is the way we come to know transcendent realities. It allows us to know love, to have some sense of powers other than ourselves. It is the seed from which religious experience grows. It has its own truth.

Science and Facts

Modern science, as we've known it in the 20th century, as we've been taught to think of the world, developed as "eyes of the flesh", according to Wilber. *We've been taught that facts are what make things true*; the facts that Whitehead quotes Galileo as insisting upon. If we can touch, feel, and see it, then - *and only then* - can we know it, is it true.

Anne Wilson Schaef describes this kind of thinking as a religion. She also attributes it to white males, but, whatever its source this kind of thinking has influenced us all:

> Its priests (of "scientific" thinking) carry out the rituals,
> and its laymen are assigned to see that the system keeps
> running smoothly. This religion is the Scientific Method.
> If one adheres to its beliefs and follows its rituals and
> procedures, one can "prove" or "disprove" anything

within the system. We are told at some point during our education that anything can be measured. All that is necessary is an awareness of which measurement or tool to use at a particular time. Measurement is seen as the key to success. If we can measure, we can predict. If we can predict, we can control. If we can control, we can be God.[3]

Ken Wilber has this to say about the scientific method:

> If the term "scientific method" has any historical meaning whatsoever, then it can be said to have been invented and practiced by Kepler and Galileo.
>
> ...Science *was not just good observation,* which had been around for thousands of years; it was a *peculiar type of observation.* [4]

He describes that "peculiar type of observation":

> ...in a scientific experiment, one desires to see if a particular event occurs; if it does, something changed. In the physical world, change necessarily involves some sort of displacement in space-time; *displacement can be measured. Conversely, if an event cannot be measured it cannot be the object of an empiric-scientific experiment; and, as far as science is concerned, it does not exist.* [5]

If some change that we recognize cannot be measured, we think it does not exist. In this kind of science we toss out the experience or discount the observation because we think it is not important. The exceptionally high or low scores on sub-tests of intelligence tests are often recorded *and ignored* by traditional scientists. Observations of common sense in an otherwise disorganized individual may not even be noted. Maybe we don't say these exceptions do not really exist; maybe we just ignore them. They don't exist according to the traditional rules of counting and measuring: the "eye of the flesh". Wilber says it better:

> ...what it (the eye of the flesh) can't see does not exist; whereas what it should have said was, what it can't see, it can't see. [6]

Many of the changes in human behavior that the soft, people sciences continually see are not able to be measured by our existing measurement schemes. When an individual moves from depression to wellness there's been a change. Do we measure it *factually*? When an individual's sense of self-esteem improves and we witness the changes that ensue, do we need to measure the what and how much of those differences to know that they happened, that they are real? Significant changes in children's learning and behavior, whether from diet, non-traditional educational environments, or visual therapy and learning therapy based on the visual model presented here, are often rejected as *anecdotal*, not scientific. Traditional scientists may see the differences in the youngsters, but they may look for some unknown trick to explain it away. They want facts, hard data, numbers, before what they see and hear is judged real; by rejecting the anecdotal evidence they often save themselves the trouble of examining and understanding what appears to be outside their paradigm. That's how empiricism works sometimes.

This reliance on the science of the flesh Wilber calls scientism. He describes how these new ideas of Kepler, Galileo etc., moved from saying, "This is an excellent method for gaining knowledge in the realm of the five senses" to "Thus the knowledge gained by mind and contemplation is invalid." [7]

> Everything science could see was viewed numerically, and since no number is intrinsically better than another, the sole hierarchy of value collapsed...[8]

In traditional science, one idea was not viewed as better than another, only different in size. Thinking of "better" uses logic, the eye of reason. We can know something is true or right and still not be able to verify it by counting. Is it better to have friends or to live in isolation? The person-on-the-street interview would get a high degree of agreement that it *is* better to have friends than to live in isolation, but this isn't science. Maybe not, but that doesn't mean it doesn't exist or is untrue. Finally, the eyes of the flesh are catching up with our eyes of reason; studies do show that people with satisfying social connections have statistically healthier lives. Their methods of counting *prove* this is a truth, as if no one knew this before their pronouncements.

Reductionism
The by-product of this Eye-of-the-Flesh thinking leaves us trying to get to the essence of what we want to know by *reducing* the object of our consideration to its constituents - parts we can count. We think about events as having causes (one part affecting another part). With no values inherent in our thought system, with numbers and counting our primary effort, we look for an *identifiable* cause when something goes wrong. We don't like it that so many kids drop out of school. Someone or something (verifiable by the eye-of-the-flesh) must be to blame! A part affecting other parts.

Our energies are then spent in trying to isolate (see and count) that entity of blame. Is it this? Is it that? Kids drop out of school because of poor parent involvement. Kids drop out of school because teachers are not paid enough. Kids drop out of school because....just fill in the blank.

In this scheme, we think we cannot fix the problem without identifying and irradicating the cause. We think it is necessary to identify The Cause before we can plan programs to eliminate it. The "causes" too often have driven the system of educational re-structuring. Some of my friends in education yawn and wait for each new, particular modification to pass. And they do with regularity, each time *another* cause gains the spotlight. We operate with a stimulus-stimulus-responsee mentality. We choose to spend our efforts and energy seeking causes identified by reducing a situation to its parts rather than think about the nature of the problem and create solutions which, to the *eye-of-reason, are right.*

NEW SCIENCE

David Bohm, physicist; Barbara McClintock, Nobel prize winning geneticist; Karl Pribram, holonomic brain theorist; Bruce Wolff and others have spent their lives showing us ways other than traditional science to look at the world; other ways to find out who we are and what we are about. Their efforts explain *how* the brain works, *how* genes work, *how* our physical world works in ways that have been dismissed by traditional science until very recently. *How* is a process: it can be described, it can be understood, it can be replicated. Counting it may be but one step in the process, not *the only step.*

The Clash of Progress and Tradition

Every break from the traditional viewpoint, in whatever time in human cultural development, has been resisted and labeled quackery by the establishment. Our current scientific and technological progress proves that past journeys into uncharted realms eventually become the established view generations later. We are the future of the past, balladeer Chuck Suchy reminds us. We now sterilize surgical equipment; we vaccinate ourselves against disease; we fly above the birds, to outer space as well as across the ocean. We now take these extraordinary events for granted, but they were once exiled to the realm of the ridiculous.

Traditional science assumed the definition of reality, and mostly we've accepted their definition. We often didn't note when it rejected anything outside that definition. But, new ideas don't fade away; it's just more difficult to hear them when we're being convinced not to listen. You don't have to strain much to hear some of the new themes floating through our changing culture; they've been so rapidly assimilated.

Holographic Paradigm

New scientists acknowledge the parts of the world; but, they don't stop there. They concentrate on relationships of the parts, not on the "eachness" of the parts themselves. No mosaics for them. This theme is: *parts have such integral relationships that changing one changes the whole thing!*

Karl Pribram and David Bohm, use the model of holography to explain their ideas.

> A hologram is a special type of optical storage system that can best be explained by an example: if you take a holographic photo of, say, a horse, and cut out one section of it, e.g., the horse's head, and then enlarge that section to the original size, you will get, not a big head, but a picture of the *whole* horse.
>
> In other words, *each individual part of the picture contains the whole picture in condensed form.* The part is in the whole and the whole is in each part - a type of unity-in-diversity and diversity-in-unity. The key point is simply that the *part has access to the whole.* [9]

David Bohm, physicist uses making a cake as a metaphor for holographic relationships. He says when an egg is enfolded into the cake batter; it remains "egg", but it is also "cake".

> In the enfolded order we see, first of all that when we've taken the droplet (of egg) and enfolded it (in the cake), it's in the whole thing and every part of the whole thing contributes to that droplet. Let's now imagine a situation where we put in another droplet. The two droplets are in different positions but when they are enfolded *they sort of mix up with each other;...* [10]

"Mix up with each other"??!! Vision, movement, language, mix up with each other to make the "cake" we call human behavior? Does it sound ridiculous, or is it the way we know it works even though traditional science hasn't yet confirmed it? When we converse with a friend we recognize that individual's unique body language, style of speech, facial expressions and patterns of thought all at once. We don't see parts working separately and independently. Yet, should something go wrong with the person, professionals (scientists) begin the search for The Cause. Is it____, or____, or____? Substitute a diagnostic label from the profession of your choice.

"Mix up with each other!" This thinking process leads in a direction opposite from the isolation and reduction of tradition. Karl Pribram states:

> In the holographic domain, each organism represents in some manner the universe, and each portion of the universe represents in some manner the organisms within it. ...the perceptions of an organism could not be understood without an understanding of the nature of the physical universe and...the nature of the physical universe could not be understood without an understanding of the observing perceptual process. [11]

Chaos Theory

Here's another theme floating in the new science air: Chaos Theory. It is the study of seemingly random events, what we ordinarily would call chaos. These scientists want to understand the implications of randomness. They have found that chaos isn't really so chaotic; that patterns are actually there, but emerge for us only in computers and mathematical configurations. They aren't apparent to us because the pattern is spread over so much time or space that we lose track of it; we can't *see* it. James Gleick in *Chaos* says of this new science:

> Believers in Chaos - and they sometimes call themselves believers, or converts, or evangelists -speculate about determinism and free will, about evolution, about the nature of conscious Intelligence. They feel that they are turning back a trend in science toward reductionism, the analysis of systems in terms of their constituent parts: quarks, chromosomes or neurons. They believe that they are looking for the whole. [12]

Another idea that has come out of chaos theory has implications in human behavior which will become clearer as Dr. Wolff's ideas are developed. The idea is:

> Tiny differences in input could quickly become overwhelming differences in output - a phenomenon given the name, "sensitive dependence on initial conditions", In weather for example, this translates into what is only half-jokingly known as the Butterfly Effect - the notion

that a butterfly stirring the air today in Peking can transform storm systems next month in New York. [13]

This phenomenon explains instances when Dr. Wolff's prescription for a patient's eyeglasses, which may have been changed only slightly, could make profound differences in the patient's reactions and, ultimately, in behavior. Traditional scientists would say that such a small change would produce only small differences in behavior and anything else is one's imagination or exaggeration. Consequently, these prescriptions often were derided by reductionist scientists: "Nothing but window glass," they said.

Control Theory Psychology

Physics and neurobiology are not the only fields that have discovered a new viewpoint. Cybernetic control theory, which emerged in the late 40's and early 50's, explains how *people use their own sensory-perceptual feedback to control their autonomous behavior.* This new science tells us we are not controlled by the circumstances of our environment, as the stimulus-response thinkers (cause and effect) would have us believe.

An application of control theory is the work of William Glasser, M.D., in Reality Therapy. He says:

> A control system acts upon the world and itself as part of the world to attempt to get the picture that it wants. When I am thirsty and satisfy my thirst by drinking some water, my behavior is that of a simple, well-functioning control system: I am in control of what I do, and what I do satisfies a thirst-quenching picture in my head. By contrast, if you could always get me to drink by handing me a glass of water, you, not I, would be in control of my life. In theory, you could make me drink myself to death if you were cruel enough to keep giving me water. This machinelike example sounds silly, but it is representative of the most common theory of why we behave the way we do. It is called "stimulus-response theory", and anything that functions by this theory would be called a stimulus-response (S-R) system.

> It is fundamental to a control system that it always wants to have a sense of control, and any way that you can gain this, even in play, is pleasurable.

> Almost all parents reading this book have pictures in their heads of their children as successful and happy. In an attempt to achieve this, we constantly tell them what to do. Our motivation is not necessarily selfish; we are

convinced that what we want is best for our children. But when we attempt to exercise some control, we almost always run into problems. *This is because as much as a control system likes to be in control, no control system wants to be controlled.* [14]

Dr. William Powers, a pioneer in control theory, says that before cybernetics and control theory were available, the behavioral scientists thought:

- The world is a mechanism, and mechanisms do only what they are made to do by outside forces.
- If organisms are mechanisms, they are operated by the world around them. (Since machines require some external control to make them work.)
- By the 1930's the cause-effect assumption was, however, far too well established to be thrown out or even seriously questioned by mainstream scientists. [15]

Dr. Powers explains that:

- ...control is something that a control system (a human) does, not something that is done to it.
- ...there is no "controller". Control is a phenomenon that arises when an active system, constructed in a specific way, *interacts* with its immediate environment.
- ...the relationship between control system and environment is not symmetrical. Even though each affects the other, *only the control system controls.*
- A control system senses its environment and *acts on it.*
- Action of system is driven by *error* signal. [16]

Such are the headlines of control theory. They are mentioned here to show the similarity in Wolff's thinking and Powers'. The last two statements above will be described in detail in other chapters since they are the infrastructure of the function of the visual system as described by Wolff.

Scientist and Science

Traditional science would have us believe there are two worlds: the objective, out there, world *and* the subjective, in here, world of the scientist. One looking *at* the other. New scientists are not so sure.

New scientists understand their own orientation somewhat differently. They understand that *where* we look to collect the raw material for our thoughts in part determines what and how we see and think. The scientist becomes a factor in the science.

Evelyn Fox Keller in her book about Barbara McClintock, 1985 Nobel prize winner in genetics, describes in detail how that kind of interactive orientation works and how different it is from traditional "eyes of the flesh" science. That McClintock's Nobel Prize was for work in genetics she had done *35 years earlier* is, in itself, worthy of examination more appropriately done in *Ms.* magazine than here. The book's title, *A Feeling for the Organism*, gives a clue how Barbara McClintock's approach in cytogenetics developed from this same orientation of *interacting* with what she saw. Cytogenetics, according to the book's glossary, is "The science that links the study of the visible structures of chromosomes with genetics."[17]

Rather than try to list in hierarchical order the points about Barbara McClintocks' approach and the novelty of her work, here is a random taste of her orientation. Quotation marks are direct quotes of McClintock's.

> No one was more conscious of the difference in focus than McClintock herself. In part, that difference reflected the continuing disparity between her own interests and those of her colleagues in genetics. *She was primarily interested in function and organization*; they were primarily interested in *mechanism.*[18]

> In her mind, what we call the scientific method cannot by itself give us "real understanding". *"It gives us relationships which are useful, valid and technically marvelous; however, they are not the truth."* And it is by no means the only way of acquiring knowledge.[19]

> "Basically, everything is one. There is no way in which you draw a line between things. What we (normally) do is to make these subdivisions, but they're not real. Our educational system is full of subdivisions that are artificial, that shouldn't be there..."[20]

These new science theories and practices show that human behavior may be much more plastic, and have much more adaptable potential than traditional stimulus-response theory and practice has told us. As with anything, from finding a lost earring or contact lens to discovering an exciting growth opportunity in the stock market, we cannot discover something unless we look for it, or recognize it when it appears. There are treasures to be found in new science thinking, if we will but listen to the explorers in our midst.

Barbara McClintock gives us a glimpse of what we miss when we ignore them:

> ...without an awareness of the oneness of things, science can give us only pieces of nature. In McClintock's view, too restricted a reliance on scientific methodology invariably leads us into difficulty. "We've been spoiling the environment just dreadfully and thinking we were fine, because we were using the techniques of science. Then it turns into technology, and it's slapping us back because we didn't think it through. We were making assumptions we had no right to make. From the point of view of how *the whole thing actually worked*, we knew how part of it worked... We didn't even inquire, didn't even see how the rest was going on. All these other things were happening and *we didn't see it.*"[21]

SUMMARY: Scientific disciplines have not been immune to the reorganization of fundamental principles and viewpoints that are currently so evident in our culture, in world governments, in political alliances, and educational institutions. Since we're caught in the cross-fire of tradition and progress, we're often exposed to ideas that have evolved from a frame of reference that is unfamiliar to us.

This chapter has focused on some of the scientific theories derived from non-traditional, scientific viewpoints. The two viewpoints, traditional and new, can be contrasted with the metaphors of mosaics and cakes. The *mosaic* point of view, the one we've grown up with, sees whatever we're dealing with as separate entities, parts of machines working together, pieces of a puzzle. The *cake* metaphor describes a view point of integrated relationships among entities, ingredients that contribute to a sum that is different from the qualities of the additive parts. These scientists are concerned with patterns, with principles, with the implications of the specific data traditional science is so good at amassing.

The conclusions of each scientific viewpoint are correct when put into the context of their orientation. If we were collecting only roses from our garden and a friend handed us a lily we would reject it. No, no, we're looking for *roses*. Judged by that criteria our friend was wrong to give us the lily. Looked at from the friend's point of view, which was *collecting flowers*, the response was right. Wolff's work in behavioral vision evolves beyond traditional science; his work becomes easier to understand, accept and use, when it is seen as an example of the "cake" kind of science.

The description of his work necessarily has to be presented in parts, language and print require sequences. As all scientists do, Wolff collected specific data; his data described the "parts" of his patient's visual process. *But the parts are of interest only because of the whole they create.* It is in the description of the whole where the new scientists excel. That recognition of the whole from the description and isolation of its parts is, at some level, the responsibility of the observer.

Chapter 3 PATIENTS: WHO OR WHAT?

THE "DOCTOR"

Bruce Wolff was an optometrist. Although others wondered whether his ideas led in directions outside that discipline, he always saw himself as adding to, not replacing, the fundamentals of optometry. He was a second generation optometrist, opening his practice in 1949 in his hometown, Cincinnati, Ohio, where his father also practiced. Like many of his generation, his professional plans had been interrupted by military experience in World War II - as a Navy pilot and trainer in the Pacific. After the war, his wife, Elaine, and young son, Bruce, returned to Cincinnati from their military home in California and Bruce entered Northern Illinois College of Optometry in Chicago, Illinois. For the next three years he commuted to Cincinnati on weekends in order to be with his family. Daughter Karen was born during this time.

By the cultural standards of those post-war times he was seen by his patients as Doctor; by that same standard people who sought him out were Patients. This doctor-patient diad has undergone change in the cultural stew of the 80's and 90's and has a different flavor from the 40's and 50's when Doctor-was-God. So most of his patients entered his office with their cultural expectations intact: the Doctor, like father, knows best. Their job as patients, they assumed, was to submit, to be "examined" - looked at, probed, measured, to be an object. In its most extreme this expectation was -and in some instances still is - that the Doctor would fix whatever it is they thought needed fixing; some weren't even sure how they were unless *he* pronounced them fine.

Their assumptions sprang from the mechanistic, scientific model that taught us all that if something is not quite right, it can be fixed by isolating the problem and doing something to it. Isn't that what we do with our cars? We expect the mechanic to know about the noise on the left when we brake. We don't really care to hear about tie rods and brake pads. We want to know the important things: Can you fix it? How much? and When? Our past experience tells us to use the same approach when we consult psychologists, physicians, optometrists, speech-pathologists, teachers. Here's where it hurts. Can you fix it? And now most of us don't even ask how much; we expect the support of a third party will fix that problem.

Often the experts themselves operate from the same fix-it manual: Psychologists give tests to find out "what's wrong", so they can literally identify *and name* the problem. That's what we accept as diagnosis. Teachers "fix" ignorance by giving out information and testing to see if we got it and call that education. We all have at least one physician story, where the fix-it approach worked wonders or when it led to an exhaustive search for just the right diagnosis or solution that would *really* solve the problem. We all look for the magic bullet.

Dr. Wolff was An Experience for many patients; an experience heightened in direct proportion to the patients' certainty that Drs. and patients came with only one set of directions and *they*, the patients, knew the recipe.

On the other hand, Dr. Wolff had his own set of expectations and certainties of who he was and what his role as Dr. entailed. Often his view of who his patients were and what, together, they might do conflicted with his patient's me-object-you-fixer view. His assumptions grew from a model different from the culturally acceptable one of the 50's, 60's, 70's, and even the 80's. It was a model that appears in the 90's almost contemporary, since our cultural understanding of what people need and want moves closer and closer to where he was 40 years ago.

So for most of his practicing years, he listened to the dissonant chords that were struck when his ways and ideas clashed with the cultural expectations surrounding him. Reactions ranged from, "It just couldn't be that something this original was in *Cincinnati!*" to "How come I never heard of this?" Emphasis on the *I*. The last comment came in two inflections. One was an accusation; could it be that these questioners really thought they had heard of everything? The other inflection was wistful; a touch of sadness that they or their child might have had the benefits of his work years earlier if only they had known about it.

Frustration, anger, misunderstanding and criticism were constants throughout his professional life, and so were awe, gratitude, admiration and loyalty. Bruce Wolff and his ideas did not engender many middle-of-the-road reactions.

THE "PATIENT"

Dr. Wolff's professional approach to his clients rested on the same principle Barbara McClintock expresses in *Feeling for the Organism*. He saw patients, not as objects to be acted upon, but as people with whom he could interact. Barbara McClintock speaks for all who strive to *interact* with their surround instead of *acting on* the world. He had the qualities she describes:

> ...one must have the time to look, the patience to "hear what the material has to say to you," the openness to "let it come to you." Above all, one must have "a feeling for the organism."[1]

Bruce Wolff had that "feeling for the organism". For McClintock the 'organism' was maize; for him it was his patients. His observations, quantitative examination, chit-chat, questioning were all information gathering routes toward constructing for himself a model of how this particular individual literally saw the world; the way vision worked for *this* person. To him, patients were simply people engaged in the act of living. Most amazing of all, he thought *children* were people too, even severely handicapped, cerebral-palsied, non-verbal pre-schoolers!

His office procedures were not dictated by x minutes per patient to produce x dollars of income or to satisfy insurance protocols. With the help of his wife, Elaine, and later his daughter, Karen, he ran his practice so he could do what he felt was necessary to get that "feeling for the organism". His major interest was always to find how he could actually help the person improve whatever symptom or process they brought to be "fixed". He once told me he felt he had a lifetime commitment to his patients. That if a person learned and changed because of his help, then he felt morally obligated to always be available to that patient if, sometime in the future, he/she would need help again. Even if the patient could not pay him. I am just as amazed as I write this as I was when I heard him say it 25 years ago.

Bruce Wolff started with the premise that vision was dominant in human behavior. Does anyone not agree that we exist in a sea of space? Or that light/dark and gravity are constants for us? Because we see, we learn to move about *independently*; we can see the results of our actions on the world; we organize our sensory-motor data within this space-gravity-light environment.

We design our world so we can see it, so important to us is that information. How hot is hot? How cold is cold? Thermometers let us *see* and keep track of what our skin tells us. Thermostats let us *see* and keep track of our selected, ideal temperature. Hunters, guns poised, scan the surround for any movement they *see*; startled by a noise, they turn in that direction so they may *see*. Toddlers creep and walk toward a shiny ball, a familiar face, toward what they *see*.

From the stock market with its moving track of lights, to astronauts with computer print-outs and screens; to scientists with electron microscopes and medical scanners, and all kinds of oscilloscopes, we humans WANT TO SEE.

Dr. Wolff and his mentors wanted to know how it is that we see. His private, professional practice was his laboratory of inquiry. His interactions with his patients were how he gathered data and tested his hypotheses. He spent his career observing people in the act of doing what they do: seeing in order to move and live.

That he did this differently from eye doctors was apparent to most of his patients. He used whatever clues from the patient's *total behavior* that were available to him. A social interchange about a recent vacation, which was seemingly outside the bounds of the examination, gave clues to how those persons organized their mental data; their posture while standing, walking, sitting, told him how those individuals organized their bodies along spatial axes. That mechanistic dichotomy of sight, visual acuity, and the rest of a person's make-up did not occur to Bruce Wolff. For him, vision was the flour in the cake of human behavior. Eyeballs without people were of little interest to him.

In his kind of practice he could be found spending hours with a very young, handicapped child trying to see what this child *could do*. He looked for what was right with the child, not what was wrong. He thought his job was to understand *this person*, not to slap on a label of particular pathology. Getting that job done might find him on a mat on the floor where the child was playing, working his 6'+ frame around to get a retinoscopic reading which could not be done in the conventional way since the child could not sit well or follow directions. He might stay on the floor, building with blocks, moving one here, one there - strategically - to see what the child's response might be. *Whatever the youngster did was an important clue to him; it told him what his next move would be.* He would proceed until he could accurately *predict* how this youngster would respond. Then he'd beam, triumphant with his new treasure: he could see the world from that child's point of view; he and the youngster then shared something precious. He was in that child's world.

Bruce's beam of recognition flashed when he read Barbara McClintock's description of how she arrived at her conclusions:

> When you suddenly see the problem, something happens
> that you have the answer - before you are able to put it
> into words. It is all done subconsciously. This has hap-

pened too many times to me, and I know when to take it seriously. I'm so absolutely sure. I don't talk about it, I don't have to tell anybody about it, I'm just sure this is it.[2]

He did not stop until he had that kind of confidence about what he could do to help this child creep toward a normal developmental sequence.

All of his patients were opportunities for Wolff to *interact*, not to simply check off the designated steps in diagnosis or therapy. An airline pilot who needed to improve his acuity in order to keep his license, a Cincinnati Reds baseball player trying to improve his batting average, a real estate agent feeling the stress of too many appointments and the varied needs of clients, all presented him with their particular personal agendas. He responded in kind, personally, summarizing his findings within the context of the concerns they presented. His examinations were like extended conversations and it was not unusual that a one hour appointment would extend to two.

Patients were not nameless, inter-changeable parts to him. Consequently, he was always *there* in a way that many professionals are not. Often that meant that one's conventional, social ways of avoiding or covering up did not pass unnoticed. His "How are you?" was not idle chitchat. His manner could be truly disarming. As a patient, you may not always have understood the detail of what he said, but you felt he was talking about *you*, not some generalized textbook case. His orientation to his patients emerged from a source of understanding described by "a contemporary (of Barbara McClintock's) who says of her own involvement in research, 'If you want to really understand about a tumor, you've got to *be* a tumor.'"[3]

Dr. Wolff wanted to "really understand" his patients and through analysis of their visual behavior he could come very close to knowing that person's world from the inside out.

THE DOCTOR - THE TRADITIONAL WAY

Following the pattern begun by Galileo (see Chapter 2), the sciences concerned with human functioning developed from the same eye of the flesh as the physical sciences: isolate the parts, measure them, look for other parts that relate and affect the parts under consideration. Today's medical model represents this point of view. A patient has a complaint, the physician looks for a cause. Usually the doctor and his instruments keep looking until they can find something that can be measured. Only then does the complaint (the patient's subjective experience) become an objective fact. The doctor can say, "Yes, you have a reason for that pain in your foot. It's broken." The x-rays said so.

Once isolated, that fact becomes a *stimulus* that produces a response from the physician: broken foot means setting the bones, applying a cast or whatever sequence the facts elicit. This model has served medicine well. It works wonderfully for trauma, when parts are identifiably broken; for specific illnesses whose symptoms are readily apparent, for mechanical pathologies. It does not do so well for functional ailments like fatigue or maintaining a state of wellness, or problems in learning or attention.

This model for organizing our experiences is so familiar to us that most of us can't think about it as only a model. It is fact to us - true reality. If we were to accept this as just one model of organizing our thoughts about the world, then there could be others. There could be realities different from ours. Few prospects are more uncomfortable. Dr. Wolff and the new sciences demonstrate, without a doubt, that there certainly can be other models, other ways of thinking; other realities. Many of these new models do a much better job explaining our actual observations and experiences than the traditional, mechanical one.

But for awhile we're stuck with this viewpoint. It is everywhere. We still apply it wholesale, even when it does not explain what we want to know. Here's how it works in education:

The complaint is a youngster is having difficulty learning to read, so procedures are set in motion to quantify his difficulty. These procedures are designed to make the complaint a fact. Then it will be real to the school and they can respond. Never mind that the child knows reading is hard, that his parents are aware that reading is a mysterious process to this youngster. Never mind their subjective experience, the procedures proceed:

(1) The school psychologist isolates the parts of the reading process (not the child's *learning* process - the *reading* process): phonic skills, word reading, paragraph reading, oral reading, comprehension, etc.

(2) The *numbers on the tests* indicate whether or not this youngster is eligible for special help. The tests are the equivalent to the medical x-ray. Instead of diagnosing a broken foot, the educators diagnose broken reading with a label according to various formulae for interpretation:

reading problems due to "immaturity", "learning disability", "developmental disability", "emotional disorder". In other words, to satisfy the model, they must look for something broken. Their reality says there must be something wrong and the model points to the child.

(3) Some decision for treatment may follow the testing. The organization and particulars of the treatment flow from the same mechanistic model. Academic work may be modified to fit the youngster's problems, compensations may be offered in order to go around the disability.

What is usually not done is to look at the difficulties the child has in reading *as his way of solving this new riddle of graphic squiggles on the page.* His errors tell something about what and how he *does* that. Using the McClintock-Wolff viewpoint we could try to understand *this youngster's way* of reading. Once understood we would know what he needs to learn next. Plans could be made for instruction that would lead to the next developmental step. Many children and their parents have no choice but to live out the self-fulfilling prophecy the mechanistic model can produce, where academic difficulties become permanent; where the child internalizes his label and becomes "a learning disabled" person, or someone who *has* attention deficits.

Education has been the example of our mechanistic model at work; but substitute an example of your choice from other helping professions to see if the model pervades. How does the doctor-patient (helper-seeker of help) relationship work? Does the professional see the patient as an object to do something to or for? Is the patient over there, with complaints and behaviors that are outside what the doctor does? Does the professional see his responsibility as *describing* the parts of the patient so that these observations can be matched to some diagnostic category and a treatment program selected from that section of his professional cook-book? Is the professional *doing something to* someone, or *to* a part of someone? Does the professional view the patient as dependent?

NOTES ON NEW-SCIENCE - OLD-SCIENCE APPROACH

The late Thomas Hanna, founder of somatic therapy and the Somatic Society describes helping professions from a point of view that Dr. Wolff would have shared in spirit, if not in particulars: Dr. Hanna speaks about his own profession, but his ideas have a broader application.

> ...the embodied process of human life can be best aided
> and improved by direct attention to this whole embodied
> process. Whatever be their differences, somatic educators
> and practioners have a similar way of seeing the human
> being as a living, integrated system that has its own
> autonomous internal laws of governance. The human
> being is envisioned as a person, as a being who is already
> self-governing and innately sensible to his own needs and
> best interests.[4]

Dr. Hanna continues:

> Whatever be their different backgrounds and viewpoints,
> the men and women of the somatic realm, in backing
> away steadily from past traditions and past attitudes
> which they saw to be unfruitful and dehumanizing, have
> converged toward a common center. They have backed
> into one another, discovering their common ground.[5]

Dr. Wolff had not "backed away from" his traditional training.
He used it as a framework on which to hang his observations and
measurements. What did this particular, *conventional finding* mean
for *this particular patient*; not, what is the current wisdom about this
finding? He most definitely was not a cook-book scientist. Formulas for him were to be tested in the real world, not applied
universally. Atypical responses from patients were not tossed out
because they didn't fit a statistical average, or textbook description.
In fact, unexpected responses often were the best clues for him.
Why did this person say that? What is the person telling about
how they see the world? How does that fit with other information?

Betty Edwards in *Drawing on the Right Side of the Brain* includes
descriptions of the two approaches described so far:

> Thomas Gladwin, an anthropologist, contrasted the ways
> that a European and a native Trukese sailor navigated
> small boats between tiny islands in the vast Pacific Ocean.
> Before setting sail, the European begins with a plan that
> can be written in terms of directions, degrees of longitude
> and latitude, estimated time of arrival at separate points
> on the journey. Once the plan is conceived and com-
> pleted, the sailor has only to carry out each step consecu-
> tively, one after another, to be assured of arriving on time
> at the planned destination. The sailor uses all available
> tools, such as a compass, a sextant, a map, etc., and if
> asked, can describe exactly how he got where he is going.[6]

This seems so usual that many of us find it hard to think of it as A Way instead of The Way. But, try again:

> In contrast, the native Trukese sailor starts his voyage by *imaging the position* of his destination *relative to the position* of other islands. As he sails along, he constantly adjusts his direction according to his awareness of his position *this far*. His decisions are improvised continually by checking relative positions of landmarks, sun, wind direction, etc. He navigates with reference to where he started, where he is going, and the space between his destination and the point *where he is at the moment*. If asked how he navigates so well without instruments or a written plan, he cannot possibly put it into words. This is not because the Trukese are unaccustomed to describing things in words, but rather because the process is too complex and fluid to be put into words.[7]

Bruce Wolff, Barbara McClintock and others can describe it. Observers could watch them do it, but many of us (who are most comfortable with written plans, who only know about predetermined destinations) cannot shift to this other mode. We want written plans; we have difficulty using a more fluid approach and its benefits in our lives. In part this is because the Wolff-McClintock approach does not begin with a cook-book, or a linear model. It's more like a jump into the pool of experience. One of Dr. Wolff's great challenges and disappointments was when he found that other professionals, once enthralled with his vision and results, would attempt to develop a cook-book. They heard the new science music but wanted to play it on an old science instrument. To shift to a new science mode it may help to remember one of Wolff's adages: Things cannot change and still remain the same.

DOING WHAT WE'RE DOING

One of the fundamentals of control theory, in fact the most basic concept, is the idea of *feedback*. When information is incorporated into what the system is controlling, then the system can continue to control, self-correcting all the way. In order to satisfy a pre-set goal of a given temperature, the thermostat tells the furnace to turn on when the information "not warm enough" enters the system and tells the furnace to turn off when "it's just right" - when the desired temperature has been reached. In voluntary human behavior, *vision provides critical feedback* to all that we do. When that feedback loop is interrupted or only functions feebly, then the phenomenon of "doing what they're doing" shows up.

An example of this process of interrupted feedback occurred while I was waiting to check out some books at a branch library. Several of us, bearing our book selections, collected around the desk. The librarian, facing our group, very methodically continued what she had been doing before we arrived: stamping check-out cards with the new date. Stamp and flip. Stamp and flip. Since I had a while to think, it occurred to me that she was just doing what she was doing - and nothing else! She was probably aware (?) people were waiting; she probably would say, if asked, that her job was to serve the patrons of the library. But, at that moment, *what she was doing* took precedence over any give and take interaction with those patrons. In the terms of visual behavior and control theory, the visual information available to her (people were waiting) was not fed back and integrated into her visual-motor (movement) process.

I once had a student teacher who was to read a story aloud to a group of young children with moderately severe learning problems. She read the story and did a good job; but that was it. What she was doing was reading a story. Never mind that the children tapped on each other, turned around in their chairs, pulled on their socks. She kept right on reading. The children and their teacher were each "doing what they were doing". They were *acting*, not *interacting*.

Once sensitized to this process you'll see it everywhere: ministers and priests who carry out their priestly duties with parishoners. Those parishoners could be interchangeable parts, their wants and needs may not enter at all into what the minister is doing. Amateur and professional athletic coaches who do what they're doing -building winning teams - may never see the negative effects of win-at-all-cost on some individual lives.

Parents who give all their effort and make sacrifices while doing what they're doing - being good parents. Punishing, driving demands are made on children by earnest, sincere parents who do what they do, 'for the children's own good', even with the evidence of unhappy, rebellious children. They look for professional help that will fix the child, so that they can continue to do what they do.

Wendell Berry, in a field seemingly unrelated to vision, learning or children describes this "doing what we do" phenomenon, this penchant we have to apply general procedures to particular people; *to ignore the feed-back of the results of our actions which would tell us something important about what we're doing.* In the essay "Nature as Measure" in *What Are People For?* he says, when talking about the interconnectedness of farming, economics and ecology ;

> The reunion of nature and economy proposes a necessary democracy, for neither economy nor nature can be abstract in practice. When we adopt nature as measure, we require practice that is locally knowledgeable. The particular farm, that is, must not be treated as any farm. And the particular knowledge of particular places is beyond the competence of any centralized power or authority. Farming by the measure of nature, which is to say the nature of the particular place, means that farmers must tend farms that they know and love, farms small enough to know and love, using tools and methods that they know and love, in the company of neighbors that they know and love.[8]

This could be a description of Bruce Wolff's particular practice of new science if "people" were substituted for "places", "professionals" for "farmers". To understand someone, even a patient, we must must get to know them, see them as unique individuals, particularize them from abstract generalizations. To do that we must interact with them. To interact we must use the responses they give us as feed-back for ourselves so that we can continue the *interactions.* This was the essence of Wolff's professional style.

We often learn best through stories. Here's one that sums up a lot about Bruce Wolff's relationship with his patients. It's *Whobody There?* by Charles and Ann Morse, a fanciful, somewhat frivolous romp through fairly profound ideas. It could even act as a cookbook. So, if you feel like jumping into the pool of new science experience, let them lead us.

> Whobodies aren't just anybodies. Whobodies are special.
>
> Anybodies stand in front of us and in back of us when we ride an escalator.
>
> When a phone call turns out to be just anybody, it isn't any fun.
>
> How do anybodies get to be whobodies? First the anybodies have to wait. You can't hurry things like that. *Then the anybodies have to look at each other. When one anybody says something the other has to look at him.*

An anybody must smile before he gets to be a whobody.
And he has to ask, *"What are you doing?" and really want
to know.*

A whobody doesn't just play with your toys and books.
A whobody plays with you. [9]

To Bruce Wolff patients were people. People who became "whobodies" as he *particularized* their needs and reactions, as he saw the individual emerge from the generalized abstraction of patient, diagnostic category, or his carefully collected examination data. *Inter*acting, not just acting, was what *he* was doing.

SUMMARY:

- Bruce Wolff began with an assumption that vision is dominant in human behavior. Vision allows us to *interact* with our environment, to act meaningfully and to see the results of our behavior.
- Bruce Wolff's relationship with his patients was *interactive*. His understanding of vision paralleled the ideas of new science (Chapter 2). To him, patients were people capable of interaction. People who operated as integrated entities; not as a sum of individualized parts. In his view patients were not objects to be "scientifically" studied.
- When potential visual information is not part of the feedback system, the phenomenon of "doing what they're doing" occurs. Specific activity is isolated from its context and relationships. This results in professional situations where the patient becomes an interchangeable part, losing particularity to the professional.
- Bruce Wolff's professional practice was based on *particularity*. His evaluations of patients and their training were planned and sustained on this principle. To him each patient was a unique individual, with particular wants and visual needs.
- The professional approach that Bruce Wolff personified can be learned. The application of this approach yields information that makes any professional more effective, regardless of the specific discipline.

CHAPTER 4 HOW DID WE GET HERE FROM THERE?

Whatever our age, wherever we are in our journey through adulthood, we carry in our bodies the signs of our adaptations: changes we've made in ourselves through movement and vision because of the social demands of our culture. Each of us bears these physical and mental marks made by bumping up against gravity, space, energy, time.

During our infancy and childhood, no matter what physical potential or problems we brought with us into this world, we began this process of adaptation to the constants we all share: *the light and gravity that are the constants of our lives.* Within this context we developed and learned to walk and run, to feed ourselves, to talk and understand, to color and write; but, we are largely unaware of the pattern of our own adaptations, *of our own particular way of moving and organizing* our response to light and gravity.

We can move. If we see, we move *independently.* We've mastered gravity, and when we interpret what is illuminated in the world - we see. These adaptations are easily accomplished by some of us and not so easily mastered by others. We are all somewhere on a continuum of visual-movement development and adaptation:

Independent Movement: from little or no independent movement to ski jumping

Efficient Movement: from laboring with every step to ballet leaps

Interpreting What We See: from the infant's confusion of color and lines to reading print or x-rays.

THE NORM

Since we have *all* adapted, then from one point of view, all of us can be considered The Norm; in that sense we are all normal. Our adaptations, physical, visual, mental, are seen within the framework of *human* adaptations; we've done what humans do with whatever equipment we had at the time. So in that sense *we didn't do anything wrong.* Our current state, the way we do things, how we react, even if uncomfortable or inefficient, is still not wrong, in fact it's right *for us.* In itself our adaptation is not a problem, something broken that needs mending. *It is simply the adaptation we've made.* Since the way we respond to the world is an adaptation, then we can adapt in a more comfortable or efficient direction; we can change. Bruce Wolff's clinical work in visual behavior began with this assumption.

We don't see the marks of adaptation we carry because we have integrated them, because they are the physical ways that we experience ourselves. Yet they are obvious to those with eyes to see. Wolff was one who saw them. He saw them as *observable clues that could point to the individual's internal process of seeing.*

So when a new patient, MaryAnn, sat down across from him, Wolff had already made mental notes of her particular physical marks and signs. When he asked if there were any special reasons she had come in for an exam, she picked a visual concern. After all, she was going to an "eye" doctor. She told him that sometimes the print blurred when she was reading. She picked a symptom related to reading totally unaware of the connection between the visual nature of reading and the more fundamental purpose of vision - *to help us locate and move ourselves independently in space.*

Wolff's Exam

MaryAnn was not aware of her postural adaptations noted by Wolff: that she carried her head tilted to the right, that she positioned herself in the chair in a rotated fashion so that her right side was tucked further back into the chair than her left, that her right shoulder was held higher than the left. His observations were guided by his understanding that vision has a fundamental purpose: to determine our position in space and to direct our movements through space. These basic visual orientations we learn through our total body activity; therefore, it follows that our bodies would show how it is that we've matched our vision with our doing. MaryAnn's postural asymmetries were uniquely hers, *the results of the way she had learned and now maintained her location and movement in and through space.*

The examination proceeded the way MaryAnn had expected until Wolff asked her to put on some polaroid filters in paper frames and look at a picture that was projected on a screen. Interpreting a picture is dependent upon the spatial-movement use of vision ("lower" function) as well as on the ("higher" symbolic function), the abstracting perceptual-conceptual process that vision allows. Seeing a picture is first and foremost a spatial task, dependent upon light sources. The picture is out there and because there is light and you have eyes, you can have the experience of seeing it.

The polaroid filters and picture (of an airplane) were designed to elicit the experience of binocularity - seeing with two eyes. If everything operated according to The Grand Design, the person would see a 3-dimensional line drawing of an airplane that appeared to be hanging out in space. It was the stereoscopic experience similar to the old stereoscope with the double pictures or the view-master and it's slides which give a "you are there" experience.

MaryAnn at first saw a jumble of lines which eventually she could identify as an airplane, but she never described it as hanging in space. The closest she could come was that it was just "out there". She couldn't judge which end of the plane was nearer to her. And most of all, she did not like the experience; her eyes started to water and nausea grabbed at her stomach.

Wolff explained that her way of organizing the visual information in front of her indicated *how* she dealt with the simultaneous, yet different information she was receiving from two eyes. He explained that her two-eyed (binocular) seeing was related to:

- visual and physical postural adaptations she had made with gravity, movement, space, light and
- the cultural demands of 18 years of the close visual work involved in her school experience.

He also reassured her that what she saw and her reaction to the experience (tearing and nausea) were not unusual.

He did not, at this time, tell her there was an easier way to do it, a way that would have allowed her to see the airplane quickly, without tearing or nausea. MaryAnn discovered this for herself as she continued visual therapy, which included wearing glasses all the time and visual training in his office once a week.

Through her experience in visual training, MaryAnn learned that, to some degree, we are all casualties of our environment and our experiences and she began to see, bit by bit, how we got that way.

Adaptation was the name of the game. MaryAnn learned that her particular cake of visual behavior was made from the ingredients of her unique genetic make-up mixed together and baked with her particular experiences of gravity, space, light, time, social demands. MaryAnn learned that tilted heads, lowered shoulders, confused binocularity were, in a sense, normal. We create our particular adaptations through our interactions with the world. *But we have all adapted.*

The paradox is that the postural deviations observed by Wolff, could be considered atypical if measured against a physiological norm of how the body was designed to work yet, at the same time, typical if measured against a statistical average. That average would have to include *all the effects of everyone's adaptation.* This is why Wolff was almost never primarily concerned with pathology. He did not consider the postural deviations as something outside normal human functioning. He was not interested in problems *per se*, he was not there to find something wrong, in the mechanical sense. Most patients did not understand this at first. He was almost always amused when people asked if they were all right, or wanted to know how serious was their problem. He operated from a different frame of reference. He stated in "About Vision" that "Abnormal individuals are rare and even rarer still are those in which there is little or no potential for any form of positive treatment."[1]

So MaryAnn began to give up her cause-and-effect, mechanistic way of thinking. She accepted, as Wolff put it, that she "had all her marbles", including eyes that were okay, and that her life could be easier, literally, if she learned to rearrange her marbles in a manner more suited to the natural way the body seems to be designed.

VISION AND POSTURE = ABC's of Behavior

Considering the concept of adaptation, MaryAnn began to understand Wolff's comment at the first exam that, for her, reading must be a chore. MaryAnn had found this puzzling, and thought he was saying she had a reading problem. She was quick to tell him her reading achievement scores in school had always been exceptionally high and she had managed decent grades through college and two years of graduate school. She began to see that Wolff's concern was with *how she read*, not with how much in the sense of comparative measurements. Once she let go of her defensive position, "The world says I am a *good* reader!", she could look at her act of profuse underlining while she read for what it was: A physical adaptation she needed to make because she was not efficient in tracking a line of print with eyes alone. Her marked up texts were not just a personal preference; there was a logical, physical explanation. She hadn't flunked some test of normalcy; she was not a bad person. The healthy, okay person she was could learn to do something a different way, could adapt in the direction of a physiological norm that would make her reading easier.

Slowly MaryAnn began to understand that her head tilt, rotated posture, reading stress were related to what and how she saw. She even began to see how her migraine headaches fit into the visual picture. At that time the medical profession had not had a cure;

heredity was given as the cause of the headaches and pain medication for the symptoms. More severe headaches? More frequent headaches? More pain medication and comments about inability to manage stress. MaryAnn had definitely gotten the idea that her headaches were her fault for not managing her life better. Other people did not have headaches. There must be something wrong with her. She definitely did not feel okay.

But now the headaches could fit into a bigger picture! They could be understood as something she *did*, not something she *had*. Even better, she found that the intensity and frequency of them could be managed by understanding that bigger picture; and, she did not have to take pills to accomplish it. Relief did not have to wait until science could isolate all the bits of physiological, cellular activity that contributed to the experience of pain.

MaryAnn, as did many of Wolff's patients, wanted to know how all of this fit together. How did head tilts, underlining, migraine headaches come to be if most of us are physically "normal". Why do so many of us need to wear glasses, if our eyes are normal? Or is the fact that so many of us need glasses proof that we have abnormal eyes?

Darell Boyd Harmon considered the same questions and concluded:

> ...it is difficult to conceive that evolution has produced, in man, a superior intelligence capable of accurately gathering data of the world around him and dealing logically with that data in solving his problems of mastery of that world; and, at the same time, accept the concept that evolution has also produced an aberrant, imperfect sense organ for the modality through which man apparently derives the greatest part of the data he uses in problem solving.[2]

So the resolution of normal/abnormal eyes and the need for glasses to see clearly requires a different perspective, something beyond cause/effect and mechanisms. Harmon, *et.al*, headed in the direction of human adaptation and developmental organization for answers that could satisfy both questions: If normal eyes, then why glasses? If glasses are needed, are there abnormal eyes?

THE PREDICAMENT OF HERE AND THERE

Not only does our planet float in space; so do we. We are attached by gravity. The particular force of gravity affecting us is enough to hold us down so we don't float off into space, but not so much that we are fixed in one place. We can move; *always against gravity*, but move is what we do.

We move in order to go somewhere else; across the room, around a chair, up the stairs. We move in order do things in the world; get dressed, eat, write, type, plant, paint, drive. We move our speech muscles in order to talk, our involuntary muscles in order to breathe, pump our blood. We are beings of movement.

We are also subjected to external energy fields: light, sound, thermal, electromagnetic energy. We have sensory systems to deal with these energies: eyes for light, ears for sound, skin for thermal.

Our predicament is that we do not come hard-wired. We are not already programmed to use these energy sources; we don't come with instructions for moving about the world independently. We do not operate primarily by instinct. What we do come with is potential. We have systems that respond to the energy, that move us against gravity; but they do not come in full bloom. *We have to learn how* in order to realize these systems' potential. We learn to develop increasing complexity in each system; while, at the same time, we practice during infancy and childhood how to coordinate all of this into complex, unified, *voluntary behavior.*

While we're doing all that, our internal world constantly shifts so that it maintains stability regardless of the changes in the external environment. We maintain our internal temperature, our fluid levels, digest our food. These internal processess are guided by a process called *homeostasis.* It's part of our total control system. When our fluid levels need replenishing we experience thirst; when they are replenished, we stop drinking liquid. There is constant movement around a sort of pre-set level: the homeostatic balance. The systems interrelate, are normally always in flux: too much balances too little. Each system seems to have its own range of balance and the inter-relatedness of all the systems has its own absolutely elegant balance that we recognize as health, wellness.

The concept of homeostasis is an important one in understanding visual/physical adaptations to gravity and light. There are optimum relationships - body parts to body parts - body to light - body to objects, that the body seems to seek (the homeostatic balance.) Developmentally our task is to accommodate those homeostatic urgings while struggling with the forces of gravity and light that push and pull us.

The process we use to resolve the homeostatic struggle shows up in our behavior. How we move, do, act results from this body/energy interplay. Said another way, watching what we do allows us to read our behavior, to learn something about our responses to the energy that bathes us. Harmon, in his discussion of vision's role in human behavior tells us:

> The primary function of vision, biologically, is related to the *determination of space relations and the space movements* of the organism. Only secondarily, as a "higher" function of abstracting and symbolizing space and space movements for later facilitation and redirection of movement, is vision an "image" function, biologically.[3]

Where Am I? - Locating Ourselves In Space

Our eyes are in our heads and lead the rest of the body's movements. In order to see, in order to find something, we must turn our heads, neck and body until our two eyes can register equal light on both retinas. We move in order to do this; to satisfy this two-eyed retinal need. We see in order to move. We start our movements *from somewhere*, a base from which we begin our movements and to which we return. We are unaware that even our concepts of up/down, right/left are related to our eyes. Try it. Point to the place in space were *up* starts, where *down* begins. Was it somewhere near your nose level (the sighting line for near/far vision)? Where does *right* begin if you're determining which things in your environment are on the right, same for *left*? Was this somewhere in the middle of your body? We develop a middle because we have two sides, two eyes.

We continuously establish a base of aligning ourselves with gravity (so we can balance and move) and with light to our two eyes (so we can see) before we do anything else. This eye-body positioning is so automatic we almost never are aware of it unless something interferes; something is in our way; we are too off-balance to continue. Then we adjust so this retina-body-gravity balance can be re-established.

We each have a home-base, a posture of rest from which all other moves are made. This posture is not static, not necessarily symmetrical. *It is dynamically balanced;* moving parts held in particular relationships, constantly readjusting to maintain those relationships when one of the parts moves. We stack our knees atop our ankles, our hips over our knees, our shoulders over our hips and our neck and heads balance on those shoulders. There are innumerable ways to accomplish this stacking.

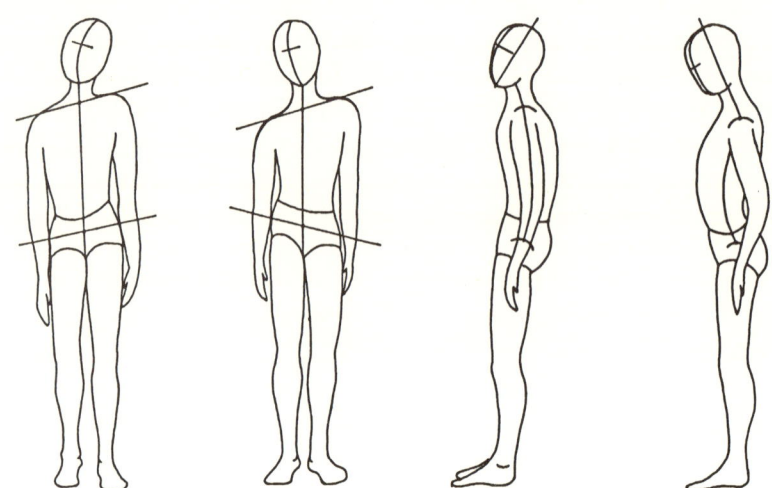

The arrangement of these body parts literally supports our eyes and determines their relationship to the light and objects in the world. It is towards those illuminated objects that we move, they are what we move around and are the objects we rearrange.

VISUAL FUNCTIONS

So we move independently because we can see. Vision helps set a direction for our movement, helps us know where we are on our journey. Vision has two functions that specifically help to guide us: our central and our peripheral vision.

Central vision is the space of greatest clarity; the focus that allows us to pick out of the environment that which we wish to regard. We look at someone's face, examine a rose, fill out a form, read a book. We keep specific parts of our world "in front of our nose", so to speak.

Peripheral vision keeps us in touch with the whole environment from which we select things to specifically, centrally, examine. This function lets us be aware of movement in the peripheral field, not the clarity of details.

We know we've come to the curb when walking down the street because our peripheral vision allows us to see the buildings going by as we walk. We have an idea of where we are in the block without having to specifically, *centrally*, examine everything along the way. It is movement in our peripheral field that alerts us. We respond to that movement, seen out of the corner of our eyes, by *centering*: turning our heads, shoulders, bodies so we can put whatever caught our eye into our central vision for inspection. We will function most efficiently, with less effort, if we keep our central and peripheral visual systems working the way they were designed.

Another job of vision is to help get us in position with the objects of the world so that we can act on and with them. When we want to pour some milk in a glass, we hold the glass in particular relation to us and to the carton which is also held in a particular relation to us and to the glass. All of this we do almost instantly, without conscious thought, *because we can see*. When we walk into an unfamilar restaurant, airport, building, it is our vision that let's us find the right person, doorway, seat, or hallway to carry out our intended business. Vision is the way we locate *where* we are now; that information becomes our *feedback* to guide our feet *where* we need to be in order to do what we want to do.

We each have our own characteristic way of aligning ourselves with the tasks of the world. Whatever is *our way*, we use it for everything we do. Maybe we line ourselves up so we are either to the right or left of what we're doing. Some of us like to be very close to things, some of us further away. But each of us has our own spatial preferences, our own comfort zone of where we are and where we want the world to be. Vision is so immediate and so much the creator of our sense of reality that we find it almost impossible to understand, at more than an intellectual level, that others don't prefer our way. The kitchen, with all its things, presents innumerable opportunities for the clash of spatial preferences should we try collaborative cooking. Why don't they know the dirty spoons go *there*, not *here*. Why do they insist upon cutting up the vegetables over *there*, when the logical place is *here*. You can undoubtedly write your own scenario. Spatial awareness, spatial alignment. Where are we? Where are the things of our world? Vision tells us.

LET'S GO - MOVING OURSELVES THROUGH SPACE

We are bilateral beings. We have two, matched sides. In order to move we push off with one side, counter-balancing with the other side. We exercise the principle of thrust/counter-thrust. In order to move in a straight line, the shortest distance between two points, we need equal thrust and counter-thrust of our two body sides. If it is unequal, each step we take leads us away from our goal, not directly toward it. We then have to correct our thrust/counter-thrust pattern and adjust if we are to reach the target. That requires more energy than if the reciprocal forces (right/left; thrust/counter-thrust) were evenly, symmetrically balanced. Have you walked on a sidewalk side by side with someone and found that slowly you were headed toward the grass? The other individual's asymmetrical steps were gradually driving you both in a sideways direction. Or perhaps you have had someone next to you comment on your frequent bumping into them when walking straight ahead. All are signs of unequal thrust and counter-thrust, of asymmetrical bilateral coordination which does not appear to be the design of our walking equipment.

Darell Boyd Harmon's work in physics, engineering, biology, human development and education led him to understand how we use our bodies and eyes as a unit to move against gravity. Harmon's work has been paraphrased above. The following is a more technical explanation: Harmon, summarized by Sheldon Rappaport:

> The eyes are a matched pair of brightness meters. They are capable of triggering an array of real or symbolic actions in response to significant light patterns occurring within their field of awareness.
>
> Before the light pattern to which the eyes are sensitive can become accurate and meaningful sources of information about the environment, the following must occur:
>
> (1) The head, which houses the eyes, and the neck, and the body, which responds to what the eyes see, must come to balance both with the light patterns and also with gravity.
>
> (2) Unless the organism establishes a balanced equilibrium with the light patterns, they are likely to be inaccurately organized by the eye's light receptors in the retina, and the receptors then are likely to trigger distorted neural signals.
>
> (3) *Therefore, one of the organism's first responses to a light pattern is to turn the eyes, head, neck and body until there is an equal amount of light on each retina.*
>
> (4) Coming to balance with the light patterns simultaneously aligns the organism with gravity, thereby providing a stable base from which to respond.
>
> (5) The organism's balanced equilibrium both with light and gravity results in reciprocal feedback among eyes, neck, and trunk as each tries to equate its activity with the other.
>
> (6) That feedback provides the organism with the opportunity for optimal freedom to perform whatever is required to cope with the task at hand.[4]

WARPS

Because of our design, there are ways to stack our body parts so that less energy is required to maintain their alignment. Deviations from this physiological norm Harmon called "warps". The norms are given at the end of the chapter.

A natural question is, "If we didn't come with these asymmetries, these warps, how do we get them?" Adaptation. Two of Harmon's favorite adages make it plain:

    A. *The child's body grows along the lines of stress induced in it by various activities, in order to reduce those stresses.*

    B. *Stress alters function; function alters structure.*

The first one tells us children are plastic, their bodies mold to fit the stresses induced by the environment. The ancient Chinese used this principle to bind female children's feet. Chairs that are too short or too tall, uneven light distribution, always being held on the same side as infants, are all stresses to which growing children *adapt*. Where the child's crib is located in the room determines the direction and pattern of light distribution for the child. Light that comes from the child's right, over time, means the child will turn more often to the right, lie on its right side. Placing the child in alternate positions so that it gets a balanced experience will go a long way in preserving balanced visual posturing.

The second adage tells us that initially stress impairs what we are doing - the function; but, if it continues, it impairs *us*. If the relationship of our chair and table do not match the proportions of our bodies so that we can easily, and in a balanced fashion, write or use a computer, then the ease with which we do something and, ultimately, the quality of what we do will be impaired. Whatever we are doing, the function will be less efficient than it could have been; and, we will use more energy than if we and our support were in a more optimum relationship. Whatever body adjustments we make to less-than-ideal arrangements will become permanent *if continued over time.*

We warp ourselves in direct relation to the stresses to which we are adapting. None of us escapes. None of us has had ideal light and furniture arrangements that support balanced, non-warped posture and movement. And we haven't begun to talk about the social-emotional components of stress to which the body also reacts and adapts. We're more familiar with Hans Selye's work on stress and the physiologic reactions that take place than with the visual/postural effects. The body contracts when threatened; we literally shrink in fear. Our shoulders go up, we lean over to protect our mid-section. Over time these can become permanent postural warps and since our eyes are located in our head, postural changes alter the relationship of eyes-to-light and consequently our vision and thinking will ultimately be affected by social-emotional stress.

Vision will be affected because it develops in both a dependent and independent relationship with our other sensorimotor development. The academic and work tasks of school require specific visual skills, and we alter our visual function in order to meet those demands. These tasks are imposed by our culture and overlay the visual functions we use to move or act independently. Reading and writing depend upon our central vision, we need to see clearly the print in front of us. Some of us, in an attempt to get this central visual job done, let go of our awareness of our periphery. We may become less efficient at keeping track of where we are when we move. We cease to pay attention to signals coming to us from the periphery; the effect of this inefficiency is that we become overly centered; we need the task to be directly in front of us if we are to attend to it. We walk down the street looking only a few feet in front of us because we can no longer rely on our periphery to alert us to potential obstacles. We don't notice someone has walked into the room when we're engaged in a conversation until they speak to us.

Or in our attempt to balance ourselves we may pay more attention to the periphery than to our central vision. We turn to every flutter, not incorporating those peripheral movements with what we've placed in our central view. The people in the next booth register in our space as much as the person across the table from us. We notice when someone enters a room and incorporate that information while carrying on a conversation, even if it is distracting. Few of us arrive at adulthood without altering the balance of our central and peripheral vision. Yet another example of stress altering function.

VISUAL ADAPTATIONS

What we commonly call *nearsighted, farsighted, astigmatism* are examples of visual adaptations that have become *permanent*. Here's where our eyes-as-a-camera assumptions make it difficult to hear Harmon, Wolff, *et al.* You mean it isn't because *we came with eyeballs that were too long or too short?* To understand what Wolff, *et al.*, mean, our eyes of reason will have to carry us through if we cannot experience for ourselves, through our eye of flesh, the meaning of this discussion.

Think about it. Very, very few infants need glasses. Most children who become "nearsighted" do not need glasses to see in the distance until they have been in school for several years.

Nearsightedness and many other vision problems were not common just a century ago. Neither was universal education and work requiring intensive near vision! Yet today, about 36% of the population is nearsighted - dependent upon lenses to see clearly in the distance.[5]

Cultures where spatial vistas are restricted because of crowded urban environments, where children are expected to spend more and more time in the near visual tasks of school seem to have greater incidences of nearsightedness.

The intimate interdependence of eyes and body shows up in postural patterns that are statistically consistent with certain visual adaptations. Harmon described them:

The correlations show that the incidence of visual and postural defects goes up significantly with increases in the differences between "norm" and actual posturally-maintained working distance in performing sustained near visual tasks. (the "norm" is the physiological optimums dictated by optics and body mechanics.) [6]

The following are paraphrased descriptions of Harmon's observations and conclusions:

- Subjects with *astigmatisms* characteristically tilt their heads laterally (sometimes accompanied by a rotation of the head).
- *Myopes* (nearsighted) tend to *incline their heads backward*.
- *Hyperopes* (farsighted) tend to *incline their heads forward*, Myopes lead with their chin, hyperopes lead with their forehead.

Some skewed positions of the scapulae are associated with visual problems.

- *Exophores* (eyes pointed away from center) tend to rotate their scapulae obliquely and upward, as if they were thrusting their arms vigorously out into space.
- *Esophores* (eyes pointed toward the nose) tend to depress their scapulae and rotate them obliquely and inward, as if they were pulling their arms and shoulders backward and away from visual space.

Although the focus of this chapter has been the biologic, physical underpinnings of the visual process, Harmon cautioned against isolating these factors from the mental and symbolic aspects of vision. He asks us to avoid the mechanistic, hierarchical thinking that puts higher and lower functions of vision in a sequential arrangement:

> In a significant respect, each is a function of the others. Full insight into a process cannot be gained by confining attention to only a single function of that process.[7]

Wolff-Harmon thinking says deviations in these lower visual funtions are present in the higher (mental problem solving), symbolic functions since the two processes develop together. *So the pattern of warps in our posture can be expected to have their correlates in the way we use vision mentally and symbolically.* Those higher functions of vision will be discussed in the next chapter.

The net effect of these bodily warps is that we maintain them at our own expense. It simply takes more energy to hold muscles in an asymmetrical balance than it does in a more symmetrically balanced position. It takes more energy to constantly correct our uneven walking pattern than it does to walk with balanced thrust, counter-thrust. Hatha-yoga exercise is based on this principle of symmetrical balance. Ancient Hatha-Yoga teaches that this physical balance relates to mental and spiritual balance.

Harmon and other "new" scientists seem to agree:

> In an adaptive organism, each part of a sensorimotor system is a function of every other part, and the functioning or structural status of any part is affected by and adapting to the functioning and structural status of every other part.[8]

MaryAnn was surprised to find that one of the benefits of wearing what she called " Wolff glasses" and the visual training was that she required less sleep. A connection between sleep and vision? Sounds crazy. But understanding body balances, warps and integrated body systems makes that jump less ridiculous.

TAKE A LOOK

Once sensitized to our postural warps, MaryAnn saw them everywhere. If you are a people watcher, you may want to do what she did. Use your waiting time at the mall, the check-out line, the Dr. office, and T.V. viewing as opportunities to observe the individual postural and movement variations that stroll by or sit next to you. Remember that what you observe physically has a visual correlate, because the body moves and positions itself so it can see! Once you become accustomed to observing posture, you can begin to think about how that person would actually move through space. As you begin to think about posture spatially, you'll begin to "hook up" visual patterns and behavior patterns with what you observe.

Head Postures: Notice characteristic tilts to the side. Rotations off the midline - turned either right or left. The talking heads on television news and talk shows are good opportunities for this kind of observation.

Body Postures: Use seated postures to note how people place themselves in their chairs: Rotations from midline, asymmetrical balances, shoulders off horizontal line. Can they maintain their posture or is there frequent shifting?

Standing Postures: Notice alignments of body parts - from the side: heads in relation to shoulders, hips in relation to knees and shoulders. How are the parts aligned? Notice the alignment of the two sides (viewed from front or back): how level are shoulders, hips? Notice placement of feet: are they rotated inward, outward? Is balance symmetrical - weight on both feet or asymmetrical - weight mostly on one foot? If so, which foot is preferred?

The postures that relate to visual adaptations described by Harmon can also be observed. The myopic and esophore posture - nearsighted - has a rounded upper back, or concave chest with chin leading. It is as if they are pulling space *inward*. Hyperopic and exophore posture - farsighted -will be in the opposite direction, shoulders back, chest forward, chins down as if they are pushing space away.

Moving Posture: Notice how the two body sides move in relation to one another: smoothly, as an integrated unit with each leg moving directly forward? Or is the walk more from side to side? Does one side move farther than the other? Do the arms swing - equally or one more than the other? Is it the whole arm or just from the elbow down? Look for restrictions, and asymmetries.

Spatial Preferences: Think of people you know. Try to describe them spatially. Where do they seem most comfortable - when they can look in the distance or when they look up close? I usually ask parents to describe their child as more of an "outdoor" or "indoor" youngster. They always know. Try to make a metaphor for how people move - like a turtle, a rabbit, pendulum.

SUMMARY: This chapter has focused on the physical base from which we learn to see. *The accuracy of our visual information - what we actually see - is determined by the body's reaction and relationship to light and gravity as it moves through space.*

We have optimal physiologic relationships - ways of moving and seeing that require the least energy to accomplish the most efficient seeing and doing. When our patterns of adjustment move us away from those physiological norms, we perform (move) less efficiently; it either takes us longer or requires more energy than to do the same things without those adjustments or restrictions. Wolff's great clinical success was his ability to know how to help people get from "here" - a state of asymmetrical balance that incorporated restrictions, physical and visual, to "there" - the place of dynamic, symmetrical balance where we all began our developmental journeys.

In a conversation during his last illness, he mused that a fundamental principle must be to "go in the direction of the norm." I think he meant not to get side-tracked by what we can't do, what we find difficult; and look instead at the underlying potential of that physiological norm; act as if it were really there. We haven't lost it. Our bodies are ready to shed our warps if we will but help them. Like Michaelangelo who said his sculpture was simply looking for the figure and releasing it from the marble, Bruce Wolff saw in us, his patients, something more than the asymmetrical sum of our parts. While other professionals and scientists labeled the warps, prescribed compensations and called it therapy, he designed and invented procedures that freed people, his patients, to live out the potential of performance they could only dream they had.

Harmon's dynamic postural norms are on the following page.

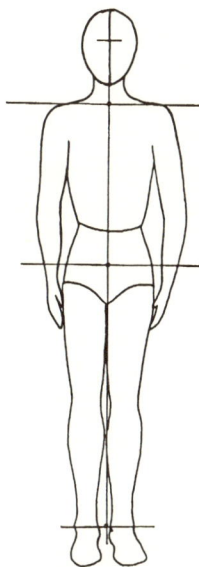 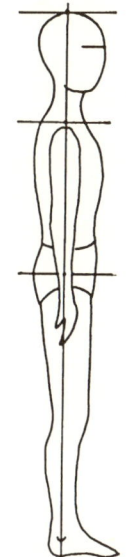

Vertical alignment, front view: Point between pupil of eyes, center of the sternal notch, center of pubic process, point midway between ankles should be aligned perpendicular to gravity.

Vertical alignment, side view: Notch of ear, top of shoulder bone, top of hip bone and front center of ankle should be aligned.

Balanced posture for close visually centered activity: For the retinas to maintain the most optically accurate relationship to plane of regard, book or paper should be about 20 degrees off horizontal. This places task parallel to the plane of the face. This relationship results in greatest optical accuracy and least skeletal-muscular stress.

HARMON'S DYNAMIC POSTURAL NORMS

Our visual information so dominates our reality that we often do not accept something as *real* until we've seen it with our own eyes. Here are two scenarios that may be familiar to you: A friend, reading the newspaper, says, "Hey, I see that a new shopping center is planned for your neighborhood." Stunned that you didn't know what was in store for your world, you ask for the paper, "This I have to see with my own eyes!"

Or on a sunny Saturday morning you find a problem and announce, "I was just down in the basement and there's water dripping from a pipe in the ceiling." What you might expect in response is some version of "Is that so? Let's call the plumber." But, you hear instead, "Really? Let me see!" And then, finally: "You're right. It sure is leaking." I'm right?!! Do you think I don't know water dripping when I see it? - you may be tempted to say. But you don't, since this is yet another variation on the theme "I need to see it with my own eyes." We've all heard it, and we've all said it.

It's just one of many common phrases we use to express this inseparable link between our seeing and our sense of what is real. "I'll believe it when I see it", "Seeing is believing", "Beauty is in the eye of the beholder" are variations of the same theme. For those of us with sight, the information gained *through seeing* becomes the raw material from which we fashion reality. *In turn, how we see actually determines the quantity and quality of the information we have available for action.* Wolff's contribution shows the linkages between the visual process and what we do - our behavior. The linkage begins with the individual as a spatial being. He said:

> Vision is a sensorimotor system that utilizes light related energy for orientation and movement in space.[1]

This physical/perceptual visual system we have for dealing with light energy creates for us *visual space*: that place, or as Wolff said, that *volume* of space where our experience occurs. He explained,

> VISUAL SPACE is that space that can be shared by those in the same place, at the same time. It involves what we see now; and what we have seen (visual memory); and what we can visualize in anticipating the future as well as in imagination.[2]

SHARED SPACE - Same Time, Same Place, Different View

You walk into a room for a meeting. The space of the room is shared by you and the other five people seated around the table. You are all affected by the light distribution in the room, slightly different for each of you depending upon where you sit in relation to the light sources: windows, lights, lamps. You are all affected by the furniture and its relationship to your particular body and to itself: is the chair seat too long or too short, too high or too low; is the table too high for the chair you're on, or too low; is there enough room between you and the people next to you, do you have enough room to write, to see the presentation. The actual surroundings within your visual space at this particular time have an effect on your visual process. Perhaps they set up physical stresses created by furniture that doesn't fit; or there is uneven light distribution which your binocular system has to accommodate.

What is your visual space at this very moment? Where are you reading this? What are the light sources, temperature, texture, furniture, noises, people in the room? How aware are you of that space while you read? The visual space of the present moment affects us and most of the time we are not aware of that surround, even though we continuously react to it. *What water is to fish, our present visual space is to us.*

WHAT WE SEE - Now, past, future

It is ridiculously simplistic to say that what we see in the imaginary office of our example - people, furniture, flip chart, we recognize because of our past experience. Simple, yes, but important to think about in a discussion of vision because what we *learned* from those long ago and not-so-long-ago experiences becomes the raw material from which we construct our present visual behavior. In our infancy and toddler years we touched, moved, tasted and made noise with chairs, tables, walls, doors, people. As we grew up we interacted with clocks, papers, pencils. And even later we flipped charts, poured coffee from the thermos, hesitated when around our bosses, and longed for our promotions.

All the while we listened to the auditory-vocal sounds our elders attached to these experiences, and we acquired the language of our culture. We grouped, coded, sorted, and organized our learned experiences with the help of words. The role of language in vision as described by Bruce Wolff will be discussed in the next chapter. *All of our past learned experience, including language, is with us when we survey and get meaning from what we see in the room.* Is it any wonder we have different points of view? The genesis of those differences starts in our total visual development, unique for each individual. It is our particular past experience with items similar to what we see now, and the meaning we derived from that experience, that *we visually project onto what we see at the moment.* Since our experiences were different and what we learned was different, early on we planted the seeds of our unique visual process.

Things this shape are "chairs", we sit on chairs, so I can sit on these. That's how we meaningfully recognize objects from the shapes and colors the light presents to us. *Our visual memory* (the bits of our past experience) *exists in our present experience of seeing.* Because I recognize chairs, see an empty one and other people sitting down, I plan my next move - I momentarily step into the future. I know what I'll do! I'll sit down. The flip chart in the room tells me what we might be able to expect in the future: probably someone will illustrate something; the group may record something. So the act of walking into a room includes meaningful seeing -vision. *Meaningful seeing uses our past experience, what we see right now, in the present, and visualization of our next moves, our future action.*

The melding of these three processes into meaningful seeing -vision - occurs instantaneously. One sweep of our eyes across the meeting room and we've got it.

Wolff reminded us that hindsight (past visual information) and foresight (projected visual action) are present in insight (what we see or know now). This is how we create the visual space in which we act.

HOW WE CREATE WHAT WE SEE

Stuck as we are with two dimensions in this medium of print, the diagram that follows is only an approximation of a complicated process within which various functions operate simultaneously.

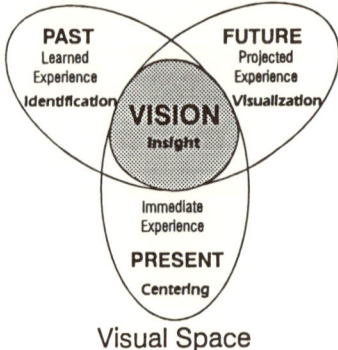

Visual Space

> It (visual space) is formed by the combination of light
> from the external world and the individual's internal
> referential framework generated by the particular envi-
> ronments within which one grew, developed and learned
> to use.[3]

Specific visual functions allow us to select what we want to look
at, to understand what we survey, to incorporate that information
in our total behavior so that we can move and act in order to benefit
ourselves through our accomplishments in the world. The labels
for these processes are: centering, identification which relate to
binocularity, and visualization.

Centering

I can hit the tennis ball because I know *where* to connect my
racquet with the ball spinning in space. I have some visual sense of
where that ball is in relation to me and where the racquet is in
relation to me. I can follow an energetic speaker and take notes
because I know *where* to look to find him up there on the podium,
I know *where* my note pad is and I can visually shift from one to
the other without missing a beat. The baby reaches and misses;
reaches, misses and finally grasps that ring above the crib. The
where of the ring now has a specific visual meaning to the baby.

> Centering is the equivalent of looking to "where it is" in
> the visual space or the ability to direct the visual system
> to a volume of visual space, large or small, within which
> identification is taking place.[4]

It's easy to understand centering in active physical movement.
You turn to face your tennis opponent. You place, center, yourself
so that you'll be free to move when you see the direction of the
ball. You line yourself up (center yourself) with the golf ball, club
and the flag at the hole.

We center ourselves at the dinner table, when reading, when
typing, when writing and even in conversation. *We place ourselves
in particular positions so that we can visually find what we want to see.*

But where is where? How near? How far? Directly in the middle
of our bodies or off to one side?

Visualize this volume of space three dimensionally with a vertical
plane, a horizontal plane and a depth plane. Envision yourself and
all the things around you as somewhere in this matrix, this space
web. Vision - centering - allows us to keep track of ourselves and
all the rest. Buckminster Fuller's definition of the universe was "All

that is not me, and me." Vision allows us to *independently* connect the "not me" with "me".

Wolff said we build this connection in "the particular environments within which one grew, developed and learned to use." *The particularity of our unique environments affects how we visually center ourselves.* As a developing child was our space restricted or free? Were we asked to attend to things more in the distance (far) or up close (near)? Were we expected to master a large or small volume of space? All of the above factors, along with our constitutional predispositions and our independent learning may have taught us that being physically close to things was where it was safest, where we had the greatest success. This may lead, eventually, to shrinking *visually* our volume of space.

Remember Harmon's 'function alters structure' from chapter 4? If we make that spatial adaptation permanent, then we *visually focus at a place in space that is nearer to us than the real object.* The real object appears blurred to us because our optical system now centers in a particular way - off the mark, so to speak. We want to pull the distance in to where we are more comfortable. Or said another way, we want to project our near orientation on the distance. Traditional science calls this adaptation *nearsighted.* Wolff called it an adaptation in centering.

This particular centering pattern may not be yours, but you do have one. Whatever your pattern, it is uniquely yours. It is where you are most comfortable when you visually hook yourself up to the world around you. *We live in the visual space we've created; our behavior is the action within that visual space.*

George was observed looking at a wall map. To find a particular town in Illinois, he very methodically examined each city dot within the state on the map from a distance of 5-8 inches, moving his whole body so he could eventually see all the dots. Further observation of George's actions showed that he consistently placed himself so that he was quite near what he wanted to see. His friends learned that they could not signal to him from across the room and always came directly up to him when they wanted his attention.

Phil, on the other hand, stood back as far as he could and still read the cities on the map. He could pick up visual clues from across the room. His friend, knowing Phil would get it, could indicate by nodding his head toward the door that he wanted to meet Phil after class.

George would always move, if he could, to sit on the same couch to converse, but Phil was more comfortable in a chair across from the couch.

People who share the same physical space over time become acutely aware of these centering differences but most often do not attribute them to vision. Two college roommates, very good friends, could never resolve when to clean their room. When Susan became aware of dust balls among the books, tapes and shoes on the floor, she thought it was time to straighten up and became very frustrated with Angela's unconcern. Since Angela was reasonably neat about her own clothes and desk, Susan could not understand this impasse.

Then Susan heard about visual centering. Of course! Knowing about her own spatial comfort zone -nearer rather than far - it made sense that she actually saw dust and belongings on the floor sooner than Angela because she looked in that spatial area much more often than Angela. When they talked about it, Angela confirmed that she just didn't pay attention to things on the floor. When she walked into the room she looked to the window, to pictures on the wall, to things on her desk. Her zone of comfort was farther away, up higher than the floor. Differences in centering; different visual space worlds.

PRINCIPLE: In order to respond or interact, *independently* with the events of the world, we must know where they are. For sighted people the where of things is determined by visual centering. "Let's see where we are," "Now where was I?", are mental equivalents of this process that begins with the immediate act of localizing what we see.

Identification

Imagine that you are presented with a photograph of an object you have never seen before. You see the photograph clearly, that is, the object is not blurred. Your sight is fine; but, in this case, your vision is not so good. You cannot *identify* what you see. Since you don't really know what it is, you might fill in from your visual repertoire (your hindsight) and see what you imagine it to be. I see it...but, what on earth is it?...I guess maybe it's a___? That is the visual process of identification. It is "seeing 'what it is' within the visual space and the continuous recognition and utilization of form and the relationship of forms."[5]

The ability to interpret what we see makes available to us vast amounts of information that would not be available if we could not see - or, if able to see - could not *identify*.

> Vision is helped by the sense of touch and the muscle sense, but the sense of touch alone cannot vie with vision, mainly because it is not a distance sense. Dependent upon immediate contact, it must explore shapes inch by inch and step by step; it must laboriously build up some notion of that total three-dimensional space which the eye comprehends in one sweep; and it must forever do without those many changes of size and aspect and those overlappings and perspective connections that enrich the world of vision so vastly and are available only because visual images are obtained from distant objects by optical projection.[6]

What Is It? Form

As in most of human behavior visual identification of shape and form is learned. We reached out, as infants, to touch the tantalizing light patterns the world presented to us. We found out what it felt like to move our hands around and over objects. That touching and moving experience occurred simultaneously with our optical experience. *The fusion of those experiences became vision.* We began to recognize similarities. When our hands and eyes moved in similar, simultaneous relationships, we put those similarities together to make a pattern of movements. Roundness emerged; squareness, triangularity, lines and limitless combinations of these patterns became fixed for us, even before we had the labels for those relationships. Young children can pick up a ball and know it will roll or that it is for throwing (they can visually identify it) even if they do not have the label - the word for it. *Their experience develops from mouth-hand-eye to identification through eyes alone.*

> Sequencing through a series of movements, either directed or by trial and error, we develop "form", a pattern which emerges from the synthesizing or grouping of parts into a whole. Grouping to a criteria is a learning experience. One learns how to move into the future. Grouping which forms a criteria is a creative experience, and a learning one as well.[7]

Sequential movements are often described these days as functions of the "left-brain". Synthesizing - pattern making - we are told is a function of the "right brain". Wolff points out that both functions - sequencing *and* pattern making by synthesizing parts into wholes - are necessary in human learning. They are simultaneously present in our identification of the form and form relationships which are fundamental to all learning. Wolff used the labels *digital and analog* to describe these two necessary, simultaneous and *integrated* functions. Digital refers to sequential, discrete data; analog to synthesizing, pattern-making.

Knowing about the shape of things gives constancy to our world. If we identify the shape of the thing, we have a better chance to know what it is and in turn, to know what to do with, for or about it. We then can take this visual form-making process used first with the concrete objects and, through our mind's eye, identify sequences and patterns that may not be physically present at the moment. *Identification becomes a visual-mental activity.*

Here's an example. Every school day Steve dropped his coat and book bag on the first chair inside the door. His mother had repeatedly told him to put them away; she had gotten angry and let him know she was not pleased. Yet, every day the same routine: Steve drops coat and bag and heads for his room; Mother picks it up and later yells at Steve that he "forgot to put his coat and bag away AGAIN!" This scenario has a sequence, it is waiting to be *identified*, to take *shape* for those with eyes to see. Some parents would recognize the form - the everydayness of it - sooner than others. Some would go a step further and put it with other *similar yet different* instances of Steve's leaving toys around, towels on the floor, glasses on the table. They would use an analog function; they would group to a criteria: Steve doesn't independently manage his belongings in a responsible fashion. He has a few holes in his self-discipline sequences. If they decided they didn't like what they saw (identified) then they could take action (find a way to teach him to hang up his coat) that would actually be connected to the form they identified. *Vision is the feedback that guides our actions.*

But a lot of us would not see a pattern. We would see the coat and book bag *only for this time.* What we saw would not serve as feedback for our actions. We might continue and continue and continue to tell Steve to hang up his coat, never identifying the *form* of what we saw. *And never getting what we want.*

How Do We Do It?

As Wolff defined it: "Identification is...the continuous recognition and utilization of form and the relationship of form." It is a constant of the visual process. We stop identifying what we see at our peril. Is the glittering surface glass or ice or water? The world around us is not static, light patterns change, objects move and are moved, we must *continuously* identify visually if we are to be in meaningful contact with our immediate world.

Often it is easier to understand something from contrast; this is especially true when trying to see something that is tightly integrated in our behavior. By negative example we can understand how it works when we see the effects of its not working. So it is with *continuous identification*. One very common experience of identification amiss is reading when you are tired. Most of us have found ourselves at the bottom of a page wondering what came before. We know we passed our eyes over the words, but because we didn't identify continuously, we missed the information available to us. Oh yes, we saw that sign back there, did it say route 56? We're not sure. We had stopped identifying. Our computer continually gives an error message until we finally identify the actual mis-spelling of the command entered. The typo was there to be seen; but we didn't see it, didn't identify it. Because we didn't see, we couldn't use the information as feedback and enter the correctly typed command. Our actions could not change. Without continuous identification we continue to repeat our errors.

Some of us visually check out even when we're not tired; we habitually have that experience not only in reading, but in social situations, in conversations. One crude, but effective description of this interrupted identification process is, "The light is on, but nobody's home." Inefficient visual identification leaves holes in our visual space world. Since we see to act, what we miss seeing we cannot act upon. The corollary is that when we don't take action, maybe it is because we didn't see (identify) what there was to do.

As ever, we each have our own degree of visual efficiency in this process; we all miss something, but what, the extent of it and where it occurs, make up our own particular way of answering the "what is it?" of what we see.

Sight & Continuous Identification: Visual Acuity

A young teacher was reading a story to her class of four year olds. After she read the text with gusto, she showed the pictures to the children and asked, "What color are the pants on Peter?" "How many other animals are in the garden?" "Where is the watering can?" Each question *centered* the children on specific details of the pictures. They leaned forward toward the text, straining to visually find those details. The questions set up a visual task which required the children to narrow their field of regard to a very small space in order to be successful.

"What is Peter doing?", "Do you see anything else happening?", "How do you think Peter feels?", "What do you think will happen next?" These are questions which present an entirely different centering/identification expectation for the youngsters. To be successful in this task the children need to see the whole picture, to relate the parts of the picture to one another and to make inferences and judgments from what they see.

Children adapt. If particular visual/spatial expectations are presented over time, they will adapt to them - visually. Ultimately many children will develop permanent centering/identification patterns based on expectations which were visually-spatially skewed. These patterns are called nearsighted, farsighted by the eye-as-a-camera people. We may eventually look closer in or farther out instead of on the plane on which the real object exists. If this tendency becomes habitual we experience the real objects as blurred. Since this is a pattern of learned adaptation, lenses prescribed for compensation often do not permanently solve the problem. Many people find that even with their new prescription, they still hold the text closer in or farther away than the norm and they continue the adaptive process, needing stronger and stronger correction so long as the demand for that adaptation continues. This is so common it is almost considered a normal progression for myopia (nearsightedness) in students.

Wolff thought *learning* was a great part of these adaptations. If we adapted because of the tasks and expectations in our environment; then *the potential exists to adapt in the direction of the norm*, provided tasks and expectations for that reversal are present. That is the basis for visual behavior therapy as conceived by him. We can learn to visually center more accurately; we can make our identifications in visual space more optically "correct". Wolff's use of lenses and visual training (see Chapter 7) helped people adapt back toward the physiological norm and the results with his patients showed *we can actually change our visual acuity patterns*. The potential exists to become less near or farsighted without surgery. PRINCIPLE: In order to respond to and interact independently with the events of the world, we must recognize - interpret what we see. We do that through a process of *visual identification* based on form and form relationships. We continuously recognize and interpret the light patterns presented to us. This identification process allows us to stay in touch with what we see. Our patterns of adaptation in this process are described traditionally as visual acuity: near or farsighted.

Direction: Our sequential movements, the raw materials of centering and identification, take us from *here*, wherever we start, to *there*, wherever we want to go. Movements by their very nature have a direction. We center ourselves - as the 'here' - and plan our moves to 'there'; the path we take is determined by the direction selected in the movements themselves. Direction is at once part of and separate from the movements themselves, an indissoluble part of centering and identification.

Behavioral efficiency requires accurate directional movements. The tennis ball is there. The doctor's office is over there, in that part of town, and I know how to get there. I need to go out this exit of the store to get to my car. I know the word I'm looking for will be here, in this section of the dictionary. After dinner I'm going for a walk and then will work on my income taxes.

Behavioral efficiency requires accurate recovery of interrupted movements. If you look away, you'll miss the tennis ball. If you start from the mall instead of your house, will you still be able to find the doctor's office across town? Do you actually find the word in the dictionary or does the attractive picture on the next page engage you instead? On your walk, does the neighbor's friendly chat change the direction of your evening? Visual direction -where we move, the path to our goals - emerges from the *sequential* matches fused in our visual movement systems.

Efficient visual skills allow us greater ease in selecting appropriate directions and maintaining our direction, regardless of interruption or obstacles, until we complete the move - get where we wanted to go. Our mental process of direction begins at this physical visual-movement level. What we learned by physically doing, we spread to our general behavior and functioning. One patient, post visual training, reported that he now responded to changes of direction in a meeting with immediate, appropriate comments instead of thinking on his way home of what he wished he had said at the meeting.

Binocularity

Stereopsis:

That we have two eyes is so obvious most of us never think about what difference this may make in our lives. Maybe one eye is a spare in the case of injury? Since things don't look much different if we close one eye, it's hard to experience the effects of binocular seeing.

Jeff had been playing around with the long cardboard tubes that come inside gift wrapping paper. He put one tube in front of each eye and saw two small, lighted circles at the ends of the tubes. As he moved the ends of the tubes towards each other he noticed that the circles began to overlap, with the overlapping section beginning to merge. He also noted that the two circles never completely became one.

The next time Jeff saw Wolff, he told him of that experience and wondered what it meant. Wolff explained that his experience resulted from the way his two eyes solved the binocular issue. In his case, Jeff could not fuse the images from each of his eyes into one complete image. The overlapping circles were the evidence that his binocularity, in this instance, was not working the way it was designed.

Like Jeff, we cannot know the difference efficient binocular function would make for us if we don't have it, because however we see, it is normal for us. But we can talk about the role of binocularity in the total visual process and listen to descriptions that hint at its influence in learning and behavior.

> Binocularity is the process that develops two eyed centering and identification within the visual space and resolves similarities and differences simultaneously into unique precepts.[8]

Binocularity is more a process of *how* rather than *what*. We have two eyes; they work independently and jointly. If through injury we had only one working eye, we would still center ourselves and identify what we see; but, the degree of binocular fusion determines *how* we center and the extent of our stereoptic experience and analog abilities. Two eyed centering-identification allows for the experience of stereopsis. The things of the world appear to stand out from one another; we feel part of what we see.

The experience of stereopsis described by someone who normally did not see the world that way, gives us a taste of the truly different visual space worlds binocularity and its malfunction create.

Jess Oppenheimer, comedy writer and creator of "I Love Lucy", did not find out until he was twenty-nine that others did not see as he did. He thought what he saw and experienced was normal, more or less the same for everyone, just as most of us normal folk do. Actually, the quality of binocular centering-identification varies greatly among people, *normal*, adequately functioning people like me and you. Mr. Oppenheimer's experience is offered here to show the unique quality of our binocular functions and to help us understand that no matter how compatible, *others literally do not see the way we see.*

Because he had had some visual disturbances while collating pages of material, Mr. Oppenheimer decided to "ask the man standing next to me about his vision. ...Pointing to a sign on the wall across the room, I asked him to turn away from it, then suddenly turn and look at it. He did.

"How long did it take the signs to come together?" I asked.

He gave me a look I won't forget."

"There's only one sign."

"I know there's really only one," I assured him, "but when you turn quickly like that, and they separate, how long does it take them to come together? It takes a couple of seconds with me.

"He managed to convince me that he only saw one sign at any time and under any conditions, and this was shocking news to me - a supposedly intelligent, grown man."[9]

That Mr. Oppenheimer said he knew there 'was really only one' sign demonstrates the limits of our language which cannot convey the actual, personal experience hidden in the words. The words "one sign" connote very different experiences for Mr. Oppenheimer and his friend, experiences they could not be aware of in normal conversation. Such is the particularity of our visual space worlds.

After he had attained some efficiency in his binocular function thanks to visual therapy, he recognized that he had had an isolated experience of stereopsis years before. Here is his description of that event.

"When I was in college at Stanford, a group of us drove to Los Angeles for the USC football game. We spelled each other on the driving. ...At about four in the morning a very frightening thing happened to me. I was driving along with everything seeming normal to me when in an instant everything before me changed. I can now tell you what it looked like in terms you can understand; I could not have then.

"The whole vista suddenly took on a strange aspect. It was on one plane horizontally as far as I could see. The road was flat and stretched out and into the distance before me; the trees suddenly rose on both sides, standing in space; the hood of the car took on a shape and stood up from the road. I could see all these things at once, and it was a most terrifying and weirdly uncomfortable feeling. It was like a fairy wonderland where everything appears unreal. I didn't like it at all and had to shake my head roughly several times before I went back to what (to me, then) was natural. I said nothing of it to anyone, fearing, I must admit, that I might be losing my mind."[10]

Binocularity Sampler

If you want a taste of your own, unique, binocular function, try Jeff's tube routine, or roll up two separate sheets of paper into tubes, one for each eye. Then move the ends of the tubes toward the center. Note what you see. Don't judge it, just make a mental note.

Another demonstration (but it gives information only for near visual space) is to take a piece of string or yarn, about 15 inches of it. Hold one end at your nose and the other end straight out in front of you with the other hand. Look at the string and out to your extended hand. What do you see? Some variation of two strings crossing each other, or coming together at your extended hand? Maybe you see only one string, (one eye working) or maybe there is a difference in the intensity of one image: one string looks real and the other like a ghost. Avoid thinking of this as a test which you either pass or fail (leftovers of our either/or kind of thinking). Rather, think of your experience as a demonstration of individual differences *within the norm.*

Binocularity and Similarities and Differences

The Analog Process of Vision

Included in Wolff's definition of binocular function is its ability to "resolve similarities and differences simultaneously into unique precepts. With two eyes we really do have two different viewpoints, slightly separated in space, one from each eye. The resolution of those two viewpoints, in addition to stereopsis, allows us to *see* things that aren't there. Analogies are an example.

Sun is to hot as snow is to ____.

Aha! An attribute of the sun is the temperature of the rays we feel. Now we have a new idea - temperature - that is not inherent in the information actually present, that which we see. Once we see the relationship between 'sun' and 'hot', we can easily fill in the blank: the temperature attribute of 'snow' is, of course, 'cold'. To the binocularly unsophisticated there seems to be only differences between sun and snow. Snow doesn't seem to have anything to do with with either 'sun' or 'hot'. According to Wolff, *we see similarities in the face of differences because of our binocular function.* We use data, originally collected by our physiological system, in our mind's eye so we can deal with what's not physically present. From our past visual experience we resolve the differences by projecting a new relationship. Here are a few more sophisticated analogies:

1. Contract is to legal as ___. Choose from below.
   A. anthology is to literary
   B. medical is to diseased
   C. check is to social
   D. disease is to contagious
2. Here's another: Explain how all the words in Group A are related to Group B:[11]

A	B
calipers	latitude
inventory	length
poll	opinion
sextant	stock

(Answers: 1. A; 2. A are instruments that measure the things in B.)

Pat wanted to improve her reading speed and comprehension. Wolff found that she had very poor binocularity, she tended to see out of one eye or the other. Analogies were presented as part of her educational therapy; but she did not get the idea of what she was to do. Her tendency was to associate with each side separately, rather than see a connection between the two. After several months of visual training and educational therapy, she began to get it. *On the day she solved her first analogy correctly and understood what, to her, was a new process, she also had her first experience of binocular vision in visual training.* Pat's life experience demonstrated the visual principle that binocularity allows us to see simultaneously the similarities in apparently dissimilar entities.

Wolff's favorite story to demonstrate this ability to take similarities and differences and make new and different forms (analogs) is this: At the time his office was adjacent to his home, which makes the cat's appearance more understandable.

"What do you see here - what does that mean?"

"A part of a circle, some slanted lines and some straight lines. Oh, those are the letters of the alphabet."

"What do they mean?"

"I don't know."

At that moment Wolff's cat walked into the room. "You've got a Siamese ca....THAT SPELLS CAT!"[12]

Principle: Two-eyed seeing, binocularity, allows us to experience stereopsis and to create new ideas from the resolution of similarities and differences. When we look, we can see something not seen. We get it; a critical skill in developing a sense of humor, understanding cartoons and jokes or finding meaning in intellectual and life pursuits.

Visualization: past & future in the present

Centering answers the question, "Where is it?"

Identification answers the question, "What is it?"

Visualization answers the question, "What do I do with it?"

I see a ball. My past experience with balls crystallizes into a visual memory which allows me to recognize (re-cognize) a ball. Just as importantly, I can use that visualized information to project *into the future* what I can do with the ball. I do all of that in an instant: see the ball, pick it up and throw, roll or kick it. We see to act.

Seeing involves our past experience and our future actions projected onto the present visual identification.

Bill watched as the ivory paint oozed out of the now open, over-turned gallon can onto the black carpet in the car's trunk. He immediately turned the can right side up and searched for a likely bailing utensil. In his split second scramble he became aware of his immobile teen-ager, Steve, transfixed by his side. During the replay of this trauma Bill asked Steve why he just stood there. Didn't he see what was happening? I didn't know what to do, was the answer. To Bill, seeing and knowing what to do were inseparable. Steve's identification of what he saw was much narrower. Even though intellectually he would have known the correct answer was 'scoop up the paint', at that crisis moment what he saw did not include the visualization of an appropriate *action*. Visualization is that aspect of the visual process that allows us, instantaneously, mentally, to know what we can do with what we see.

With inefficient visualization skills we are tied to the present. We will tend to act only if all the information is currently in front of us, plainly visible. We will not be good planners or mental problem solvers. Students can pass reading comprehension tests when the questions about the passage are on the same page as the passage by continuously looking back to the passage to find the answers. Questions and answers are present at the same time. Poor visualizers have difficulty reading between the lines, and have more difficulty answering questions when they cannot refer to the passage. Inefficient visualizers find it difficult to bring their past experience to the issues in the passage, and have fewer hooks in their heads on which to hang new information. This paucity of mental hooks makes interpretation difficult whether the material is read or heard. Jane, an unmotivated student to her parents and teachers, demonstrated poor visualization skills. She described school as boring. She said she didn't get anything out of the lectures, so she worked on her homework for the next class instead.

Without seeing in her mind (visualizing) the connections within the lecture and hooking them to other information she had, there was no reason for her, she thought, to mentally look for anything in what was going on at the moment; so she mentally checked out.

For Jane to become an independent problem solver she will have to:

a. be able to see what the problem is (form recognition);
b. select (visual memory) and
c. effect appropriate solutions (visualize the future).

When she is able to do that she will then know what to do with the lecture she hears. Competence begets confidence. She would not need special courses in self-esteem.

Wolff's terms of hindsight, insight and foresight capture this integrated visual process *where past information (hindsight) merges with the visualized future (foresight) to interpret the visual present (insight)*. These are the ingredients of the cake called meaningful seeing: vision.

PRINCIPLE: Interpreting what we see requires seeing (visualizing) what is not physically present. When we talk of people with vision, we usually mean those who know what to make of what they see (identify) and who can project some future course of action from what they have seen. We want leaders who see more than we do, and because of that, know what to do. Prophets are efficient visualizers.

Observation Sampler: When we see in ourselves or others behavior that is less efficient than the tasks of the world require, consider the *visual connections* those tasks demand. Ask yourself, if I or the observed individual were to be successful, or to work with less stress, what would we have to do that we are not now doing in this specific situation? Try to stick to a physical description of the task and the behavior involved instead of feelings or attitudes. Try to see the *Where Is It?*, *What Is It?*, *What Do I Do With It?* connections and decide which of those processes are least efficient.

SUMMARY: Harmon explained how we use our skeletal-muscular system to get ourselves in position to see clearly, to act on what we see. Wolff explains what we do when we interpret our lighted environment, when we see. We do not just open our eyes one day and the world appears whole to us. It only seems that way because we have learned to interpret this light stimuli through our moving doing experience. Wolff tells of the results of a study that showed "Monkeys reared with their eyeballs sewn shut have *no* sensible reaction to the light input when their lids are released. It is the result of extreme deprivation of experience." [13]

Because we *learn* to see, we do not have to live with symptoms and effects brought about by visual problems. We can learn to see more clearly, to see more of the information available to us, to do more with what we see and do it with less stress. We can change the way we see, which will affect what we do.

Wolff's working definition of vision packs the focus of this chapter into 68 words:

Vision is a sensorimotor system that utilizes light related energy for orientation and movement in space.

It is ordered by the process of *centering identification* and confirmed (or denied) by translation into action.

It develops and maintains itself by continuous self monitoring.

It produces visual space within which its processes can be assessed to define the person.

It is fundamental in the interaction of all those who have it. [14]

CHAPTER 6 FLAVORS OF OUR BEHAVIORAL CAKES

A recurrent theme of new science and Wolff's work is the dynamic, *interactive* relationship of human organism/world. All that we do in the world happens reciprocally; we act, we see the results, we act again. We react. It happens almost instantaneously; an integrated experience of doing and seeing. But to understand it we have to take that whole apart and look at visual behavior *as if* it had parts; we have to separately arrange them - somewhat artificially. In this chapter we'll consider the *tasks of the world* - what the world requires of us - and the *visual-behavior* that results from and creates our relationship with those tasks. The parts are arranged:

Introduction
Tasks
Visual-Behavior Connections
  • New Science view
  • Behavioral options
Behavioral/Visual Components
  • Sensory-Perceptual Integrity
  • Language
  • Spatial Comfort Zones
  • Sensory/Perceptual Mode Organization
  • Feedback - Error
  • Digital/Analog Integrity
  • Visualizing
Vision/Behavior Loop Diagram

INTRODUCTION

Behave we must. We cannot survive without action. From birth to death we live out a symphony of behavior, actions, composed by the organization of our physiology, our thoughts, actions and feelings. All of this constitutes our responses to our lighted, spatial world of gravity. We learn to live in this world through a series of tasks. There are stairs to climb, food to cook and eat, books to read, cars to drive, projects to complete, golf scores to improve, children to raise and teach. As we grow we gradually find out which of these tasks are the ones we want, which do we need, which can we actually accomplish. Our behavior is the plan and execution, *what we do*, to get what we want or need, what we *see*. We're successful when our behavior matches the tasks involved and gets for us what we want. We get positive feelings. These positive feelings are part of our total feedback system, telling us yes, this behavior works.

When what we do does not produce what we wanted, and we see that our actions don't work, the feelings produced (frustration, disappointment) become *part* of the clues available which tell us this is not the thing to do; to try another approach. Simplified control theory psychology.

> When we sense that what we have is not what we want, we generate behaviors that act on the world and, of course, on ourselves as part of the world[1]

A 12-15 month old toddler stood next to her mother while waiting in line at the post office, contentedly sucking a bottle she held. She did not seem to notice that her mother had moved to the counter 20 feet away from where she had been standing. The toddler didn't move, she was still in line. Then, apparently aware her mother had moved, she ever so slowly headed in that direction; her want to be with her mother pushed her visual-movement buttons: she visually located her mother out there in space (centering and identification) and used her visual feedback to guide her walking so that she ended up next to her mother. *Her visual want created her walking behavior; her accurate visual-movement match allowed her to get what she wanted.* She found out that she could do what she needed; one more step toward independence.

The game of everyday life for all of us follows these basic rules; but as we grow to adulthood our experiences gain greater complexity. Many tasks are at the level of visualization and thinking rather than at the physical level, but the fundamental principles remain the same.

TASKS

We have visual-movement abilities that can match certain events and forces in our world. Most of us have the necessary equipment to *potentially* get the job done. After all, it is human arms, hands, fingers, legs, thinking, and language which have created all that we see and know in the world outside of nature; our physical structures, buildings, roads, computers, our human institutions, family, government, education. Our task is to match our bodily equipment to the demands of the task. That match creates success. *When our behavior doesn't work - we can't do the task, we still have the potential to learn what we need to do to be successful.* That potential resides in our recognition of error, our feedback system. It is because we remember exactly how we did it so we can do it again or so we won't repeat our errors that we develop meaningful, productive behavior.

Wolff's professional task was to determine the quality of the match people made between the tasks of the world and the organization of their responses to those tasks. His framework asked what would a person need to do in order to be more successful? What was it about the way they organized their visual-movement action system that produced their errors?

Emily, a college student, was bothered that she had trouble finding her car in the parking lot; that she often got lost in a department store and didn't know which entrance she had come in. From an assessment of her visual abilities, Wolff related her spatial concerns to inefficient *visualization* skills, particularly with form and form relationships, and to her preference for wholes, rather than with the parts of things or situations.

Wolff used the *analytical, numerical examination data* he gathered along with *his observations and the symptoms Emily described* to construct his conclusion. The visual-spatial template he used gave the data a new form. He asked what visual-spatial demands do our tasks make on us? What skills, body equipment, and level of organization do we need to meet those demands?

He understood Emily's symptoms as *visual demands inherent in the task.* To know which door to go out requires visual notice of it; visually hooking it to some landmark - the name of the street it faces, the men's department where you entered. These are skills dependent upon the visual processes of centering and identification, form and form relationships, digital processing. Visualization, whether of land marks or the specific sequence of movements (two rights and three lefts), determines how we find our way out, mentally visualizing the car in the parking lot in relation to the entrance.

Wolff looked at Emily both through the "eye of the flesh", his analytical observations and the symptoms presented, and through his "eye of reason", the sense he made of his scientific observations *in light of the behavior of his patients and the tasks they attempted.* Many professionals look only at the human behavior side of the human/world relationship. They analyze, count and describe what and how the person performed; they do not consider the nature of the *tasks* involved in that behavior and their inherent *visual-spatial demands.*

Tasks and Behavior - A Reciprocal Arrangement

To add the awareness of the visual-spatial component to your repertoire try some of these:

1: Think of a maintenance activity at home that you either like or dislike: _____ or Think of an activity that is part of your work world that you either like or dislike: _____

2. Try to describe the actual, physical/mental task requirements. Write them down and save your description so you can add to it with other exercises in this chapter. For example: Where are you when you do it? Where do you have to look to do it? Is it loaded with sequences, does it have a high degree of visualization, does it require judgments and generalizations, is it more visual or auditory, etc.

3. Take specific time to observe *someone else* doing a particular task, fixing a snack, making a bed, a child getting ready to do homework.

Using the same frame work as above, try to describe exactly what *the physical/spatial parts* of the task are.

VISUAL BEHAVIOR CONNECTIONS

When patients in visual training experience the transfer of more efficient visual processing into their everyday lives, they often have trouble connecting the observed changes in what they can do with their improved visual skills. Yes, they admit, the skills in the training room are certainly better: their tracings are more accurate, they can maintain stereopsis on the slides, they see differences at far and near with the training lenses; they can process larger amounts of information, but, is that *really* the reason they aren't as tired at the end of the day, that they need less sleep, that they now accurately balance their checkbook, that they can read a map and actually get somewhere? They have an even longer stretch to make the connection that their improved visual skills are the reason they can now follow a complicated conversation, come to decisions more quickly, lay out an efficient strategy for reorganization of their department at work with little stress.

People bring to visual training a wide variety of explanations and metaphors for how their behavior came to be; but almost no expectation of the *behavioral enhancement* visual training can provide. From their old science frame of reference they try to plug in new science answers to their queries of "What will visual training do for me?" This inevitable incompatibility creates confusion until their experience in everyday life catches up with their experience in visual training. Cause and effect, linear thinking does little to ease the confusion. It gets in the way of understanding how vision influences and drives everyday behavior. A brief review might be helpful.

The "New Science" View of Behavior:

Linear descriptions of the visual influence in human behavior such as sensation/perception/concepts/vision◄—►behavior misrepresent the point of view from which Wolff's model developed. David Bohm, physicist, offers a metaphor for visualization that comes much closer to describing how vision influences all of behavior. It is the idea of a cake. Instead of thinking about our sensory information, our mental activity, our actions, our emotions operating as if they are separate systems within the same machine (body), Dr. Bohm invites us to use as a metaphor the relationship of the ingredients in a cake. The flour, eggs, sugar, chocolate do not change into something else, but they become *integrally related* to all the other ingredients in the mix and that *new relationship* is what we recognize as cake. The separate ingredients are all present in the new cake, but only in this *integrated way:* what a fitting metaphor for vision and behavior, as viewed from Wolff's point of view.

The unique, personal flavor of our own "behavioral cake" results from the mixing of our genetics/physiology + experience + learning. Once our cake is baked, we can still find the predominant visual ingredient within our total behavior, just as we recognize chocolate or lemon cakes. Our behavioral flavor includes what we *don't do* as well as what we actually do.

Behavioral Options - *A Fully Baked Cake*

All of us want to be effective. We feel better when we get what we want. We come closest to getting what we want when our abilities match up to the demands life presents. If we find that our best efforts do not get us what we want, we may momentarily find comfort with clichés: We're only human; people make mistakes after all; we're just people, so what can we expect?, it's okay. *Rarely do we see our mistakes as behaviors (cakes) that could be modified if the ingredients were arranged differently.*

Wolff highlighted this human predicament of task-behavior matching one morning when Karen, his daughter, professional colleague and author of the next chapter, visited with him in the hospital while he recovered from surgery. Getting ready to leave, she gathered up some papers with the comment, "I should get started on the quarterly tax reports for the office, but I'm afraid to start; I don't want to make a mistake."

"Then don't," said her dad.

WHAT! 'I don't want to make a mistake;' is a common enough scenario; but, *'Then don't.'?!* Of course! Literally, it's just that simple. If we could look at what a task required, gather up the necessary information, anticipate what has to be done, look at what we're doing so our product matches the intent, we'd have it. We wouldn't make a mistake. Cinchy! - as Katie, Wolff's grand daughter, would say. Cinchy... and overwhelming. Who can do this?

By his 'Then don't' comment Wolff was neither suggesting that we should try to live error free lives nor that it is possible. But in his way he put Karen's wish - I don't want to make a mistake -into a perspective most of us never see. If you don't want to make a mistake, it is physically possible to increase your chances for success: to have a choice. We can do what the task requires and be successful; or we can ignore some part, forget to plan the next move, stop interpreting what we see and we will be certain to make a mistake.

What a burden if we think the only way we could increase our chances for success would be to manage this with conscious, deliberative effort. In reality, our success is instantaneous and outside our direct, conscious control, *yet it is accessible for modification and adaptation.* We can learn to see more, to see more accurately, to interpret more clearly what we see, to increase the likelihood that we can match the tasks to be done.

Wolff's comment puts us square in the middle of the idea of responsibility (response - ability). How do we respond to the demands of the world? If we really do have a choice in the accuracy of our responses, would we be satisfied to excuse our inattention, to shirk the effort of planning alternatives and comfort ourselves with, we all make mistakes, or nobody's perfect? As comforting as those clichés are, most of us would still choose fewer errors and greater success in our lives *if we could!* By his "Then don't" comment Wolff highlighted the essence of his work: that there is a greater possibility for success, for getting what we want than we've imagined; that by enhancing what we see, by literally looking at what we're doing, we can do more and do it more easily.

Megan, an 8th grader, received 4 F's and 2 D's on her most recent report card. She had struggled with grades like this for a great part of her school life. Her parents had made special efforts so that

Megan did not describe herself solely by her school performance; but her most fervent wish was to succeed in school. When, after a few months of visual training and educational therapy, F papers changed to D's and occasional C's, Megan was certain she was finished with training. Her goal had been to get rid of the F's. She could not envision anything better than that. She was introduced to a bigger picture: that this improvement (which she had thought would never be possible) could continue, that she *could actually learn to do what was required* to get A's and B's. Her beaming face spoke the words she couldn't find. Megan didn't want to make a mistake. Wolff's work with her said, then don't. The change in her visual status and academic behavior responded, okay, I don't have to anymore.

To increase your awareness of behavioral choice try this:

1: Think of a task you would like to be able to do better, or learn if you don't already know how. It might be gourmet cooking, golf, getting places on time. Task:_____. Think about what a person would have to know how to do in order to do this task. Begin with the end in mind. They would have to:

1.____; 2.____; 3.____, Be as specific as possible.

2. OTHERS: Observe specific behaviors in someone you see frequently. Pick a particular situation: specific sports performance, interpersonal relationship moment, a student and an assignment. What did the person actually do? Try to describe what a video camera would see. If they were not successful (in your mind), *what did they leave out, what didn't they do?*

VISUAL BEHAVIOR COMPONENTS

What did Megan *not do* that produced F grades? What did she *learn to do* to create educational success? What are the behavioral ingredients we can improve in order to increase our chances for successful doing in the world?

Sensory/Perceptual Integrity

If we know of no physical or mental impairments in another person, and we have few of our own, it's easy to identify with them. They are like us - normal. We explain whatever differences we recognize as personal preferences or learning styles, and allow that we each have different past experiences. Rarely do we glimpse that the behavioral differences we recognize are related to how we do things; how our experience of ourselves, our experience in the world and what we've done with it are truly unique. Most of us don't see the dominance of vision in the organization of our sensory/perceptual modes in our everyday behavior; but, it's there all the same.

Vision seems to coordinate, to direct the symphony of human behavior. Because it is so automatic for most of us, we are not aware of the meshing of our separate-yet-integrated sensory-perceptual systems. It takes someone like Jess Oppenheimer to let us see how it is when one's systems do not mesh effectively. Mr. Oppenheimer, as you may remember, discovered as an adult that he did not have binocular fusion (see Chapter 5). Here is his description of how that distortion of his visual-spatial knowledge affected and controlled his *spatial awareness of sound.* It's helpful to remember that Mr. Oppenheimer was as normally functioning an adult as most of the rest of us. His atypical experiences were just not observable to others. But he says it better:

"As my space world began to take form with relation to sight, a similar effect became apparent in sound. I was becoming stereophonic also, and in the same relationship as the sight.

"Before the improvement began, I could not tell where a sound was coming from. I could not carry a tune and I could not listen to music. I could hear it, but it did not become music to me."

As his binocularity became more efficient..."Sound began to have a position in space, instead of happening at my ear. That is right, happening at my ear. ...If it (the sound) was a sharp or very loud sound, I would hear it as though the eardrum was an overloaded speaker, with a harsh edge of distortion to the sound that was physically painful. ...it had no position in space. I knew it came from the right side because it was loud in my right ear...my senses did not tell me where it was in space. ...If there were two sounds at the same time, I would hear one with one ear and the second with the other ear, but I did not fuse them, just as I did not fuse the vision of the two eyes, but tried to keep track of them independently. ...I used the same system for listening to music. One ear, for instance, hearing the singer and the other the accompaniment;...

"...as the mental ability to handle the images from the two eyes improved, due to the lessening of muscle imbalance, so exactly did this aural condition improve, and voices started coming from people's heads and from loudspeakers, rather than having a separate existence..."[2]

The article provides more detail than is given here, but from this excerpt we get a sense of how the distance sensory/perceptual modes of *vision and audition are linked in their spatial organization, and orchestrated by the visual process.* Mr. Oppenheimer lets us see the *visual* connections to seemingly unrelated behavior, inability to sing or listen to music.

Usually we observe only the net, behavioral, effect of a person's internal sensory-perceptual organization. We tend to project our own experience onto others. If we see no evidence to the contrary, *we assume the inner experience of another is similar to ours.* Mr. Oppenheimer lets us know otherwise and the insight gained from him helps explain what is often, to us, inexplicable behavior. Instead of saying, "I can't understand what makes a person do that!", we may be able to know that a person's internal world could be truly different from ours. The other's behavior becomes logical if we understand its sensory-perceptual genesis.

To increase your awareness of the integrity of sensory-perceptual systems:
1: Identify situations where you use two or more sensory-perceptual systems when the task seems to require only one.

Such as: Putting on your glasses (visual) when talking on the telephone (auditory), because you *listen* better. Preferring music or TV as an auditory background when reading or studying (visual); find you do not *listen* as well as you would like when you cannot *see* a lecturer (a crowded auditorium and someone blocks your view). Ability to integrate background noise, (traffic, children playing, etc.) with whatever visual task you're doing.

2. OTHERS: Notice when people read aloud - signs along the road, directions on the bottle. Observe the degree of hand and body gestures when someone is speaking.

Visual - Verbal Matching: Language

Jamie, a 4th grader, brings the connection of language and vision in the cake of human behavior from the theoretical to the observable. Jamie scored well on achievement tests; he was pleasant and well-behaved. But his papers did not get handed in; he did not put his name on them; he almost never followed class directions without error or individual repetition from the teacher. These behaviors have a high value in most school rooms. Jamie's mother added her own tales of what she considered to be noncompliance with verbal directions at home. The conclusion by all, teachers and parents: Jamie had primary difficulties with *language, with "auditory processing*". The logic is strictly traditional, since the symptoms involved words and Jamie did not have a hearing loss, he must not understand what he *hears;* hence he has an *auditory* problem. Another example of natural cause and effect, linear logic.

During the evaluation of his visual skills Jamie did not comply correctly to verbal directions for movement sequences, i.e, "Hop to me on one foot, turn around and go back on the other foot." When pressed, he could repeat the directions; he had heard and remembered them. What he did not do was translate the words into meaningful movement sequences, behavior. From this point of view, his "auditory processing" problem took on a much broader behavioral pattern. It related as much to visualizing and movement sequences as to listening. Maybe that's what meaningful listening is.

Because language seems to be auditory/oral phenomena, its role in visual processes and development is usually overlooked. Since we hear words, many of us focus primarily on that auditory base when we think of language. There are think-with-words enthusiasts among language experts just as there are eyes-as-camera buffs in the professional disciplines dealing with sight and vision. Words are vocal sounds attached to *experience. It is almost impossible to separate the visual-movement experience from the spoken or written word.* But in either/or fashion we habitually use "visual or verbal". In reality, it's both. Words (language) *and* vision have an *integrated* relationship. And what affects one affects the other.

Wolff used the terms *visual - verbal matching* to describe these relationships. When a task requires a higher component of visual information the label "VISUAL-verbal" applies; when the task is led by auditory demand, the description would be "visual - VER-BAL". For people with sight, there is almost no time when pure auditory experience occurs without simultaneous visual experience and vice versa.

Rudolf Arnheim, in *Visual Thinking,* comes closest to describing the intimate connection of our visual experience with our language abilities. He says:

> Nobody denies that language helps thinking. What needs to be questioned is whether it performs this service substantially by means of properties inherent in the verbal medium itself or whether it functions indirectly, namely, by pointing to the referents of words and propositions, that is, to facts given in an entirely different

medium. Also, we need to know whether language is indispensable to thought.[3]

The baby's first utterances of "mama", "dada", "ball" are sounds that only become meaningful, representational words to the child *when they connect* with that child's physical, visual/movement/tactual/gustatory/olfactory experience. Otherwise they are just babbling sounds. The speech syllables of *ma,ma* come to stand in for the physical, *visually recognized form* of the person our language denotes as mother. All the sensory, perceptual information experience that person has hooks onto those sounds. The sounds become meaningful *words which evoke the memory of that experience in the absence of its physical presence.* Without the visual, movement, sensory, perceptual experience, words would be collections of sounds only.

At the same time, verbal labels help us group similarities and differences so we can expediently organize multiple experiences under one label (concept). The word "fruit" stands in for a wide variety of experiences - visual, tactual, gustatory. The label allows us the luxury of economy; one label stands in for all the members of the group sharing similar attributes.

Another example of the integrated visual-verbal connection is the role of language in arithmetical computation. It critically sequences the mental operations involved. Whether one says "Twenty-seven *divided* by five" to represent $27 \div 5 = ?$ or "Five *divided* by twenty-seven" matters. The sequence of the words literally tells us what to do. For many beginning students this distinction of word order is irrelevant; consequently, they are apt to confuse the computational sequence and get an answer that's not appropriate to the visual sequence of digits. Arithmetical skills are neither visual *or* verbal, but visual *AND* verbal.

As Dr. Arnheim states:

> The visual medium (as contrasted with the auditory medium) is so enormously superior because it offers structural equivalents to all characteristics of objects, events, relations. The variety of visual shapes is as great as that of possible speech sounds, but what matters is that they can be organized according to readily definable patterns, of which the geometrical shapes are the most tangible illustration. The principal virtue of the visual medium is that of representing shapes in two-dimensional and three-dimensional space, as compared with the one-dimensional sequence of verbal language. This polydimensional space not only yields good thought models

of physical objects or events, it also represents isomorphi-
cally the dimensions needed for theoretical reasoning.[4]

More than one volume could be written on the nature of
language, thought and vision. Students of these fields, if not already
familiar with *Visual Thinking,* by Rudolf Arnheim, will find there
an extensive discussion of the theme that the realm of visual
experience is intimately, indivisibily available in language and often
allows for non-linear thinking which language tends to limit because of its linear, time-bound structure. David Bohm, physicist,
explains this organic mix of language, sensory-perceptual data, and
experience in *Thought As A System.* He says all are inextricably
bound together as thought and that they function almost like a
reflex; all there, all the time.

A real-life example of non-linear visual behavior is Barbara
McClintock's experience in genetics. She found she could project
her vast scientific experience onto her visual identification of
genetic changes, and could tell *by looking at the plants in the field* what
their genetic changes would be when she examined them in the
laboratory.

> Before examining the chromosomes, I went through the
> field and made my guess for every plant as to what kind
> of rings it would have - would it have one, two or three,
> small or large, which combination? And I *never made a
> mistake, except once.* When I examined that one plant I was
> in agony. I raced right down to the field. It was wrong; it
> didn't say what the notebook said it should be! I found
> that...I had written the number from the plant adjacent,
> which I had not cut open. And then everything was all
> right.[5]

Language serves us best when we have rich, experiential connections with the words we utter and read. The experiences originally
are largely visually driven. We understand the meaning of "deep"
and the concept of "depth" in the phrases, a deep topic, a deep
person, out of our depth, because we have experienced the physi-
cal/visual deep of water in the pool or a hole that we dug or saw.

*The form and structure of what we see become the raw materials of our
thinking and non-visual experiences.* More abstract concepts like *happy*,
and *democracy* carry within them a structure that can be visualized.
Happy is a relative term; happier than..., happy vs. sad - *visual,
sequential relationships* that we organize on a continuum, a balance
scale, a visual structure. We can make visual/graphic marks on

paper (neither signs nor symbols) to stand in for the ideas of happy or democracy; *visual forms* that correspond to those experiences. Try it: on a blank sheet let your pencil make marks that represent *happy* to you. Do not use symbols or letters, just happy marks. When Betty Edwards and Rudolf Arnheim did this activity with many of their students, they found greater similarity than dissimilarity among the marks people made. [6]

Contrarily, we can learn the sounds of language without strong experiential connections; as most of us non-French speaking children did when we sang "Frere Jacques". We uttered melodic syllables only, unconnected to meaning or past experience. Many children, and not a few adults, exhibit this mismatch between their visual and verbal behavior. What they say and what they do truly are two different things. They learn the melody, but not the meaning. When Mom asks Jack if he will be sure to put the garbage cans out by the curb and he says, "Yes", she tends to assume that means she'll see the cans at the curb at the appropriate time. Jack, on the other hand, knows the tune and inserts "yes" right on cue. His utterance does not necessarily connect to his action behavior. The cans will not make it to the curb.

When others present us with a mismatch, we most often rely on what we *see,* rather than on what we heard. Psychology tells us children learn what their parents do, not what they say. Parents who tell their children not to smoke more effectively convey that message if they, themselves, do not smoke. At some level we know that the cliché actions speak louder than words implies that it's the actions *seen* that are imitated; that it is vision that speaks louder than words.

This fundamental, reciprocal relationship between language and vision, shows up in everyday language behavior. Gwen, an adult who wanted to improve her general organization skills at work, happily reported just such an experience. She had been working on visualizing relationships and strengthening her visual analog processing skills, not on language per se. Yet one day she found she could understand a conversation between two other people, her daughter and her daughter's friend, as she overheard them while in another room. Gwen explained that the reason this was remarkable was that she had always found it so difficult to make connections, identify referents, keep sequences straight, when she listened to others converse, that she had long ago given up trying to understand. She was delighted when, *with seemingly no effort on her part*, she understood what her daughter and friend were talking about.

Principle: Language can be understood from a visual-spatial perspective; as a matching process of the visual and verbal systems rather than as a function of the auditory-language system alone. Words and their syntactical arrangement relate to the way we manage the visual-spatial characteristics of our experience. The thinking process itself goes beyond words alone, using visual-spatial modes and all perceptual data. The visual process and the auditory-language-process are *reciprocally* related.

To increase your awareness of the visual - verbal connection; try these:

1. SELF: Using the words below, close your eyes and see what mental association you make with them. *Notice what perceptual-sensory modality you use.* Even though the real experience of "chimes" has a very high auditory component, many people visualize playing chimes, with no auditory accompaniment, or seeing someone play them, also without primarily re-auditorizing the sound.

Check your mental imagery of: **fire engine wind children**

2. OTHERS: Observe someone giving directions or describing an event. What kind of words do they use? What perceptual modes do they emphasize? Are they actually descriptive or do they substitute, this, that, something, somewhere ? Often this kind of substitution indicates weak visual-verbal links.

Behavioral Space - Comfort Zones

You've undoubtedly played the familiar group game of Where-Shall-We-Sit? when you go with friends to the movies and restaurants. You, who prefers to sit in the back third of the theater, inevitably will be with someone who prefers the front third. The rules of this game require civility: Oh, it really doesn't matter; wherever you want to sit, you say while thinking, why would anyone want to sit so close (or so far away)? We each have our own place that seems so right to us; the location where we are the most comfortable. Unless confronted we often are not even aware that this is a choice. We just sit down, it seems. But when our right place and another's right place are not the same, we have to negotiate. We may accommodate; we may give in. We usually compromise; but, *we don't change our spatial preference.* Our spatial comfort in the tasks of everyday life reflects our visual orientation.

Our spatial preferences are part of our construct of what we call reality.

Restaurants and theaters are not the only places where our visual-spatial judgments and preferences affect our everyday behavior. Driving, especially with another in the car, can glaringly remind us of individual differences. Haven't you found yourself mentally muttering, 'Why must she drive so close to the car in front?', 'Why doesn't he stop behind the line instead of in the cross walk?' and other less factual comments. We each drive as we see, we each see differently. Intellectually we may know that we all do not see in the same way; but, most of us still find it hard to accept when others' behavior differs markedly from what we see.

If our warp rotation is to the right, we may have to keep correcting to stay in the middle of the lane; if we ignore our peripheral vision, changing lanes and crossing intersections may not be one of our strengths. The way we align the car, too far from or too far over lines on the pavement, matches our spatial preference in other tasks. If we visually pull space in towards us we will tend to stop short of the line; if we visually push space away, we'll probably stop with our front wheels past the line. No matter how diplomatic our back-seat driving, we'll have little influence in changing another's spatial orientation in driving. They, as we, literally drive the way they see, regardless of their "corrected" visual acuity.

Ray Barsch, clinical psychologist, used the terms *near-space*, *far-space* to describe those spatial areas where we seem most comfortable. Where do we retreat to consider a problem? Do we look at the ceiling or down at our knees? Which activities do we prefer, the near-space ones of knitting, painting, accounting or the far-space ones of golf, spectator sports. Do we want to sit in a booth or do we prefer the table in the middle of the room? Of course these behavioral preferences are not black and white. They result from many factors, but they *are spatial preferences.* The pattern of our preferences is reciprocally related to basic visual processes.

To increase awareness of your own and others' spatial comfort zones; try these:

1. A. Imagine yourself entering a movie theater, church, auditorium. You are early enough so that you have your choice of seats. Where would you automatically sit if you had your choice? If you were with others, recall the conversation in selecting seats. Did you give in to another's suggestions or was it your suggestion that

resolved the impasse? Think of the last three times you were in such a space, how consistent were your seating preferences?

2. Observe yourself the next time you drive and stop at an intersection. Are your front wheels over the line (if there is one) or did you stop so you can still see the line? When you pull into an angle parking place, look at the alignment of the car between the lines. Describe its spatial position.

3. Notice the spatial area of concern in people who visit you. Do they comment on the view out the window, what's on the walls, the carpet, the coffee table? Do they ignore the space around them and engage in conversation totally unrelated to their surroundings?

Modality Organization

Ears to hear with, eyes to see with, muscles to move us. It's common to think of each of our body's sensory-perceptual systems as separate entities - modes, working away at the job of processing the energy for which they seem designed. But in real life we use these modes of processing information in an integrated fashion, not one at a time. An example of how this works is what many of us do when faced with putting together an object from printed instructions such as a child's wagon, a mail-order lamp or an outdoor grill. You know how it goes: You line up the pieces and start to read. What's that again? You re-read, look at the pieces and read again. If it still doesn't make sense, what do you do next? Most of us will read it *out loud*. We'll move from an *eyes alone* task to an *eyes and ear* task. We may even read, say and touch the words, one at a time, trying to find a way the information can make sense to us. *Each task we face in this world calls upon particular sensory-perceptual-movement syntheses.* The most efficient completion of the task uses whatever sensory-perceptual modes the task requires.

Reading is an eyes only task. It's the fastest way to get information from the printed page. Listening is for ears. To do it we really don't need to swing feet or doodle on paper, although many of us add those supports. Listening and translating what we hear into meaningful chunks of information require less energy if we do it with ears alone.

To understand how these processing modes influence our total, everyday behavior we need to see the hierarchy of development we lived out in infancy and early childhood. As we grew, we practiced organizing particular sensory-perceptual (mode) combinations at special times and in given sequences. Our organization of a given mode moved from the simple to the complex; from dependence to independence. Sucking turned into chewing; random grabs turned into finger-poking, and later thumb-finger opposition; balancing the head led to sitting, rolling, crawling, walking. Babbling turned into words, sentences and paragraphs. All occurred while our *eyes were turned on.* We matched what we saw with everything else we did.

But we didn't do this all at once. Each sensory/perceptual mode flowered for a special developmental time. We practiced finding things with our hands, passing things from hand to hand, touching before we became involved in moving about independently through rolling, crawling, walking. We turned our early babbling into words and sentences after we moved independently. It took some time for us to be able to look and know and tell.

Our developmental energy, like a laser, concentrated on certain modes in particular sequence: gustatory, olfactory (mouth and nose); tactual (hands-skin); kinesthetic (moving about); auditory (listening, talking) and visual (gathering information with eyes alone). Each new developmental stage took us farther out into space, where we practiced ever increasing independence. Eventually, as independent visual processors, we connected ourselves visually to the horizon, to the stars and, through visualization, beyond our immediate space and time. Infancy is a developmental symphony, first the violins carry the melody, then the woodwinds, then the brass, *but they're all playing all of the time.* All of the sensory-perceptual modes operate simultaneously, organizing around the predominate theme of the moment. For those with sight, vision is ever present, a kind of glue to which the meaning of the others attach. The sight of the bottle lets the baby know food is on the way; the sight of mother across the room signals reaching and smiling.

This developmental hierarchy appears to be V A K T (O/G): Vision, Auditory (listening/talking), Kinesthetic (moving), Tactile (touching), Olfactory/Gustatory (smelling and tasting).

If the tasks of the world call for combinations of modalities that our skills cannot match, then we call upon developmental support. This may be systems from a previous developmental level, or systems that are more efficiently organized. When we cannot put the toy together from reading alone, we add audition - talking. When we cannot sit still and absorb the information in a lecture through listening alone, we add movement - doodling, fidgeting. When we're not sure if the flowers we see on the table are real or artificial, we add touch. *Whatever modality is insufficient to match the demands of a particular task calls forth support from earlier developmental modalities*, whether or not they are well organized.

The term *learning styles* commonly expresses this fact. In our growing up years many of us found a particular modality that worked well for us. So well that we substitute or add it to tasks that do not require it; we specialize. If we're very comfortable with listening and talking, we tend to talk our way through activities that are primarily visual-motor: following directions, reading, crafts, balancing a checkbook. If movement is our thing, we might gesture, rock, swing our legs, tap the table, underline and take notes so we can know what we see.

According to the concept of learning styles some of us are *auditory* learners, some *tactual,* some *kinesthetic,* some *visual.* This idea recognizes that *regardless of the demands of the task many people tend to process the information the world presents through a preferred modality.*

This is logical as far as it goes; but, the concept does not look at the cost to the individual: the limitations of time, energy and degrees of success caused by these adjustments. If the shortest distance between two points is a straight line, then a detour from that path takes longer and requires more energy. If reading the directions and doing what they say requires vision and movement, then saying them aloud, underlining, or asking somebody else, slows down the process and we use up energy that could be available for other things. It's inefficient.

Tasks in school are predominantly visual-movement with secondary demands of audition (listening and talking). There are few primary demands of specific movement (except in gym) and even fewer for touching. So to describe a student as an auditory or kinesthetic learner, tells us the degree to which this student does not easily match the demands of the classroom. They are *inefficient visual learners.* Wolff's work stood the idea of learning styles on its head. The consensus of the day puts many of us in the permanent boxes of auditory, or kinesthetic learners, as if we came that way and will remain there.

Wolff said these learning patterns were adjustments we had made to the visual-movement demands of tasks. We behaved that way because we had not learned how to do otherwise. We would continue those behaviors until there was some expectation that it could be different. Instead of offering a label or a crutch, his work presents the opportunity of sensory-perceptual flexibility: competence, because our modalities *can become efficient enough to handle whatever tasks we meet in the world.*

The sensory-perceptual modality organization most efficient for most tasks is VAKT. Many of us have other patterns. Someone who prefers to talk their information processing and likes to move - gesture, write, underline - may have AKTV as their modality organization. Once an individual's modality pattern is described, it can be used predictively to select tasks which that person will more easily accomplish.

To help increase your awareness of sensory/perceptual modality preference; try these:

1. You are at a party and meet someone with whom you exchange phone numbers. What would be the best way for you to remember the new number? Would you repeat it over and over to yourself? (auditory). Would you write down the number, knowing that the act of writing helps you remember? (kinesthetic). Would you associate the numbers or parts of the sequence with a familiar idea? (visualization). Ignore the whole process, have the person write down their own number and glue yourself to the paper, knowing there's no recalling the phone number without it?

2. OTHERS: Observe someone getting ready for a meeting, dinner party or some event where there's a bit of pressure. How do they stay on track? Mutter and describe out loud, but to themselves, that they've put the flowers on the table, the nuts in the serving dishes and now will put the ice in the glasses... (auditory). Or do they have a checklist to which they constantly refer and the loss of which would create panic? (visualization crutch). Or do they just go ahead and do all that is required, operating from some unobservable mental design, able to get it all done, even with interruptions of phone calls or children? (efficient visualization/movement).

Feedback

The bump of your car's right tire on the gravel of the shoulder of the freeway breaks your mental reverie and you quickly turn the steering wheel to the left. Your newborn's wails subside as you rub her back and your relief is palpable. Backrubbing was the fourth behavior on your list of what to do, right after food, dry diapers and walking the floor. Your success in keeping the car on the road and attending to a new baby depends on how you use your built in system of feedback.

Feedback is the sensory-perceptual information we use to *continually guide our movements.* The visual, auditory, tactile information of the tires hitting the gravel jerks our kinesthetic system into action. We know just how much to turn the wheel because our visual feedback tells us yes, the car is in its proper position in the lane; our auditory information tells us, yes, this is how tires-on-pavement should sound; our tactile-kinesthetic information says, yes, this is the degree of smoothness we expect. All is well, no further adjustments necessary.

Many people who are perpetually late often express bewilderment at how others can get ready and appear on time. Even though they value being on time, they often feel or are told that their lateness is because they just don't care enough. If they really wanted to, they'd be ready on time. That's a judgment based on looking at their behavior only from the outside. Getting-ready-on-time behavior looks different from the inside-out.

Getting ready on time means *matching what you are doing to an external time sequence.* If one just starts getting ready and follows an internal-only program (bath, pick out clothes, personal stuff) without looking at the clock, then punctuality will be left to the fates. It is the feedback information the clock provides that directs the actions of people who get ready on time. They know how much time they have, *what part of their sequence they may have to alter.* They weave time and actions together. They utilize feedback.

Powers and Glasser explained in Chapter 2, that people function as independent control systems. Behaving something like a thermostat, we FEED the information *that results from our action* BACK into our action system. This information acts as guide, sensor, director of our future actions(feed forward). We use feedback to know whether or not we're on the right track or should try an alternative. But we can also ignore it and not modify our behavior.

E.W. Deming's concept of total quality so much in the business management news these days grows out of this control theory concept. It relies on collecting data that can be used as feedback to show whether or not decisions and procedures actually produce what they were designed to do.

One of the primary premises of Wolff's work is that improved visual processing and behavior depend upon *efficient utilization of the feedback information that vision provides to the whole organism.* Visual training patients have prisms, various lenses and machines that help create stereoscopic experience. These activities, described in Chapter 7, are designed to help them recognize the visual feedback signals that are naturally there. *Vision guides our movements, our movements verify what we see.* The way we use our feedback information affects our total behavior. We've already met the librarian who ignored the visual information of patrons approaching her desk to check out books while she continued her solitary stamping of date cards. Children ignore parts of their visual field and the information available to them when they continue their work after the teacher has given a general direction, such as "Put your social studies away and take out your math book." They may require their name to be called to know what's going on in the room. The phrase *paying attention* means that we use our feedback data to guide our behavior. This youngster was paying attention - to the work in front of him; but, he did not incorporate what he heard in his spatial surround (feedback) to guide new actions.

Errors

We know, we know: To err is human... and err we do, usually with great chagrin, anger and occasional profanity. David, a nine year old, said out loud what many of us think. "If I don't play, I can't make a mistake, and then I can't lose." Since winning, being first and best, is so ingrained in our culture many of us whistle some form of David's theme song. But few of us can take David's extreme position literally. We do play; we have to, the world and our developmental energy demand it. A paradox: We want to be successful - a state where we don't make many, if any, errors; where we can rest, sure that we can do it! But, the only path to this kingdom of confidence goes through the land of *ERROR*. It is there where our tools of feedback let us discover what works and what doesn't. Only in this land of error do we learn! Success only emerges from what we've learned. So our kindergarten maxim of if at first you don't succeed, try, try again, comes full circle. The way we deal with error is determined by how efficiently we use our feedback system. It doesn't matter if we're trying to feed ourselves, pour milk in a glass, adjust our rear-view mirror, improve our golf swing, calm an upset child, close a business deal, the path to success is the same: try something, *see what happens*, modify what was tried the first time and *see what happens*. This is totally impossible without sensory-perceptual feedback which relies on error to work.

Control theory explains that frustration and negative feelings are part of our error-signal system, telling us we're on the wrong track, to change course. Satisfaction and pleasure tell us that what we're doing works; our path is one we want; so we continue. Too often we separate these emotions from the behavior that creates them. Then we see them in isolation, outside the context of sensory-perceptual integrity. Linear thinking says it is an event that causes us happiness or unhappiness. Control theory says these feelings are signals from our internal process and our own actions. From the reductionist stimulus-response framework, we tend to deal with the emotion separately, thinking that how we feel is the main event. We don't pay as much attention to the information feelings give us about what we're doing.

For error information to help, it must actually be integrated into our sensory-perceptual-action systems. If it isn't, we do not learn new behavior. Since our total behavior has such high visual direction and operates so reflexively, it follows that much of the error information available to us is visual. Enhancement of our visual feedback system allows us to incorporate error information much more efficiently. It makes learning new behaviors much easier. If we do not see the error, we may not visualize a more appropriate response and may stick with behavior that doesn't get us what we want or take us where we want to go.

Digital/Analog Processes

"We left home at 3:00 p.m., arrived at our hotel by 10:00. The next day we visited with my sister and then we went to Disney World. And then later we went to the beach." This was Vicki's response to "How was your vacation?" In order to tell about her vacation Vicki listed in sequential order the *specifics* of what they did. Her husband Bill, on the other hand, answered, "The weather was awful; the people were great. I hated to come home." Same trip, different sensory-perceptual-action organization of the experience. Vicki looked for the bits, the sequences; Bill saw larger chunks of experiential data. Both organized their vacation experience according to the way they saw it.

Vicki's and Bill's different styles of organizing sensory-perceptual-action information highlight two functions of the visual-movement process that Wolff termed *digital and analog*. Vicki's sequential description emerged from her emphasis of the digital function; Bill's leaned toward the analog. He packaged his information according to main ideas, and probably could retrieve sequential information if pressed; but, his use for that data was as a support for his bottom line.

The digital process can be understood best by thinking about the information we get from a digital clock. It shows us only the present, a minute at a time, ever sequencing those minutes in linear fashion. The digital process allows us to do that, to see one thing at a time, to focus on the parts, to line up those parts in sequential, one-at-a-time order so that we can make sense (analog) of what we see.

We instantaneously compile that data to make generalizations - combine perceived similarities. Aha! When I see four lines of equal length arranged so they enclose space and are in the relationship we call right angles, I'll call that configuration *square*. With this new idea of squareness I won't have to digitally process those four lines and their relationship every time I see them. The new idea is an analog (an expression of similarities). I can use it instantaneously to describe other relationships. "My book is square", "My room is square", "That field is square." Dissimilar things can have something in common that is not immediately observable until that mental generalization is laid on them. *Squareness* is something *we do*, not an attribute that is given to us by the environment. The analog process allows us to create new ideas from the bits and pieces of digital data lying around in our experience. Aha!, we can say Aha!

We create analogs from our experience and we have organized the tasks of the world within these functions. Wolff always asks us to see *task demands and our response as reciprocal*, never as one or the other. To describe that kind of relationship he preferred the labels: DIGITAL-analog or digital-ANALOG, depending upon the primary demand of the task. DIGITAL-analog tasks/behaviors include arithmetical computation, following directions, describing the plot of a story, devising an action plan for business. Those with a digital-ANALOG demand - derive meaning from the observed parts; seeing similarities and differences: arithmetic word problems - mathematical thinking; finding the theme of the story, the quality of the characters; creating a vision of what strategy will best meet the demands of the current business climate.

We use both processes. We don't operate with half a brain. We can have no generalizations without data to generalize; we will know very little if we have only sequential bits of information and cannot see how they fit together.

Much has been written about right/left brain behavior which taps into the digital-analog functions; but the right/left brain descriptions emerge from the traditional, part-thinking of linear science, itself a process weighted in the digital direction. That view ascribes behaviors to one side of the brain OR the other. People often describe themselves as "right brained", meaning they are not so good at mathematical computation, prefer art, music, as expressive modes; or "left brained", good at sequential patterns, language based activities, poor at metaphors, visualization. Wolff saw these functions differently, as reciprocal rather than discrete, human perception and thought require both, working as a complimentary, unified process. "Right/left brain" or "digital/analog" the human actually functions indivisibly.

In real life we find that our make-up, our experiences, our visual warps conspire to make many of us more comfortable when our digital-analog scale tips more in one direction or the other. As with modality preferences, we often specialize. But that leaves us at a disadvantage since the tasks of the world require from us more nearly equal digital/analog skills; BOTH/AND not either/or. So we choose.

For those more comfortable with DIGITAL-analog tasks, professions with a heavy sequential component are probably a first choice; engineering, law. Those preferring a heavier digital-ANALOG dose would be more comfortable with professions where planning, identifying pertinent issues, seeing patterns, projecting, making connections were the requirements. As in his descriptions of other human behaviors, Wolff's work helps us see that we cannot fully understand human behavior without understanding the sensory-perceptual-action demand of tasks that people are trying to do. What is the visual demand (in the broad sense) of those tasks? How do the people match their sensory/perceptual/movement systems to those demands?

People who have become myopic, (nearsighted), who pay great attention to information in their central visual field often can find detail upon detail in a task or situation. The parts of the task may be most important to them. Wolff once described that way of seeing as "Lots of angels dancing on the head of a pin." It is no accident that professions with heavy loads of sequential detail in their practice often have as practitioners a high percentage of people with myopia. Some come with that particular visual adaptation which made that profession attractive to them in the first place; they were good at those skills. Some acquired the myopia as a permanent adjustment to the heavy near, digital visual demand inherent in the preparation and practice of these professions. Either way, the world/behavior interconnection cannot be severed.

Visualization

"How am I supposed to concentrate on driving when you keep asking me where I'm going?" says the caption in an editorial cartoon picturing an irritated political leader addressing his back-seat hecklers. All of us can know where we're going because we can visualize.

The role of visualization was discussed in detail in chapter 5. *Visualization is that foresight which allows us to bring past, learned experience into the present and combine it with a projected plan of action.* Not only do we know where to look (centering) and recognize what we see (identification), we know what we can do with what we see. Visualization behavior allows us to function independently and with relative confidence. It is the hallmark of leadership, whether personal, corporate or political.

Max DePree, president of Henry Miller Corporation and author of *Leadership is an Art*[7] says, "The first responsibility of a leader is to define reality," and "The only kind of leadership worth following is based on vision." Humming a Renshaw-Harmon tune on the importance of movement, DePree says, "Leaders are obligated to provide and maintain momentum." He explains, "Momentum comes from a *clear vision* of what the corporation ought to be, from a well-thought-out strategy to achieve that vision..."

The leadership skills Mr. DePree describes above are equally important in personal development, in attaining genuine maturity and independence. The degree to which we reach these developmental goals rests on our knowing what to do - our ability to visualize behaviors that solve life's problems.

Did you, like most of us, harbor the teenage fantasy that once you got to the land of adulthood you'd be free of the *I don't know what to do* anxiety? No more would you have to agonize over how to start a conversation, what fork to use at a banquet, how to break off a relationship, what college or career to choose. You'd know! How long did it take you to discover that the nirvana-like state of certainty and assurance you assumed went with the right to vote, drink and pay taxes dissolved on the horizon? Adulthood carries its own challenges to our need to know; the struggle and anxiety seem to remain but now it's who can I marry, is this the right job or career, how do I become a good parent, how can I help my aging parents?

That need for confidence, that need to know you know what to do seems built into the human condition. We'd like to have it ourselves and we certainly want to find it in others. We call it effectiveness; we call it leadership. But whatever we call it, we want the people we consult and rely on to have it. We assume our doctor will know what to do when we bring our aches and fevers to the office; we want our attorney to know what to do when our youngster calls from the police station; we want our congressional representatives and president to know what to do when international strife or domestic threats appear. We feel overwhelmed when we or those we rely on do not know what to do.

Joe thought his problem was anxiety. He described to his psychologist feeling overwhelmed, too much to do, too many time pressures, judgments from his boss for things that were falling between the cracks. If he just didn't feel bad, he could handle the job pressures, he thought. As he described what his job entailed and how he handled the day to day routine, it became apparent that Joe did not know what to do with many of the papers that came across his desk. He had no system for dealing with interruptions, priorities, seemingly unrelated stacks of papers. Joe was not in charge; his paper work bossed him around. Joe's psychologist taught him some anxiety-reducing behaviors; things he could do when the feelings associated with anxiety appeared. In addition to these coping skills, Joe began visual training and learning therapy. This gave him the opportunity to strengthen his visualization skills.

With structured guidance he could begin to visualize one piece of his job puzzle at a time. What did he want? Longer work times with no interruptions. What would that entail? Doing something with the interruptions. What system could he invent to handle it? A schedule, a list to keep track of interruptions to be handled at a more appropriate time, closing his office door. How could he learn to ask himself these questions about other tasks? By understanding visualization and its roots in the total visual process.

The practice of visualization has become incorporated into the training for developing human potential. Sports performers visualize themselves flawlessly going through their routines. Patients with illnesses visualize themselves having mastery, actively altering their illness's course. Sales personnel learn to visualize themselves successfully closing a sale. Spiritual meditation relies heavily on visualization. It seems that in the cake of human behavior, vision and its powerful visualization component are major ingredients.

Visualization depends on the ability to see, literally, events/objects related to the larger visual field (context); to hold what you see and relate it to what you already know. Wolff designed visual training activities that allowed patients to experience feedback in the visualization process, to check their progress, to learn it as any skill can be learned.

Most of us have the potential to visualize; many of us do not employ the skill when it could be effective. We say, "I don't know," and move on as if that recognition is the end of a cycle instead of the beginning of a visualization process.

Stephen Covey tells a graphic story of the role of visualization in leadership.

> Envision a group of producers cutting their way through the jungle with machetes. They are the producers (the problem solvers). They're cutting through the undergrowth, clearing it out.
>
> The managers are behind them, sharpening their machetes, writing policy and procedure manuals, holding muscle development programs, bringing in improved technologies and setting up working schedules and compensation programs for machete wielders.
>
> The Leader is the one who climbs the tallest tree, surveys the entire situation and yells, "wrong jungle"![8]

We hope and wait for leadership; we yearn to live more satisfying, effective lives. Visualization as the keystone of our visual behavior will help us stay out of the wrong jungles.

It is possible to intentionally learn, practice and teach visualization and to know its power in our lives.

THE BEHAVIOR VISION LOOP

The diagram that follows is a digital, linear attempt to show the continual regeneration of behavior and the integration of all systems:

TASK

MOVEMENT/vision (incorporates all aspects of visual-movement process)

RESULT (task is successfully completed or an error is produced)

FEEDBACK this information determines the next TASK (error = try alternative MOVEMENT; success = select alternate TASK)

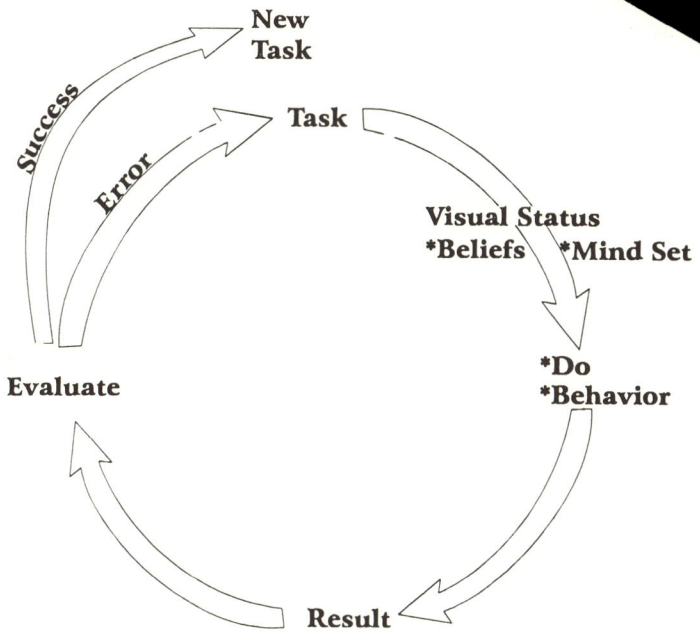

THE BEHAVIOR VISION LOOP

MMETRY AND DYNAMIC BALANCE

before Bruce Wolff passed away, he was asked "If y_ _ate just one thought from all you have learned, what woul_ _?" He replied, "symmetry, balance, everything in its place". Those who were with him at the time heard a few elegant, simple, but powerful words. He was referring to the dynamic balance within the binocular visual system and the bilateral motor system, as well as the dynamic balance between them. Powerful words, because these systems are inherent in all of us and affect all human behavior.

The transformation of the individual toward reorder and restructure, and having everything in its place and balanced, began in 1946 during the years my father called "The Skeffington House". "Dr. A. M. Skeffington," said Wolff, "was a master of ferreting out and disseminating information from other disciplines."[1] Though Skeffington's background was the eye and its ability to resolve, he began the:

> marshaling of the mind and body into ever broadening concepts by orchestrating the developmental concepts of Arnold Gesell, the perceptual concepts of Sam Renshaw, the intellectual concepts of Halstead, the environmental concepts of Darell Boyd Harmon, and the educational concepts of Newell Kephart and Emmett A. Betts. [2]

Through this remarkable integration of information from these men, Skeffington spent his lifetime developing a holistic theory of vision, bringing it from a singular sensory system, to a dual effector motor sensory system. He saw that vision had emerged as the dominant process in man, pervasive in all human behavior.

Equally important was Skeffington's concern with the biologically unacceptable nearpoint demands which led to the clinically derived *non-corrective* nearpoint plus *lens*. This change in thinking provided an alternative viewpoint of the traditional refractive error and acuity as the sole criteria for lens application. Wolff said "research facilities were unavailable to Skeffington at that time, and so he insisted on clinical verification from all his associates. It was from this clinical application of his theory that behavioral optometry was born."[3] Bruce Wolff had entered into the

"Skeffington House" at probably one of the most exciting of times. He began his clinical practice in 1949, in Cincinnati, Ohio, and it became a hotbed of creativity and research.

My life began in 1946, during the beginning of the "Skeffington House" and, as a youngster, I remember traveling around the country to various cities where my father and others lectured at seminars or optometric congresses. A special treat was gathering and spending time at the "shack" as Skeffington's home on the Merrimac River was called. Wherever these men met the scenario was always the same; late night bull sessions where theory was debated, formulated and rehashed some more. I remember falling asleep listening to these conversations night after night and wondering if these "working vacations", as they were called, were typical of everyone's vacations. Eventually my father's world enveloped me and became an inseparable part of my life. To step away and write about what has become so much a part of me has not been easy. My journey from the "Skeffington House" to the "Wolff House" has brought back many memories of a family that worked together for many years and truly believed in what had developed into a new way of thinking.

The transformation of the individual toward reorder and restructure with "everything in its place" and balanced could only be accomplished, Wolff said, with the "reasonable adherence to and support of the treatment program prescribed." More specifically, this involved the appropriate lens application and/or visual behavior training (VBT) and recommendations to other disciplines when appropriate. In this chapter I will briefly discuss lenses but will give particular attention to VBT which has been my life's work for 27 years.

The end result of these bull sessions that lasted into the wee small hours of the morning represented unparalleled growth in the field and a shift in: (1) how the optometrist used lenses, (2) how he viewed and interacted with the patient, and (3) how he related his ability to extrapolate from the case history, observations and measurements, the patient's performance to and for real life situations.

PERSONAL NORM

The interview of the patient now took on new meaning. The purpose of the case history was to gather pertinent information which established the *personal norm* of that individual — *how everything worked and fit together for him so he could hook into the real world and function*. Wolff said "the personal norm is totally unique to that individual and is the most important, yet the most neglected viewpoint in clinical management."[4] Personal norms are derived from the patient's complaints, his ocular, health and developmental histories, and educational, social, occupational and recreational demands. These relevant bits of information become pieces of a puzzle that gradually begin to fit together forming patterns of behaviors. Historically, the complaints of the patient were concerned with the elimination of certain uncomfortable symptoms or the awareness of seeing differently since the last exam. This contrasted with the need to do things differently or to do the things they would really like to do, but had considered beyond their reach. Wolff had always said it was up to the optometrist to address both the patient's wants and needs and to let them know that alternatives existed which would bring results, at some point, along the path of restructure and rebalance. He always felt "abnormal individuals were rare, that the vast majority were just normal people in difficulty who could be helped in varying degrees depending on:

1. The available potential of the individual;
2. The extent of substitute and compensating behaviors;
3. The value placed on different, but better performance to the individual and those immediately involved;
4. Reasonable adherence to and support of the treatment program prescribed."[5]

1. THE AVAILABLE POTENTIAL OF THE INDIVIDUAL.

We are all, for the most part, born with the essential parts and necessary pieces we need in order to develop this bilateral-binocular visual-motor system to its fullest potential. But still, there are no guarantees that this will happen in any of us. Pathology accounts for only a small percentage of the population where it may affect the available potential. The gene matrix, or heredity, that which makes us unique unto ourselves, provides the general direction in which that person will develop. Even when eye pathology is involved, or birth defects such as Down Syndrome or cerebral palsy, the available potential of that individual may surprise you. Bruce Wolff said, "Never underestimate the intelligence of a child." As Darell Boyd Harmon explained,

> The child at birth is neither complete in size or in the
> structure of each of his bodily systems that will eventually

work together in making him a coordinated and integrated human organism. The growing up process from infancy through adolescence gives that person time to literally 'grow' and fill in and complete all those sensory, nervous, bony, muscular, and visceral structures.[6]

There can be many pitfalls along the way. Wolff said "one had to be careful not to create an abnormal from a normal by improper labeling, and testing that concentrates more on what the individual can't do, rather than on what the individual can do."[7] In today's world of wanting everything labeled, categorized and convenient, this is an all too common pitfall and many children suffer because of it. They never receive the help they need because the available potential was never properly diagnosed.

My older daughter, Katie, was a perfect example. After her birth I was told by a prominent Cincinnati pediatrician that I could put her in an institution and never had to see her because she was born with Down Syndrome. And that was just the beginning. It has been, and still is, a battle with the "experts" as to what she can and can't do. So far she has defied all of them by graduating from high school and the Strauss-Kephart Institute, which is part of Indian Hills Community College in Ottumwa, Iowa. She has become a certified nurse's aid and currently is working in that capacity. She played soccer, swam competitively in the summer at the local swim club, skis, ice skates, windsurfs, was in ballet and gymnastics, plays the piano, cooks and sews. She was voted Student of the Month and Most School Spirit in high school and managed the cheerleaders. Katie had her first pair of training lenses at five months old and has done her VBT since she was a toddler, continuing through high school. She still does some every now and then just to keep up her range of skills.

On the other hand, my younger daughter, Kristin, was noticeably bright from the very beginning, with a world of available potential — potty training herself very early, speaking in complex sentences at 15 months, always asking those in-depth questions at 3 years, and reading at age 4. What more could parents ask for? Except I noticed her avoidance of certain gross motor activities — not that anything had been amiss or out of sequence in her development, but rather a reluctance to participate when her larger visual field was involved. She was highly verbal at a time when she should have been more motor-minded — a definite mismatch. To counterbalance these possible areas of deficiencies, I pushed for better visual awareness by enrolling her in ballet, gymnastics, swimming and VBT. She had already been wearing her training lenses since the age of 15 months to counterbalance sustained nearpoint activities.

Kristin's Montessori teacher, Jane Maher, also noticed a hesitancy with math and digital skills, which were also addressed in VBT. Kristin continued her VBT into high school as time would allow, making sure there was a reservoir of flexibility in her ranges of visual skills. No "sight" problems occurred — myopia, the most common adaptation, had been avoided by someone so persistent to achieve academically. Kristin graduated from high school a member of the National Honor Society, Cum Laude, and was also voted Student of the Month. She played varsity soccer and basketball, swam and competed successfully, is an excellent skier and windsurfer, plays the piano and is currently attending The College of the Holy Cross in Worcester, Massachusetts. Because Kristin's available potential was so obvious, the mismatch could have been so easily missed if I hadn't known what to look for.

2. THE EXTENT OF SUBSTITUTE AND COMPENSATING BEHAVIORS.

The importance of the concept that vision is both bilateral and binocular became evident in the clinical experiences of Wolff and his colleagues. "It soon became evident that these concepts being formulated and the procedures being used in the analytical examination and VBT had reached a level which required them to be reformatted into a more efficient system."[8] Wolff followed in Skeffington's footsteps by disseminating information from other disciplines and wrote these postulates which have become axiomatic in his model of vision. They became known by my father as the "Wolff House".

1. Vision is capable of monitoring itself within the same system.
2. Vision utilizes the past in the present to anticipate the future.
3. Vision is ordered by the process of entering identification and confirmed or denied by translation into action.
4. Vision is both bilateral and binocular:
   a. Bilaterality providing thrust and counter-thrust for movement and sequencing.

    b. Binocularity providing an analog for recognizing similarities and differences simultaneously.

5. Vision can be assessed by observing in the present the responses to visually oriented demands in a comprehensive structured environment. [9]

Wolff was aware that people tried to meet life's cultural demands the best they could with the experience and skills they had developed up to that particular time. *Changes and interference within the balance of the binocular bilateral visual-motor system result in adaptations of substitute and compensating behaviors, many of which are negative in nature.*

MOVEMENT

When considering the origins of these adaptations that were taking place, Wolff noted that children aren't as flexible as adults think they are. It's assumed that they can adapt to almost anything with little or no negative consequences, but this is not necessarily so. In the infant, patterns begin immediately after birth and progress rapidly. Early learning patterns that take place are extremely important, so if any changes and structuring need to take place, there's not a lot of time that can be wasted and still keep the natural development in sequential order. The established pattern, good or bad, perseverates because it's the only one the baby knows. This is what is meant by inflexibility. Often these negative patterns or lack of patterns continue beyond childhood and into adulthood becoming embedded and even more difficult to change. It's now known that there are definite changes in the physiological system in relation to the stress demand of the task. *The harder the task is and the more demanding, the more tension is generated, the more tendency there is to pull in, tighten up and restrict movement, create limitations, and begin eliminating information to make things simpler and easier to cope with.*

Harmon said that "the actual form or adaptation that takes place during development depends on the specific environments provided for the child and how well those environments fit the growth and developmental process."[10] This is the uniqueness of homo-sapiens . . . its ability and capacity to adapt and change. Harmon went on to say that

> The organism will adapt literally, physically and psychologically according to the demands, limitations or stresses of the environment. This growth pattern is inherently a balanced bisymmetric process. The child is constantly

undergoing modification and change in order to maintain integration of all parts and pieces. Interference with any of these parts distorts or limits the growth and development of the whole organism.[11]

A mismatch between the center of environmental activity and the growth pattern activities creates a conflict. The child grows along the lines of stress in order to reduce that stress. *A match between the environmental activities and the growth patterns creates simultaneous growth of the organism with maximum efficiency, and is the pattern desired.* But modern man has deviated immensely from what he was like thousands of years ago as a hunter and gatherer. Then he used this visual-motor system for what it was intended: survival, for movement and orientation in his three dimensional visual space. Movement was and still is the key to survival. *Society's demands now are often so stressful that they are more than the person's flexibility, capabilities or skill level to resist them.* "This results in the breakdown of the muscles, bones, body chemistry, and neural pathways, etc. of the whole organism."[12]

A balanced system that is totally symmetrical is static in nature. The natural state of rest is asymmetrical, such as the TNR (tonic neck reflex) of an infant, or one's lounging and sleep postures. Cross-patterning appears to be a natural tendency, Wolff thought. A person's orientation and posture have two frames of reference: balance and movement, which affect each other reciprocally. The primary purpose of bilaterality is that it is the mechanism of movement and out of movement, balance is generated. Balance becomes the relative constancy for judgment, understanding and abstraction of movement . . . hence the reciprocity. Three given stimuli to which the individual reacts and postures himself to are: light, gravity and experiences within the environment. These demands occur during one's work, recreation, sports and academic nearpoint tasks, such as reading, writing, drawing and manual manipulation. Also included in these environmental demands are T.V. and the now omnipresent computer, whether it be for work or play.

In order for the individual to move, this static balance must be broken by the reaction to these stimuli and by the bilaterality itself which allows for two balanced movements in opposite directions (thrust and counter-thrust) to happen simultaneously. The side of preference leads this action and initiates the sequencing of movement.

BINOCULARITY

Vision is also binocular. Wolff described binocularity as "the process that develops two eyed centering (where it is) and identification (what it is) within the visual space and resolves similarities and differences into unique precepts.[13] Harmon stated that "for practical purposes, the two eyes are matched optical systems."[14] Being bilateral they must function simultaneously in near and far space in order to organize that space into useful visual information. The ability to separate foreground information from background information (figure-ground skills) and to restructure new patterns from the selected information, is dependent on binocularity. This is the analog process. Negative adaptations of substitute and compensating behaviors limit the ability to select available information which allows for change, restructure and rebalance within the binocular visual system. *The dynamic balance within the system allows for the digital and analog skills to become integrated functions.* Synthesizing parts into wholes becomes possible. Similar yet different functions happen simultaneously.

3. THE VALUE PLACED ON DIFFERENT, BUT BETTER PERFORMANCE TO THE INDIVIDUAL AND THOSE IMMEDIATELY INVOLVED.

Most individuals, regardless of their mental or physical abilities, want to please and do well for themselves and others. They initially want to do well in school, be well liked, accepted and ultimately lead full, productive adult lives. There are many intelligent, highly motivated individuals who have not developed the appropriate level of visual-motor skills, but, who are still high achievers. They expend an enormous amount of energy, effort and time do so. Then there are those who aren't as highly motivated and may have only one or two visual-motor skills that are not developed fully, but, that's enough to create a frustrated, stressed non-achiever. I said initially because as the child progresses in school and the demands become greater, more abstract and more visually oriented than his present skill level, the adaptations and compensating behaviors develop, and learning becomes harder and less fun. Self esteem lowers and everything seems to snowball out of control, culminating in the mismatch between potential and performance.

Youngsters must rely on adults to help them through this crisis, and find the appropriate care. This in itself is no easy task given the enormous amount of information available through T.V., news stories, books, magazines and other printed material. The choices for solutions are overwhelming and often contradictory. Most youngsters don't intellectually understand why they aren't doing well but are usually quite aware when they don't fit in, can't do what the other kids do, and are generally unhappy. It then becomes the responsibility of the care-givers to recognize the value of better performance and to commit to following through with the treatment plan. The more mature and sophisticated the individual becomes, the more the responsibility for recognizing the consequences of a better performance and for selecting the direction they want to proceed, shifts to that individual.

Adults seeking care for themselves are faced with a similar situation. The majority aren't initially aware of the alternatives available to them, but once they do become aware of their problem and seek help, they become confused and overwhelmed with contradictory advice. All care-givers involved, parents, tutors, teachers, psychologists, psychiatrists, optometrists and other professionals, must be on alert to recommend and guide these people toward a solution to their difficulties.

4. REASONABLE ADHERENCE TO AND SUPPORT OF THE TREATMENT PROGRAM PRESCRIBED.

This involves the proper choice of lenses, and/or VBT, and recommendations to other disciplines when appropriate. The formula is really very simple and is the same for any learned skill. Maximum adherence to and support of the treatment plan will bring about change. Minimum or no support or adherence to the treatment plan will produce little or no change. But again in this world of "I want it now" and quick fixes, people expect miracles to happen when, in fact, that will not happen at all and they will be truly disappointed. These skills take time to acquire, especially if the substitute or compensating behaviors are fairly well embedded.

Lenses

As previously discussed, Skeffington provided an alternative to the traditional viewpoint of lens application. The usual procedure of prescribing a lens solely on what was measured was now viewed differently. *The goal was to induce movement with a lens toward internal change in order to eliminate internal interferences and bring about balance within the binocular system.* This need to prescribe either greater than or less than or differently from what was measured became clinically supported. Minus lenses were prescribed in certain cases for those who were not myopic and even a combination of minus and plus has been used simultaneously in order to induce an oscillatory movement in a youngster who didn't move or crawl. A traditional lens represented the view of the external world as it should be, which in turn, matched the internal process and *didn't provide the necessary impetus for change to occur.* The desired lens provided for the restructuring and rebalancing of the internal system, allowing the person to develop an expanded awareness in order to deal with more information with less stress. It's as though the lens pushed the nearpoint task beyond arms length and past what Skeffington had called the "biologically unacceptable" near-point distance. Wolff suggested thinking of this type of lens as a tool used to enhance and direct the primary skills of development. More recently, some lens applications have been used to create a certain amount of stress in order to induce a change in the overall visual behavior — the person has to react to it.

While some restoration of balance within the system can be achieved through lenses alone, and a certain amount of change can also be achieved with VBT alone, for the maximum results in the least amount of time the combination of lenses and VBT prescribed simultaneously is the ideal treatment plan. The following example illustrates change with lenses only after a 4 month interval. The task item is from the *Developmental Test of Visual-Motor Integration.*

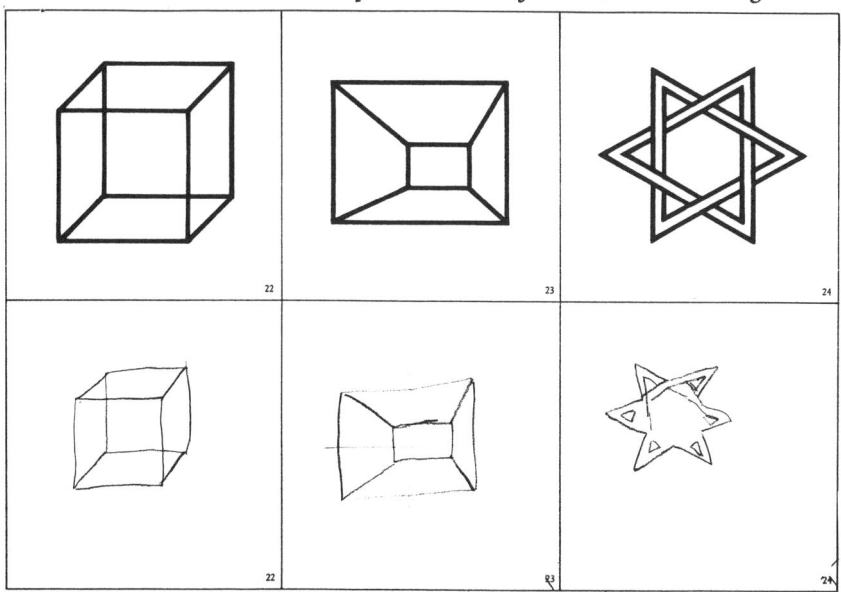

Before Lenses

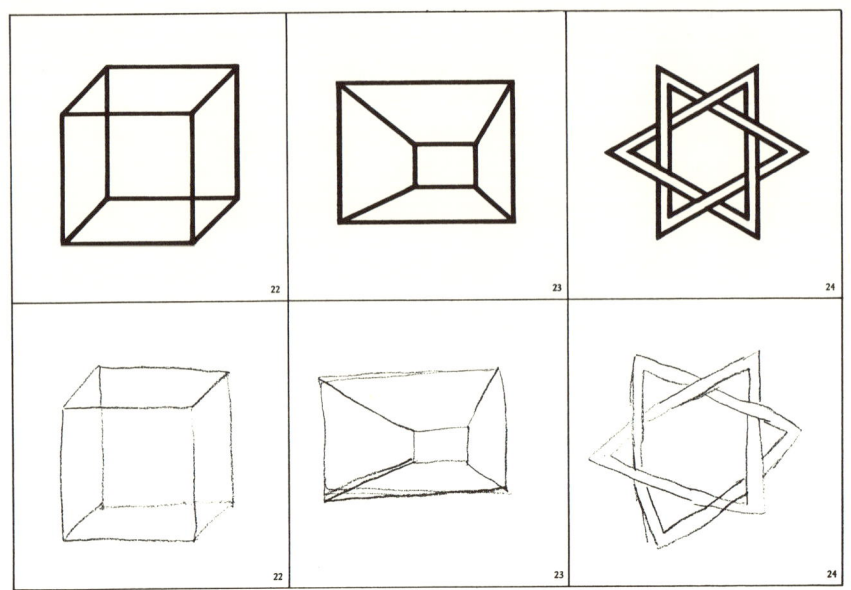

After Lenses

The following example illustrates change in binocular integration before and after 3 months of VBT only.

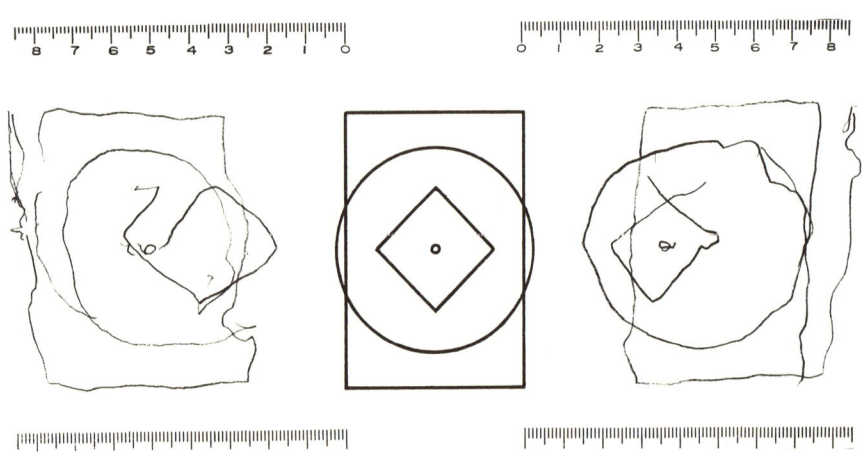

Cheiroscopic Indirect Tracing *Before* VBT

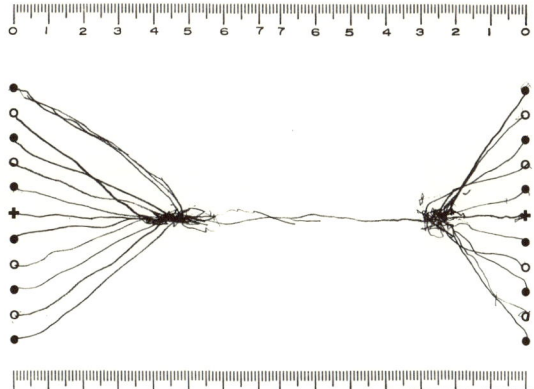

VAN Orden Star *Before* VBT

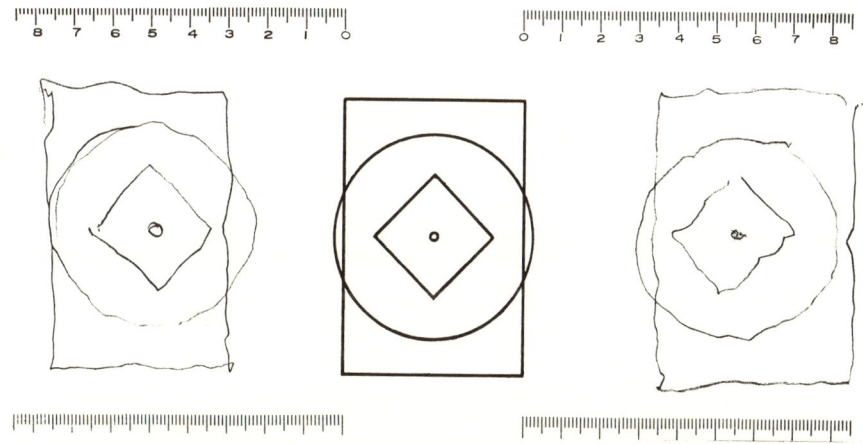

Cheiroscopic Indirect Tracing *After* VBT

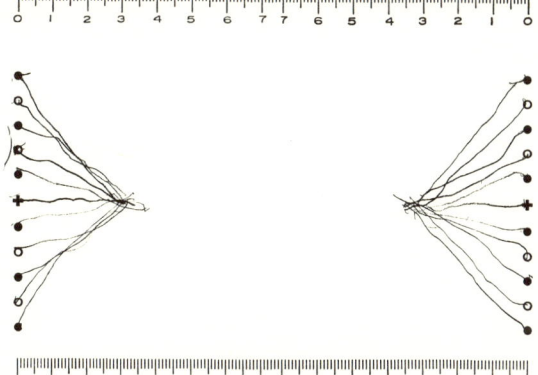

Van Orden Star *After* VBT

VISION AS THE EMERGENT

Wolff said that vision is a private world. We can only infer how someone else sees. *How a person interprets what is in his visual space is totally unique to him; it becomes his own frame of reference.* We teach babies to talk and how to move but not much on how to see. We assume that it's always been there, that it is a given. But this is not true, Wolff said. Most people think that we just open our eyes and automatically see, but in fact we see to do, to move, to act; it's a performance that's integrated with all the other sense modes. The integration loop that goes on in the brain, Wolff said, is a total circuit so there is what is called feedback. "Twenty percent of the retinal leaves go back to the muscles, tendons and joints and not back to the brain. Bits and pieces of information are fed back into the central nervous system."[15] Information goes in, is integrated and goes back out. Any interference with the initial input through the visual system will interrupt the flow of the loop and affect the processing and output of the information.

This feedback process is fundamental to all independent human learning. Visual abilities and skills need to be learned and this learning process begins at birth and continues throughout a life-time. Many children learn these by chance, trial and error, or by sheer strength and awkwardness, but many don't. A visual-behavior assessment opens up this private world by observing the "integration of the visual with the body postural and movement mechanisms, the visual-motor, visual-verbal, visual-auditory, and visual-perceptual systems."[16] This assessment will identify the individual's potential, personal norm, compensating and substitute behaviors, how and to what degree information is processed, symmetries and asymmetries within these systems, lags and omissions in the visual development, digital and analog abilities, binocular integration, bilateral motor equivalence, tracking and locating skills, visual-motor adaptability, convergence/divergence and fine and gross motor skills. Characteristics of the individual's visual space are also assessed, as well as the functions of Centering, Identification and Binocularity. Results from the total assessment determine what can and should be done.

Wolff described vision as "an emergent from sight, experience, learning, doing, sequencing, analoging, and visualizing."[17] A holographic paradigm . . . these ingredients become synonymous with sight, (the given), hindsight, foresight and insight. Vision is past, present and future . . . it supersedes time and space. It is a TOTAL processing system. Visual-behavior training deals with that total person and all these functions. It provides the environment for these visual abilities and functions to develop.

MATCHING VBT PROCEDURES TO CONCEPTS

Soon after Bruce Wolff began his practice he quickly became one of the leading creative thinkers and contributors of not only theory, but also of testing and VBT procedures as well. Following the framework of Skeffington's philosophy, Wolff and his colleagues created a well-rounded set of procedures over the years that are still used successfully today. Visual-behavior training is designed to deal directly with visual problems and indirectly with "sight" problems. A *visual problem* is an habituated limitation of movement patterns used to scan and retrieve bits of information. A *sight problem* develops from the visual problem. Sight problems are commonly known as myopia (nearsightedness), hyperopia (farsightedness), strabismus (crossed or walled eye), amblyopia (lazy eye) and astigmatism (eye warp).

The goal of VBT, as well as lenses, is to change the internal environment of the individual. VBT procedures should be designed to free people from the skews, warps, inefficient adaptations and asymmetries within that internal environment. It must be remembered that the human organism is always in a perpetual search for, and in a state of flux in order to maintain balance, homeostasis and constancy within all the systems. This uniqueness of the human organism to be able to adapt and change in a negative way, *also allows it to adapt and change in a positive way.* That unique quality makes VBT possible. In VBT a person embarks on a journey from his **PERSONAL** NORM with all its baggage, to a more **EFFICIENT** NORM of better visual-motor skills that allow for the gathering of more information and eventually a greater ease in selecting appropriate directions and maintaining that direction (sustaining skills).

DEVELOPMENT OF VISION PROBLEMS

Parents have often commented they feel guilty that they didn't catch their child's problem sooner, or that they could have somehow prevented these visual problems from happening. But they must remember they're also doing the best they can with the experience *they* have. Wolff had always said that children are raised by amateurs. No one literally teaches us how to do it. We learn from how we were raised, through common sense, trial and error, and from what we incorporate from what we read and are told by professionals. The earliest development which is the most critical is usually the most baffling because how many of us have been around infants? And even if we were, how are we to know what is important and what isn't? Dr. Arnold Gesell was the first to explore and write in depth about child development from the perspective of all sensory modalities. His primary skills of development for the first five years of life provide an excellent general framework and guideline of the sequential progression and integration of these skills. Any omissions and lags in the developmental visual-motor systems need to be learned as soon as possible. An abbreviated list of Gesell's primary skills are as follows:

Approximate Developmental Progression

Womb	Subject to gravity and environment
Out of womb	Subject to gravity light and environment
0 - 2 mos.	Past 8" is a blur
	TNR - head to one side, not midline
	Fists
	Eyes lack coordination
	Eyes and head move together
	Stares
2 - 4 mos.	TNR more symmetrical/
	comes to midline
	Less head movement with eyes
	No eye drifting
	Finds hands
	Less staring - space is expanding
	Oral
	Eye-hand coordination begins
4 mos.	fovia fully developed,
	depth perception
	Lifts head - arches back
	More social
	Rolls over - CW, CCW from stomach
	to back
4 - 6 mos.	Can direct gaze, Space is expanding
	Grasps objects/explores and expects
	Fly-arms and legs up and extended
	On hands & knees/rocks
	Rolls as mode of transportation
	Pushes chest off with arms

6 - 8 mos.	More control of body movements
	Rolls back to stomach CW, CCW
	Binocular
	Visual inspection paramount
	Visually spans room/space is expanding
	Sitting
	Transfers objects from one hand to another Crawls - first time bilateral system is put together as a unit, with eyes guiding him through expanded space
8 - 12 mos.	Crawl is perfect - used as transportation
	Perfecting eye-hand coordination
	Convergence
	Will hold objects close
	Stands with support/wide stance
	Walks with support/wide stance
	First words
	Explores space
12 - 18 mos.	Good leg control
	Visually guided hand activity - blockbuilding
	Imitates well
	Words
	Egocentric, contrary, non-conformist
18 mos. -	Walking, climbing, all visually guided
2 yrs.	Very motor minded
	Jumps 2 feet
	Stands 1 foot - no hop
	Speech increases
	Conceptualize, abstractly builds
3 years	Less motor, more visually oriented
	More finger manipulation
	Much more organized and sophisticated
	Gallop
	Sentences
4 years	More verbally sophisticated
	Perfected gross motor and finer motor skills
	Hop 1 foot
4 1/2 years	Becoming well equipped

                              Matching visual with other senses
                              Can trace well
                              Can draw vertical and horizontal lines -
                              circular
                              Oblique last to master
                              Knows a diamond but usually can't make
5 years   Well on his way in all areas
                              Readied for school[18]

WHEN?

One question often asked is at what age can VBT be started. Wolff always said the earlier the better, so the developmental sequence is a natural progression of learning with "nothing seemingly amiss". Otherwise, the substitute and compensating behaviors can take hold the longer one waits. The longer one waits, the more embedded these behaviors become. Then it will take longer to take them apart and put them back together again as new patterns. This process of change can often be very disconcerting to the individual. When these skews, warps, inefficient adaptations and asymmetries have been a part of an individual's learning pattern and behavior for so long, any move in a different direction can be quite uncomfortable for some people. Headaches, dizziness, and even nausea are sometimes part of what Wolff describes as "critical empathy". To what degree and how often it occurs varies immensely from one individual to another.

VBT procedures should be introduced only as they can easily be absorbed. Too many at one time or too many too soon will diminish the rate of learning. The learner progresses only as quickly as his unique learning curve and patterns allow him to. Learning is not automatic; just because you tell someone to do something doesn't mean they're going to learn and respond appropriately then and there. Guidelines and clues can be given by the therapist during this learning process, but the individual must understand that, ultimately, it is he who is responsible for the learning and seeing.

ERROR AND LEARNING

The learner must also be told that it's okay not to know how to do something. After all, that's why they're in VBT in the first place; to learn. From my experience, the majority of children I have worked with are almost afraid to learn because they're afraid to make mistakes. They've learned in school that errors are synonymous with a bad grade. In order to avoid errors and make it look as if everything "comes out all right", some youngsters even resort to cheating as a solution; but, they quickly find out that all they have learned is how to cheat, which is a dead-end solution. They learn in VBT that there are no grades, and that mistakes are learning tools. This is a novel concept to most of them. Errors tell us if we're on course or not; they're a necessary part of learning, not an evil. *One must know what is incorrect to know what to change and do differently.* But the individual must learn when practicing in VBT, that errors shouldn't become habitual and embedded as a pattern. The cycle of repeating errors indefinitely must be quickly broken.

Another roadblock in the path of learning is that people tend to seek out what they do well and eliminate those things they don't. People simply don't like what they can't do. It's the same with seeing. If an individual is uncomfortable with what they're seeing, they'll become selective with what and how they see. This cycle must also be broken by letting them know that even though the procedure may be difficult initially, there isn't anything they will be doing in VBT that they aren't capable of doing eventually. These procedures take time to learn and acquire. It doesn't happen overnight. The "I don't know how," and "I can't," are common phrases heard far too frequently. Rarely do I hear "I don't want to,"; and if it is said, it's usually out of fear of learning. The learner must also know that they aren't in VBT to be entertained. Nine times out of ten they would rather be watching their favorite cartoons, or be playing with their friends, just anyplace else. They need to know it's okay not to like everything in VBT, and it's okay to get a little bored. Wouldn't it be wonderful if we could all do only those things we wanted in life and always had fun doing it? The solution in this case is not to practice too much at any one time.

Ideally, VBT sessions should last approximately one hour, but may vary depending on the individual, especially initially. With very young children, for example, three year odds, a half-hour session may be more appropriate. There should be a reasonable closure with each session, if possible, with everything completed unless there's a particular problem that's being solved that may overlap sessions.

THE ENVIRONMENT AND STRUCTURE OF VBT SESSIONS

Wolff preferred VBT be done in a group setting rather than on an individual basis because it's more typical of a classroom and one's natural learning environment. However, one-on-one sessions are certainly appropriate for special needs children and adults and should be encouraged. Those who are familiar with the Montessori approach to learning will find many similarities. Everyone works as an individual within a group setting, but in VBT the group changes during those few hours with the comings and goings of the day's participants. Children feel more comfortable and less ostracized knowing there are others in the same boat as they are. They quickly realize they can learn a lot from each other, too. Observation is a great teacher.

The organization skills and inner discipline of the individual become important factors in how he progresses through the VBT session. Good manners are required and mutual respect for the therapist as well as others in VBT is expected. Unruly behavior is not acceptable or tolerated. A certain degree of socializing, talking, interaction and freedom or movement is certainly allowed and encouraged, as long as it doesn't interfere with the individual's learning or anyone else's. Instructions are simple, concise, and consistent and it's important to make sure they are completely understood with all questions answered. All procedures can be tailored and modified to the sophistication, physical abilities and available potential of the individual. It's extremely important to find the variable that works with that *particular* person so he begins to have a positive learning experience.

Each procedure in VBT represents one or more slices of life's everyday demands. They put in a nutshell an array of skills and experiences that need to be learned and stored in visual memory for future use. VBT provides a framework of experiences that continually keeps the individual in *meaningful contact with his immediate everyday world.* The more information and experiences learned and stored, the more choices that are available for solutions to the problems and demands of everyday life.

Wolff organized the VBT procedures according to how they most appropriately related to the following functions: CENTERING-identification, centering-IDENTIFICATION, VISUAL-motor, visual-MOTOR, and Field Structuring. Binocularity is a universal category and is inherent in all procedures. Even though these functions of vision were thoroughly discussed in the other chapters, a quick review will help to understand these interrelationships because an *efficient learner depends on the simultaneous and instantaneous integration of all of them.*

VISUAL SPACE - is that space that can be shared by those in the same place at the same time. It involves what we see now; and what we have seen (visual memory); and what we can visualize in anticipating the future, as well as in imagination. It is formed by the combination of light from the external world and the individual's internal referential framework generated by the particular environments within which one grew, developed and learned to use.

CENTERING -is the equivalent of looking to "where it is" in the visual space or the ability to direct the visual system to a volume of visual space, large or small, within which identification (what it is) is taking place.

IDENTIFICATION - is the visual process of seeing "what it is" within the visual space and the continuous recognition and utilization of form and the relationship of forms.

BINOCULARITY - is the process that develops two eyed centering and identification within the visual space and resolves similarities and differences simultaneously into unique percepts. [19]

The following are the categories and groupings for VBT procedures. The detailed discussion of the procedures in bold type can be found in Appendix B.

I. CENTERING -identification
   A. Procedures
      1. **Rotations and Fixations**
      2. Stick and straw
      3. Rotoscope
      4. Prisms near-far
      5. Rope
   B. visual - MOTOR
      Procedures
      1. **Body Balancing**
      2. Balance board
      3. Board BME patterns
   C. VISUAL - motor
      Procedures
      1. **Walking Rail-Prisms**
      2. Floor-prisms
      3. Prisms-dowels
      4. Prisms-pegs and rings
      5. **Cheiroscopic Tracings**

      6. Cheiroscopic Van Orden Star
      7. Cheiroscopic stereo slides and pointers
      8. Pegboard
      9. Prisms-blocks
  II. The centering -IDENTIFICATION
     A. Procedures
       1. Tel-eye Trainer Rock
       2. Loose Lens Rock
       3. Window Rock
       4. Plus Flash
       5. Board Tach
       6. Near Point Tach
       7. Craig Tach
     B. Accommodation facility (focusing)
     C. Recognition of form and the relationship of form
     D. Visualization - the process of instantaneously knowing what to do with what we see and what one can do that would apply to a particular situation - what alternatives and consequences does one see?
       1. Memory
       2. Anticipation
 III. FIELD STRUCTURING
     A. Procedures
       1. Deep Wink
       2. Ellipse
       3. Rivalry
       4. Stereo Ranges
       5. Visualization
       6. Visual - Verbal matching
       7. Visual - Auditory matching - Aural span

The session begins with the routine of coming in, taking off and hanging up coats, taking off shoes and glasses and putting them in their proper place, and finding the VBT book in the IN compartment. These behaviors must all be learned in sequential order and then reversed when the session is over. The individual must then learn how to use the VBT book which is usually an ongoing process for several sessions. A discussion and copy of the VBT book can be found in Appendix B.

HOW LONG?

    The question most often asked is also the most difficult to answer: How long will VBT take? The initial answer Wolff gave was how long does it take the individual to learn anything? One of his patients asked him if she were ever going to be finished with VBT and he said literally no, that the process of learning and the interaction between learning and vision begins at birth and ends at death. Realistically the individual is "done," Wolff said, "when he is no longer acutely aware of posture and how he is seeing; but, is now transferring from the set into the kind of performance we want." Each procedure appropriate for the individual should be learned well, with consistency to the point of becoming habitual; second nature, yet spontaneous. (S)he should now be well organized, moving comfortably through the session with confidence, efficiency and independence. The individual begins to become aware of the patterns of their performances and how they are related to the VBT program as a whole.

Wolff said one of the abilities they have to acquire is to begin to see the relationships between various training procedures and what they did that day in relation to what they did last week and the week before that. Then they will soon be able to know what still needs to be done in the future. It must be remembered that through VBT individuals deal with changing the way they process information and with their habitually embedded patterns of behavior from previous years. VBT is unique because it is self monitoring so progress can be assessed weekly.

Because of all the factors involved in vision and the fact that it's such a private world, VBT shouldn't be compared to physical therapy which is often done. In physical therapy the arms, legs and body can be literally manipulated to get the desired result. In VBT the desired effect is from movement and feedback through the integration loop. It's also important to keep in mind that in VBT, when the individual is moving from asymmetry to symmetry and balance and the old habitual behaviors are being broken down, it may appear the individual is getting worse rather than getting better. Performances may be in disarray for a time and the critical empathy factor may click in. This is a necessary part of restructuring; the undoing to redo. Eventually the old behaviors are replaced with the more efficient ones, so it's important to stay with VBT through this critical period.

Visual problems are either stress, environmentally or developmentally related. If the problem is complex and involves a combination of these, or is developmentally related, as with my daughter Katie, then the person will spend more time in VBT than if it were only stress or environmentally related. The average length of time is approximately 4-12 months. For those individuals who only need to enhance their visual skills, the length of VBT is usually less than 4 months. VBT can be used at any time during the course of one's life when we feel or know that the cultural demands have exceeded the flexibility or skill level of the total system. As I get older, I still do certain procedures to ensure flexibility within the visual-motor system.

A dream come true would be if every youngster could benefit from this powerful tool, whether through the incorporation of VBT within the school systems or privately.

THE FUTURE

A few years before he died Wolff discovered and was introduced to the writings of others who were traveling his philosophical road: William Powers and William Glasser and perceptual control theory; Thomas Hanna, somatic body theory; Karl Pribram, holographic model and holonomic brain theory; Barbara McClintock's dynamic view of science.

It was apparent that their ideas were parallel and mutually consistent. A few of the next generation of new scientists thought it was time for these parallel tracks to converge and were eager to learn from whatever would happen at the junctures. Karl Pribram and William Powers had agreed to participate in a symposium with Bruce Wolff in October, 1989, sponsored by the Cincinnati Center for Learning, The Midwest Region of Reality Therapy and the Ohio Valley Congress of Behavioral Optometry. Bruce Wolff died in July, 1989 and the symposium was canceled.

We still feel the loss that this interchange of ideas could never take place. I remember my father saying this opportunity reminded him of the excitement of the early days when Skeffington and his colleagues spent hours, and eventually years, exchanging their ideas. This dialogue eventually evolved into the contemporary discipline of Behavioral Optometry. The opportunity for this symposium to stimulate new ways of thinking and to contribute to the momentum of a post-traditional science which could more accurately describe human behavior has faded for the moment. When it reappears in the future, I am hopeful *Visual Behavior* will be in the minds of those who pave the way.

CHAPTER 8 LIVING THE THEORY

People invariably want to use what they have learned about visual behavior once acquainted with the principles or having seen changes in their own or their children's or students' lives. This chapter focuses on transforming the intellectual theory into daily life. Whether for ourselves, or as parents, counselors, teachers, or therapists strategies are presented that focus on experience, the most profound teacher of all.

"I have so many students who struggle. I see now that they have visual problems. What can I do to help them?"

"At work I have to delegate tasks to people in my department. Knowing how they learn and function would help me assign tasks that would have a higher degree of compatibility. How can I do that?"

"I want to be a positive influence in my children's lives. I want to help them grow to be effective and happy adults. It makes sense that how they see and move impacts their choices and performance. What are the most important things I can do, as a parent?"

When Bruce Wolff answered such questions, fog often obscured the view. Many seekers gave up, letting either their embarrassment at not understanding the answers they heard or their anger at what they thought was the lack of an answer get in the way of comprehension. As parents, therapists, employers or educators, their attempts to apply the principles often hit the insurmountable road blocks of HOW. Because Bruce Wolff creatively stirred in his personal, novel, non-linear observations with information that was already known about vision, psychology, philosophy, body mechanics, many found that mix unfamiliar and obscure.

ASSUMPTIONS

It sometimes seems difficult to apply the theory because the assumptions of Wolff and his listeners are often so different and are rarely articulated. The chasms of misunderstanding and misapplication, if they happen, form here, at this level of unexamined assumptions. Many of us open our subject-object, stimulus-response, linear bags in which we try to pack the new, non-linear ideas. It doesn't work very well. A common response is to give up in frustration, often blaming the message as well as the messenger, without recognizing our own role in a teacher-learner relationship that is truly reciprocal.

A better match between knowledge and application occurs when the assumptions can be brought to the surface. *Effective replication of Wolff's work requires that these assumptions be incorporated into the application of the knowledge.* Experience has shown that when they are not included, the mechanical model reappears; people expend energy attempting to find the check list for therapy, and, not surprisingly, the results are not the same as Dr. Wolff's. When this happens a logical conclusion seems to be that it is his work that is at fault, rather than the recognition that *this* model was not actually followed. Here is a brief review of some of the assumptions from which applications to everyday life can be made.

Particularity

Certainly Bruce Wolff made generalizations; but, he resisted forming bottom line statements when it came to his patients. Unlike many professionals, he did not see patients as interchangeable parts, or refer to them by diagnostic labels. He had not developed a script from which he played his professional role.

To him patients were interesting *people*; each one a variation on the human theme. Because he assumed that variation would be unique, he always found something new in his clinical practice, even after 40 years. For him, the patients and the twists and turns of their visual development were potential surprises; these surprises were his teachers. He assumed he could and would learn something from them; that only through them would he see facets of the visual process that would have been impossible to find if he had tried to define that process intellectually, academically, independent of his patients.

So he observed and generalized principles, not people. He winced when he heard others say, "Most myopes.....", "All amblyopes...". The general principles he derived that explain the human visual response to light lived, for him, *in the particular pattern of response presented by an individual.*

Wolff had fundamental differences with medical physicians, educators and psychologists who applied to patients generalizations formed from statistically averaged data and who neglected to use the *particular data presented by the individual client*: "Children with I.Q.'s of X can only learn Y"; "patients with x cancer need y treatment". He made many a professional uncomfortable by pressing them to explain those cases who were exceptions to their professional rules. He assumed that any principle worthy of that label must allow for the very apparent individual differences he met every day.

He urged his patients to look at generalizations from their particular vantage point, not to cut off their feet to fit the bed; or, one of his favorite clichés, throw out the baby with the bath water. He expected them to translate professional dogmas in the *light of their own experience* before evaluating them. Many a parent of a child with handicaps learned that it was just as important to *read their child* when making decisions about education and treatment as it was to read the pamphlets describing general diagnoses, treatments and programs handed out by other professionals.

Reciprocal Interaction

All that we do and know in the world is a *relationship between ourselves and the world*. We act on the world; *the world acts on us*. We sit down on a selected chair, turn on our selected computer and use it to do our work - acting on the world. The chair, table, light, computer screen force us into postures that have the potential over time to cause us permanent physical adaptations, some of them injurious -the world acting on us. We ask a question and respond to the answer. We tell our troubles and are comforted by the response.

We do not function apart from this unified, indivisible phenomenon of reciprocity. *Vision is the link that allows us to participate independently in that reciprocal relationship.*

Integrative Processes

The world and we, as part of the world, function integratively. What we see, hear, touch, and move becomes one, integrated, experience. We do not act from or in parts. All of our sensory-perceptual modalities function as one dynamically balanced, integrated system.

We generalize our experience. Not until we may need crutches because of an injured leg do we suddenly see physical barriers that were literally invisible to us before our injury. Taking an art course alerts us to form and shadows in our world that we had not seen before. What we perceive as parts are intrinsic to and integrated with our grasp of the whole. To change a part, changes the whole - to change the whole, changes the parts. All of our systems - the whole of us - work together so we can effect change in the world while maintaining our internal stability. *Vision both drives and is driven by the dynamics of the total sensory-perceptual system. Vision can be modified by changes in sensory-perceptual experience; sensory-perceptual experience can be modified by visual changes.*

Parts and Wholes

It is through our understanding of the relationship of parts/wholes that we can both know and influence the tasks of the world. *Vision allows us to see the big picture*; to create a context within which we derive meaning from the parts. Examined in isolation Susan's non-compliance may be something other than just being obstinate when she consistently refuses to act on perfectly logical, useful suggestions her mother gives her to solve a current problem. "She just won't listen to me," her mother complains. The bigger picture, unseen at the moment, may be that Susan is attempting to use her own systems, to discover what she wants and what she can do as part of her developmental independence.

Vision allows us to pick out the parts, to put them together to create form and meaning. Inefficient students often leave out a crucial part when they study for tests: they neglect to commit the material to memory. They think that because they've gone over it (read their notes) that they know it. They don't understand that knowing something is not the same as knowing *about* it.

See More; Do More

Our internal reality will more nearly match the external reality of the world if we use the visual data that is available to us. We can all learn to see more than we do now. Children inexperienced in jigsaw puzzles often are stumped because they literally DO NOT LOOK at the model or look only at pieces that are nearest to them, insisting that the piece they need isn't there. How often do people stay in unsatisfactory jobs because they literally do not see options for retraining, and job searches?

Efficient visual processes allow us to see more, quantitatively and qualitatively, - to increase our chances for success. The feedback process is fundamental to all independent human learning. Because we see what happens when we attempt to effect change in the world, we can *independently* choose our response: alter our course, complete our act, select other tasks. Stephen Covey says this is where genuine personal freedom resides, in that space between the stimulus and our response; it is our "freedom to choose".[1] What we recognize as error is actually information that appears in that space of freedom and is vital to us if we are to know whether or not to proceed. It lets us know whether or not our actions accomplished what we wanted; error tells us when we're on course. In that space between stimulus and our response we can, *if we attend to the information,* choose alternate actions, behave independently and creatively.

Our ability to act independently will be quantitatively and qualitatively affected by inefficiencies in our feedback systems. Reduced feedback information means more instances of dependence in our lives. We tell pre-school children what to eat. We and they accept their dependence. As independent adults do we revert to an expert to tell us what and how much to eat, or do we act from a picture of health that we've developed and made our own? Dependence vs. independence. The quality of our lives depends upon using the signals we have, feedback. Do we independently pay attention to tight necks and sore arms and take a break from the computer, or do we wait until the pain is chronic and intense and then consult an expert for a cure? Do we independently pay attention to our internal feelings of unease with a co-worker and initiate action to resolve the differences, or wait until we are so fed up that we say or do something we regret?

Faulty feedback means we'll have to rely on others to tell us if what we've done has hit the mark and to discover alternatives. To act with an inefficient feedback system means we will need some kind of script, some external guide. If we only imitate - our parents, our teachers, our mentors - we have compromised our independent function. *Independent human activity depends upon visual-movement feedback.*

Go In The Direction of The Norm

Wolff assumed that most people wanted to enhance their performance, to lessen their errors and inefficiencies. He assumed the best chance for that lay in attempting to reduce physical and visual warps, to let the human system come to the state of dynamic balance that seems possible by design. If we have two eyes and a bilateral system, then efficient binocular function seemed to him to be the direction to go. So, rather than be satisfied with compensation for the warps that our adaptations have produced, he looked for a niche where some change in the direction of the norm might have a chance. If most three year olds can follow simple directions, then he would talk to this hyperactive, non-responsive three year old *as if* she, too, would follow directions. He'd keep testing, looking for the *response that was in the direction of the norm.* When he detected a glimmer, he knew he had a place to start.

His lens prescriptions were made from this assumption. Yes, this individual needed compensatory lenses in order to see adequately in daily life; but, where in the complex could he change it so that some adaptation could start in the direction of the norm? He worked to reduce the lens power for patients with accommodation problems, to balance the difference when asymmetries appeared between the two eyes.

When incorporated, this assumption leads to a different view of medication, of compensatory therapies in many disciplines. If my arm hurts from too much computer work, do I get a brace and take pain medication or do I use the pain *as feedback* and go in the direction of the norm - what are these muscles and movements designed to do and under what conditions?

Joseph Campbell's advice to "Follow your bliss" for spiritual integrity when making your life's plan seems to have this same root. Find out the norm, whether physiological or philosophical, and head in that direction to find the greatest comfort, satisfaction and enhanced activity.

Being true to the application of Bruce Wolff's ideas of visual function requires particular attention to this assumption of the norm, so fundamental is it to his work.

WHAT WOULD IT BE LIKE?

Many people find that these assumptions and principles contrast sharply with their own views of who we are and how we get along in the world. They ask SO WHAT? What difference will it make to me and the quality of my life if I were to see things differently; if I saw different things?

A Different View of The World

To understand vision and its particular nature in individuals can explain a lot that, at first, may seem inexplainable, or that traditionally is attributed to an unknowable source.

I just don't understand why Susan's room is such a mess, I've told her time and time again to clean it up. She just doesn't care. Not necessarily. It may be that she has poor visual-spatial organization, particularly in sequencing.

I just don't understand why Frank takes so long to tell a story, why doesn't he just get to the point? Frank may not ramble by choice, he may be weak in the analog function.

With the understanding of behavior as *visual*, we can let go of blame and punishment. *People don't make mistakes on purpose; they make mistakes because of some glitch in their vision-movement-spatial-feed-back system.* We can let go of punishment and emphasize consequences. Punishment inflicts pain for some mistake already made; consequences provide *feedback which can guide future independent behaviors.* In frustration many parents of low achieving students use punishment as a last resort attempt to motivate their youngster. What? F's again! You're grounded until we see these grades improve; you can no longer have the car! This is punishment for past actions. It does not address whatever behavior produced the low grades. It does not highlight specific behaviors the child needs to change nor does it offer the encouragement people need to learn and apply new behaviors. *Punishment ignores the child's learning process and possible inefficiencies.* Its intent is to inflict pain. Consequences act as feedback and allow for growth because they provide information the individual can use. Consequences can involve others in what was meant to be an independent activity: Your interim report card says you have missing assignments. What system will you use to see that this doesn't continue? When can I see it? How can I help you devise a system if you don't have one? Let's track your system for a few weeks and see if it's actually working.

Punishment diminishes and constricts; it hurts. *Telling me not to do something does not let me know what to do to change it,* to avoid censure or punishment in the future.

To understand behavior as visual lets us accept the differences we see in others, knowing that they are doing the best they can with the information they have, just as we are. There is a Boynton birthday card with a group of cows at a lecture. In the front row is one horse. The presiding cow says, "Okay, all in favor say 'Moo'. All opposed 'Neigh'." The caption of the cartoon: *Just because you're outnumbered doesn't mean you're wrong.* Each of us is outnumbered because no one else sees the world quite the way we do. But, the good news is *we're not wrong.* For some the bad news is *neither are the points of view of others.*

To understand behavior as visual gives us an alternative view of our own behavior. We are not stuck with only a psychological or physical/genetic model. It's no wonder I'm not good at math, no one on my mother's side is either. The teacher says Philip has low self-esteem and that's affecting his school work. These become chicken-and-egg routines. Who knows which came first? What we do know is that math and school work depend upon efficient visual processes and that fact is often ignored.

Perhaps it isn't nature or nurture, but the reciprocal integration of the two, each affecting the other that creates human behavior. Emotional responses are *part* of our dynamic system, not the predominant determiners of our actions. We can be free of the behavioral determinism hinted at by genetic explanations of behavior. Nurture vs. nature battles become irrelevant. Our behavior results from a dynamic process, not either/or - not fixed solely by genetics or conditioning; *therefore the potential for modification at any time in an individual's life is much greater than common knowledge would have us believe.* People over age 60 often make positive changes in their visual status with training based on this model.

A Context For Our Experience; We Can See Similarities

If all human beings do the same thing - create behaviors from the visual-language-movement-feeling ingredients - then whatever I'm doing, whatever you're doing, whatever they -over there - are doing is not *outside the usual experience of human beings,* whether contemporary or historical.

Jeff, a 45 year old professional, admitted sheepishly that he found himself shaking, and on the verge of tears now and then. He wondered if something was wrong with him. When his behavior was put into the context of his recent acceptance of a new job in a different city that had added responsibilities and would uproot his family at a critical time, his loss of control looked very different than when he described his behavior as an isolated, worrisome experience. The lens of context makes the concepts of normal and abnormal look very different. With only their own experience as context, many people find it difficult to understand or modify their reactions to a particular experience. Without a big picture to which they can relate the parts of that experience they find little interpretation or meaning. They may think that they are the only ones who have had that experience. *If we cannot see our experience in a larger context, we will probably not see any similarities between our own and others' experiences.* In that case we would see only differences. We might even go so far as to call what we know normal, and that which is different, abnormal, or the other way around.

Because of this lack of context many of us do not see the similarities among people of different color, religion, gender, I. Q., physical abilities. Many of us don't see the unseen analog for vision and learning: that we all learn to use our physical equipment to effectively act in the world in order to get what we want. Pre-school children with Down Syndrome use their physical equipment to gain mastery over their world, just as the CEO of a corporation has only his physical equipment to carry out his particular visual organization. Their behaviors differ in complexity, developmental stage, and task selection, but *not in kind*. Their learning and visual processes are the same: based on the information they have, this is what they do.

It is paradoxical that when we look at an individual's visual-language-movement organization, we find that we are similar because we are all different! We are alike in our differentness.

Doing Things Differently - Doing Different Things

Most of us learn early on to accept the way things are for us. I love to read; but it makes me sleepy. I'm usually late. Writing a report wears me out. I'm not good at math. I don't play sports. I love people; I'm not a book worm. I'm afraid of water. We dare not hope things could be different because we see no way of undoing the status quo. *What if?* What if you could learn what you needed to know in order to do some things that are currently not within your view of yourself? Would you begin to hope? It's one thing to make choices from genuinely possible alternatives and quite another to be stuck with choices because you didn't have any other options. If reading is hard for you, you're not likely to become an avid reader or a professor of English Literature. If you have no idea how to connect spatially with a ball in flight, you'll not pick tennis as your favorite sport. But *what if* reading could become easier. What if you could know where the ball is and how to get yourself to it? Might your preferences be different? Would you like to have the freedom to choose?

From physical skills to mental problem solving, improving your visual efficiency means that whatever you do will feel much easier. Perhaps you'll be able to read without going back over paragraphs or falling asleep. Maybe you'll find yourself finishing a report in about the same time as it used to take to get organized. You might find yourself coming to conclusions and making choices with less agony and in less time. Instead of walking a developmental treadmill, you'll continue on your way building more and more complex skills.

Where's The Help

One way to begin is to find a professional in behavioral optometry and explore what that contribution could be for you. The Optometric Extension Program, Santa Ana, California, can tell you who might be in your part of the country. Optometrists learn the specialty of behavioral optometry at the post-doctoral level through seminars and mentoring; consequently, there is *wide variety in the depth and breadth of their application of visual principles* in specific human activities. Enhancement of sports performance and reducing visual stress are areas where some behavioral optometrists have specialized. Very, very few emphasize vision's role in thinking and general behavior.

WAYS TO BEGIN

Whether or not you have the opportunity to work directly with an experienced professional, the following suggestions may help you incorporate increased visual efficiency into your life. These suggestions can in no way substitute for the kind of improvement you could expect if training lenses and visual training *were done appropriately.* But the principles work regardless and can set a direction for greater efficiency, less stress reaction and increased awareness.

Dynamic Balance

The idea is to bring symmetrical balance, alternations, alternatives into your process.

POSTURE: The principles are explained in chapter 4. Try to use furniture that fits you, especially when doing close, visually centered work. Check out your postural alignment in the mirror, front and side view, note asymmetries. Make an effort to position yourself in a more symmetrical fashion. Straighten your head, put the small of your back against the back of the chair, the paper you're working on directly in front and not off to one side. You won't be able to maintain it, but at least you can let your body have a taste of symmetrical balance. If you're really serious about working at this try a Hatha Yoga class. You'll increase your internal body awareness and do exercises that will put you in dynamically balanced postures that can have a lasting effect.

ACTIVITIES: Balance your activities; alternate tasks that occur at near and far distances. Take frequent breaks when doing close work. These need to be breaks from continuous visual activity as well as movement and posture breaks. Rather than wait till your neck or wrist hurts, build these times of respite into your work segments. Get up from your chair and walk somewhere, stretch and bend in the opposite position you've been in; look out a window, down the hall, somewhere in the distance. Try to have some general movement time built into your daily or weekly schedule, when you move yourself through space. Try looking straight ahead when you walk, incorporating the periphery at the same time so you know when it's time to turn the corner, step off the curb without having to look at it.

MENTAL ACTIVITY: Turn things over in your mind. Look at a problem or situation from a vantage point that's 180 degrees from your current position. What would the opposite situation be? If you're thinking of doing x, what would it look like if you didn't do it, or you did the opposite? If getting a plan of action started is difficult, look at the other end: what would you like to have if the plan worked? That big picture often makes clear the parts that would be necessary to create it.

Error

Many of us expend lots of energy trying to prevent errors or defending ourselves against expected censure when our efforts fail. Try an experiment for one day, or one time. *Let the error just be there.* Don't feel bad about it, don't justify it, don't blame it away. If you can do that, then look at the error *as if you didn't cause it.* What were the components, what actually happened. Factually. The oversimplified spilled milk analogy will do. What happened? The milk landed on the table instead of in the glass. Why? I didn't keep the carton over the glass. Why? My arm was cramping and I had to move. That's all there was to it. Try the next step which relates to the suggestions in dynamic balance: What would it have taken not to repeat the error? Do I need to think about why my arm cramped? What could I do next time?

For error to work for you, let in the information it brings you. Several frustrated customers were observed dealing with their errors when attempting to use newly installed check approval machines in a local grocery store. After following what they thought was the suggested button-pushing, card-inserting sequence on the instruction panel, nothing happened. They'd start again, follow their same sequence, repeat the same error they had made the first time. Eventually they walked off muttering that these new machines were already broken. So, after your usual reaction in an error situation, take a second look. What can I learn here? What other things can I try?

CONTEXT

Where are the parts in relation to the whole? Where is this in relation to that? Can I think about both at the same time? When looking at the picture you've just hung, see it in relation to the other things around it. What effect do the sofa, lamp and table have on the picture and the picture on them? Is there a connection between behavior in your pre-schooler and what may have happened just before? An adult's laughing and talking may be the context for 18 month old Michelle's increased activity, squealing and the resistance she gives when you try to constrain her. She thought she was entering into the merriment and you want her to stop? You thought she was disturbing the guests and just acting like an 18 month old, unaware of the contextual connection.

Am I just rubbing a tool on a surface or am I peeling carrots or am I making dinner or am I contributing to the health of my family. What am I doing? What is it related to? When you run into a problem, usually you deal with only a part.

Task: Change the air filter on the furnace.

Problem: Where does it go?

Many of us stop right here. A common solution is to ask someone else; to reduce our independence. The next time you find yourself thinking "I don't know" as the end of it, ask yourself:

What is that part related to - the air intake system. Where is that? - some duct going in. This gives you a place to start -the WHERE part of the visual process. You will then, more than likely, see the information you need to proceed. Since nothing actually exists in the world in isolation, begin looking for the context, the actual objects or factors that are connected to or surround the piece you're examining. The next time you don't know, try an alternative before you give up.

Analog/Digital Processes

If you've already identified your preferred process for organizing information, you might want to increase your efficiency in the reciprocal mode.

To Practice Digital Skills

Tell yourself to list the parts of something: an incident, a story, a problem. Add on to the main points or your reaction to a situation. Think about the sequences of what you'll do. Make specific lists so you can see the parts of a task. Make an effort to pay attention to parts and how they're organized: in maps, telephone books, proof-reading, recipes, directions, etc. Do it as a specific practice, once a day or week. It will be uncomfortable at first.

To Practice Analog Skills

When you hear yourself telling something by starting at the beginning and going through every step of the event or story, try skipping to the end, actually leaving out some steps. Or give your opinion first, or start with a summary before you tell the parts. When you have analyzed a situation and listed the factors involved, go the next step and formulate the therefore. Put those factors into some ballpark, give them an interpretation, create an analogy or metaphor. This situation is like ____.

When you hear yourself giving bottom line statements like "I liked it...I didn't like it", try to list two reasons or factors that go with the conclusion.

Put like things together, when organizing your kitchen cupboards, closets and dresser drawers, office space and procedures. Remind yourself to put things back in that order of similarity.

Again, set this up as a specific practice: do it at certain times.

Where? What? What Do I Do With It?

Use the structure of the visual process (centering, identification, visualization) intentionally to solve problems. Ask *and answer* yourself when pondering a situation. Is this a time when I don't know *where the problem lies?* My daughter reports that the kids in her class don't like her, call her names and talk to other kids about her. I don't know if the problem is my daughter's perception or her own behavior that precipitates the situation or even if it's factually true. To help her I need to locate the basis of the problem.

Identification

If I know where, can I put my finger on *what the factors are?* The teacher explained that my daughter's perception is accurate, that another youngster told the teacher she heard some kids teasing my daughter on the playground.

Visualization

Once I've found the factors, do I *know what to do?* Should I insist the teacher intervene, should I teach my daughter some defensive behavior, should I ignore it? Try visualizing consequences to various solutions. What would happen if... mentally try behaviors on for size before you actually do something. What's a best or worst case scenario.

See More By Looking Less

What do you see? What do you see on the coffee table in front of you, on the wall full of pictures opposite you, in the panorama outside your kitchen window or your car's windshield? "Whatever I look at," was one person's answer. By that she meant that she looked at one thing at a time. To her, seeing meant a constant shift of her eyes from this to that and that and that; rather like pointing a flashlight to illuminate specific items in the dark.

There's another way; one that gives you more information with less effort. Instead of picking out something to look at, try looking through the space out there. Look at the whole coffee table at once. Let whatever is on it come to you; be aware of individual items without isolating them from each other or the background. Don't stare, but just let yourself see instead of purposely looking. Know that the space in front of you goes out indefinitely. It does not stop at the person across from you, or the car in front of you. There is space beyond that person; that car. See the person and that space by looking through the space. Let all that is in front of you line up for you; some things closer, some things farther away; some appearing smaller than, some appearing larger than.

When looking in the mirror, try to see your whole face at once, without looking at each feature. See both eyes at once.

Give yourself a chance to experience the paradox of seeing more by looking less.

Visualization

From placing the living room furniture in your new house to algebraic word problems, life is easier if you develop your visualization abilities. Some people are more in tune with this faculty than others, but we all can use and improve this skill. It saves us energy when we don't have to physically try things out and saves us agony when we bump into obstacles we didn't see in our mind's eye.

There are lots of sources for developing these powers; books on memory improvement, organization, meditation, etc. But most sources are oriented toward visualization of particular data and do not address ways to use it in everyday life.

A way to call on this skill is *to wait*. If you don't know what to do, if you don't have an answer, or can't seem to make a connection, try waiting a few seconds before you give up, ask someone else or start the trial and error approach. Often something will bubble up; some hint will emerge that you were not aware of in the pressure to make that fast response your parents and teachers taught you to make. If you wait, you may be rewarded with the solution or a reasonable attempt in your mind. The visualization may not be a photograph-like image; it may just be an awareness.

Try to represent ideas and situations in pictures. This is one of the powerful and popular tools for improving memory. It also works to clarify issues and situations that are difficult to formulate or put into words. Use shapes, lines or stick figures to draw your reactions. As part of an exercise to personally connect with the environmental message in Dr. Seuss's story of *Lorax*, one adult drew two circles, one very small, the other very large. This was her visualization of her feeling of impotence in the face of environmental destruction. She was the small circle; the seed of responsibility was the large circle.

Betty Edwards in her book, *The Artist Within,*[2] describes the use of analog drawings for mental problem solving. In a rectangular format use lines, dots, shadings (symbolic graphics) to represent your problem or issue. One of her students had drawn a wavering, continuous, connected line around the perimeter of the rectangle and titled it, "Problem: Career going nowhere. Life heading nowhere, in no one direction."[3]

Use visual images as metaphors for problems, clients, children, issues. Connect to the metaphor and issues and solutions will appear that cannot be seen when only real life situations are considered. This is one of the techniques for thinking creatively. Timmy was seen by his teacher as a *scared rabbit,* always trying not to be noticed, not to be held accountable. She had been trying, unsuccessfully, to get him to assume some responsibility by putting him in the spotlight, praising him, giving him jobs to do. For every advance, he countered with a retreat. When she thought about how she would handle a scared rabbit, she got some insight into what she might try with Timmy. She waited instead of calling on him, put out some non-threatening bait in the form of games and books he could use when certain work was finished, and watched without comment as he tentatively changed his direction from hiding to doing.

Any improvement in visualization seems to have an exponential effect in general behavior; a little goes a long way; some begets a great deal more. Intentional use of visualization in your life can certainly help ease you through your day.

Change is hard. Most often we don't start that journey until we can no longer stay on that shore of habit and safety. One patient said it for all of us, "I'm not against change, so long as it's imperceptible." Bruce Wolff often would tell patients who wanted the benefits of improved visual processing but found it difficult to add change to their old habits to try doing *any small thing differently;* walk up the stairs one at a time, walk down the hall backwards, eat with your less preferred hand. Because we function as an integrated unit, introducing small, seemingly unrelated changes into the system seems to send a signal that the total system generalizes. The internal base has been modified. It's then easier to introduce changes of a greater magnitude, new behaviors that relate more directly to what you want to do or learn. If you decide to change your direction and attempt some of these suggested activities, you may be, as Betty Edwards described,

"...surprised to learn how much of the language of visual, per-ceptual thought you already know, right at this minute, perhaps without realizing it. And it is my hope that you will also discover that this new language, when integrated with the language of verbal, analytical thought, may provide the ingredients essential not only for true creativity -that is, new or novel ideas, insights, inventions or discoveries that have social value - but also for useful creative solutions to the problems of everyday life." [4]

Bon voyage!

CHAPTER 9 HELP THAT HELPS

Parents and Educators: guiding children's sight toward vision

Many parents read to their preschoolers every day and bake cookies or do other extra things on weekends because this fits their idea of what good parents do. As William Glasser, M.D. (Reality Therapy, Control Theory) says, we design our behavior on the basis of the pictures we have in our heads: pictures of what we want, how we want to be, and what we need to do to make those images come true. If my picture of a good parent includes reading and baking cookies, then that's what I'll try to do. If, on the other hand, my picture of a good parent means strict discipline for most of my children's infractions -the world is a tough place and I'm doing them a favor by letting them know that - then discipline strictly is what I'll do.

Whether business executive, parent, teacher, physician, psychologist, or other healing professional, we, too, have pictures in our heads that guide what we're doing, and how we do it. We've pasted these pictures together not only from our childhood experiences, but from our professional training and experiences as well. Our mental pictures and our visual pattern influence each other: our behavior emerges from that integration. No matter how they are created, *we cannot function without mental pictures*, visualization of our behavior road map, or thought reflexes as David Bohm would say.

Bruce Wolff's pictures show vision in a new context. We can intentionally increase our effectiveness as parents or professionals by pasting some of his pictures into our own mental albums of how children learn and people function.

Many of Wolff's pictures, summarized in Chapter 8, were not original with him. Any parent, teacher, or healer whose results are exceptional employs many of the principles of vision often unconsciously. *What Wolff did was to uncover the fundamental visual processes that explain how and why these principles work.* With that knowledge the success of talented teachers, healers and parents can now be available to the rest of us. We can deliberately *and intentionally* use the principles that produce success for our children/clients/patients. With these added pictures of visual behavior we can articulate what the clients need in order to be more effective in their lives. We will then be more effective in the help we provide. To review: Here are the principles that cover the basic tenets of Wolff's work: See Chapter 8 for discussion.

• Reciprocity
• Integrative Function
• Parts/Wholes
• See more/do more
• Feedback
• Particularity
• Go Toward the Norm

These visual processes are fundamental in all who have sight. *Your children's or your clients' visual processes actively influence their response to your work with them.* Place the template of these visual principles over your activities to make a profound difference in the lives of clients, students, employees, patients. We can add a rifle to our professional armament that allows us to *hit specific behavioral targets.* Without these principles we rely on our familiar, eclectic shotgun, spraying particles we hope will meet specific client needs. Incorporating this template of visual behavior lets us see relevancies that were hidden before; specific parts of our eclectic approach that brought about positive results. We can see how to employ them intentionally in other situations. We may see more clearly teaching/therapeutic opportunities that before were in shadows.

To add your understanding of the visual process to your professional expertise means you would have another ingredient added to your cake of professional/parenting behavior. It is not intended as a substitution. You don't have to set aside any knowledge or techniques. Whether parent or professional, blending knowledge of the visual process with your own parenting/professional skills increases your potential to help.

To begin, look at Wolff's description of the factors that influence atypical development in the visual process. By looking at the negative we often begin to understand the positive. If you fix a broken bike or solve a plumbing problem you have a deeper appreciation of how bikes and plumbing actually work. Explanations for your greatest successes or failures in teaching, healing or parenting may reside here, in his description:

> Interference in the development and maintenance of vision is accountable to some form of deprivation, or, stressing the system beyond its current capabilities. Under those conditions adaptations made within the system

in order to cope are negative in nature, and restrict performance in various ways or another, the most frequent and easiest to recognize being a loss of visual acuity. Other adaptations may not be so easily recognized unless one understands the diffuse extent to which vision affects human behavior. 1

Said another way, if we want to reduce interference in the development and maintenance of vision in our clients/children we need to help them:

- reduce the restrictions on their growth, (stress) and
- increase, if possible, the capabilities of their systems, (their learning).

This holds whether it's our own seven year old son learning to manage his morning get-ready routine, our high school English student developing better study habits, our office manager implementing company policies, our young adult patient seeking meaningful relationships, or our parishioner in the midst of a spiritual conflict. *Whatever our connection to them, we help when they can reduce restrictions in their lives and increase their coping and learning abilities.* We cannot increase their coping ability. It is something they must do. We hinder their development if we add more restrictions, and/or cannot provide opportunities for helping them *increase their skills.*

How does it work? How can understanding vision affect my interactions with those I'm trying to help? Isn't their visual pattern their own internal process, not accessible for external manipulation?

It works because you introduce factors at will that reduce restrictions in their visual process. By design you can prevent their current capabilities from over-extension. Intentionally you can help them increase their learning capabilities in ways traditional approaches overlook. With these additions you may find that the stalled progress or atypical responses of some of your clients or students may resolve into forward movement.

Many patients of Wolff's found their counseling or physical therapy progress accelerated as their visual processing improved. Some who tried lenses and visual training reluctantly, and only because traditional methods had brought less than hoped for change, were often truly surprised when their improvement could not be denied or attributed to any other factors. Even though they had lived it, they still found it difficult to accept that the visual approach actually influenced their behavior. They'd wonder why they didn't have headaches anymore and what might have made a positive difference in their daughter's grades. Such is the dissonance when tradition meets a new reality.

Reciprocity in The Teacher-student, Healer-patient Relationship

The traditional, mechanistic model of relationships teaches us to focus on each part of this dyad, teacher or student; doctor or patient, separately. Stimulus-response, cause-and-effect explains the way each reacts to the other, reciprocity almost never. So we learn and practice in our professions *only what WE should do*, as if we function apart from our client, student, etc. We learn what to get from them (histories and fees, answers), do to them (examine and test) and do for them (prescribe, suggest, teach).

To that end we learn task analysis, lesson and unit planning, symptoms and remedies, sermon writing and liturgical planning, the sequences of academic content. *We become experts in what we, not the clients, are doing.* The child or client could be interchangeable, necessary parts that we manage. As professionals we've had training that included methods of one sort or another. As parents, on the other hand, we have only our own experience as children, our observations of our parents' childrearing practices, and a host of conflicting experts to guide us.

If we see our role in the teacher-learner dyad as prescribers, we tend to offer information and expect the client to put it to use: we're the stimulus, they're the responders. We do not usually see it in reverse: they as the stimulus, we as the responders. So from a mental picture of Us/Them we pronounce: take these pills, follow this diet, do these exercises, study this way, read Chapter 3, make your bed, clean your room, do your homework. What's wrong with that, you may think; it's all so familiar.

With the addition of the visual model, we have an alternate context into which we place those parent-child, student-teacher, doctor-patient, us-them interactions. They function *dynamically,* one side affects and is affected by the other side *at the same time.* Since the design of most professional preparation grows from a mechanical, not a reciprocal model, few of us have had courses to learn the signs of the client's environmental situations that create restrictions, or to see the limiting adaptations our clients and children have made.

Rarely did we learn how to create situations (task demands) that intentionally call forth positive adaptations designed to create change for our clients. We were usually not trained to involve the clients-children-students in discussions and decisions about their wants, goals, fears, restrictions; and we were not accustomed to use their information as guides for what we might do differently because of that knowledge.

When we operate alone, on our side of the equation, we know only our own information about the other person. We do not know them as they experience themselves. We do not have a clue about their visual-space worlds, their reality. We are often surprised by their reactions of non-compliance, indifference or vocal complaints. Both sides feel isolated. The Experts, with one-sided knowledge, are left to themselves, to pull tricks out of their professional bags. The learners-patients tell the pollster they want a doctor who will listen to THEM. They resent being treated as group-identified parishioners, kids, heart patients, clients with depression, senior students, rather than as the individuals they and their friends know them to be. We have all heard some form of the complaint that professionals don't care: "I'm just a way for him to make money," "You don't care what I think, you only care about my grades," "She handed me a diet and didn't even ask what I already eat," "He makes me do 20 problems that I already know how to do."

Understanding vision and its reciprocal nature moves us beyond a segmented, one-sided concern with our own professional/parenting behavior. *We can be of more help to our children and clients if we learn from them something of their internal world.* Then we will have a chance to place ourselves into that world in a manner they will find acceptable and helpful. What we do in response to our students-clients-patients behavior matters. *If we incorporate their behavior into what we do, we will more likely get what we want* - the opportunity to make a significant difference, to provide help that actually helps.

If we cannot, then people often feel like objects and may acquiesce to our plans but not carry them out. When the help offered exceeds their capabilities at the time, they are caught in the Catch-22 of unilateral therapy. In order to get better he needs to do x; he cannot do x because of the restrictions in his behavior. Low grades in chemistry, interim notes of poor test scores may signal us as parents to insist on more study time. Jim is obviously bright, he must not be applying himself, we reason. Jim may even agree with you, and add another 45 minutes chained to his desk. If he cannot decode the formulas, has not a clue about the periodic table, and thinks moles are found only in gardens, another three days at his desk will not help. *What he knows and doesn't know needs to be put into the parents' and Jim's equation for solution. Unless we include the information from the patient or student in our considerations and deliberations, we cannot know their capabilities for participation.* We set ourselves up to be less effective than we might be.

What follows are a few descriptions of strategies to try. What's offered here does not cover all the principles of vision; the suggestions do not cover all possible interactions. They are not recipes from a cookbook of methods. They are simply descriptions that act as analogs, ideas to stimulate your ideas. Let them flow over, in and around you. Don't be concerned that you don't get a sense of what to do. If you hear the melody, you'll find the words. As our students, children, and clients regain unrestricted behaviors and increase their learning capabilities, their sight will become vision. They will be able to see possibilities for themselves and have confidence in their genuine ability to match more effectively their behavior to whatever the world puts in their path. Such is the gift of vision. Such is the goal of healers, parents, teachers.

PARENTS

Parents new to parenting soon find that children come in two paradoxical modes: dependence and independence. Infants who stay awake regardless of the rocking, bottles and hour; toddlers who run the other way; adolescents who go steady no matter what, all launch their bewildered parents into the choppy seas of their emerging independence. Whether or not the parent-child life boat capsizes depends upon the quality of the parents' management of this dependent-independent paradox. Effective parenting rests on a base of reciprocity, feedback and the balance of what they see in their children, their own mental pictures and what they do about both.

Children come with hardware that works: physical systems, sensori-perceptual systems, as well as cognitive, emotional potential. The world, parents included, acts as the laboratory where they combine and refine these potentials. Whatever difficulties arise in managing this developmental journey are magnified exponentially for parents and child if the child's basic hardware malfunctions - cystic fibrosis, deafness, cerebral palsy, Down Syndrome.

Regardless of the status of the children's learning equipment, it is their parents, or primary care-givers, who literally are the world to their children. They provide the software the youngsters use to

script their own development. Sighted children who develop efficient vision gradually write their own programs, picking and choos-
ing pieces of their experience that help them maintain,
independently, their developmental momentum.

Parenting Strategies That Help Sight Become Vision

1. *VISUAL-motor/visual-MOTOR* : Within the guidelines of safety,
children need maximum opportunity for movement: crawling,
walking, climbing, running. Within the context of appropriate
ability, they need equipment that they can move; tricycles, wagons,
wheelbarrows, peddle cars, swings, slides, balls, bats, skates, jump
ropes. These activities need not be encouraged at the expense of
quiet, controlled activities; but young children need movement in
order to learn how their bodies work, where they are in space, how
objects work and how they can make them work. Through movement they practice the laws of physics; they match what they see
with what they do and say. They store up the foundations of
sequential thinking, problem solving, visualizing.

For growth without restriction, close visual work, coloring,
writing, TV, video games, need to be balanced by movements
through space. A grandmother, meeting the idea of visual development for the first time, said, "You mean my mother was right?!
That I might not have become nearsighted if I had listened to her?
She always said sailors were not nearsighted because they spent so
much time looking in the distance while at sea, so I should go
outside and play instead of doing what I preferred, reading, and in
dim light, at that."

Tasks and encouragement need to be developmentally appropriate and in sequences that follow the usual progression: i.e., simple
to complex; large to small, center to periphery. Then you can be
happy with the circle and square drawn by your 4 year old and not
be concerned with the diamonds or diagonals that are beyond his
developmental stage. You'll understand that reversals in beginning
writing are usual or when they indicate lags in developmental skills.
You won't pressure your youngster to play soccer if she hasn't
mastered standing and hopping on one foot, running and skipping
or doesn't visualize well enough to see herself in relation to the
field, the ball, goals, and rules.

Outside is not the only arena for visual-movement development.
Playing in water with cups, funnels, bulb-basters, etc. is wonderful
eye-hand coordination and applied physics for pre-schoolers. Bak-

ing, clay work, sorting, stringing, putting together, taking apart all require matching what you see with what you do, and are more fun than just coloring within the lines, and these activities develop sustained near visual skills. Video movies are fun, and excellent stimulators of language; but they do nothing to help youngsters build a repertoire of visual-movement or the sensory-perceptual matches that are the foundation of their future efficient learning. Video games usually require very small movements - finger or wrist motion matched to fast-paced visual changes. This kind of visual-movement behavior may be more of a splinter skill than a foundation on which broader learning is based.

2. *VISUAL-verbal/visual-VERBAL:* Receptive language (understanding) develops before expressive language (talking). The quality of one depends upon the quality of the other. Words are symbols - they stand in for experience - but first *they have to be attached to that experience.* Pour in the language. Talk about what you see, what you are doing, name things even before children can talk. Ask for simple responses, pointing, looking, going to, rather than asking the child only to pronounce words. Talk about relationships, behind, next to, above, right, left, in front, bigger than, smaller than. Tell what is happening, what you are doing, so the youngster has a chance to see the world in action, to understand cause and effect, to see analogs and sequences, to know the reasons why.

Many children figure these things out for themselves, but many, many children do not. Those youngsters bring to academic tasks a paucity of understanding of how the world and they work. The tasks of reading and math assume projection on the part of the learner. If, in the story, Jane and Dick play with a wagon, go shopping, or build a tent, the readers' comprehension dawns because they have internalized what it's like to pull a wagon, push the cart in the supermarket, haul blankets over chairs to make a tent on a rainy day. Without that visualization of their own experience, students read words only. The academic world stays outside their real experience and becomes head knowledge only; or for some kids, not even that. Many children see school work only as something to do to get a grade tomorrow or to avoid detention; non-integrated, stimulus-response behavior.

Visual information can be a powerful tool. So *show* your children as well as tell them. Drawing a picture on the calendar to show when it will be circus time makes a much bigger impression than only the words, 'we're going next Saturday'. Make charts, lists, draw stick figure scenes. Represent visually whatever you want the youngster to learn and to notice. Don't just talk. With pictorial clues the information won't disappear as words do. The children can go back to it, use it as a reminder in the future, begin to see how visualizing helps us to know and think.

3. *Visualization:* Glasser lists power as a fundamental human need; personal power that supports competence, confidence and achievement. Visualization is the vehicle that empowers. It is here where the life lessons learned are brought to bear on the immediate problems of living. So expect your children to remember, to think up solutions to simple problems, to come up with alternatives, to anticipate, to see possibilities.

Most parents understand that for children to learn to throw a ball accurately they must practice. Parents will gently position themselves so preschoolers can get the ball to them and get the idea of throwing successfully to a target. They will automatically increase the distance between themselves and the youngster as skills improve. *Few parents use the same strategy to teach their children to think, to visualize.*

Most often a query such as "Where's my shoes?", brings forth an automatic parental answer. Rare is the parent who can let youngsters experience the natural consequences that occur from failing to remember, to anticipate, to find alternatives. The results of their behavior provides the feedback information they need to self-correct. This kind of learning requires guides, not pedagogues who tell them exactly how to do it. *"What do you think?"*, *"What have you tried?"*, *"What do you want help with?"*, "Are you satisfied with how this worked out?", "What's your plan to fix this?", "Are you ready to talk about a plan?" are all ways to indicate you'll support and help when needed, and, most important, that you confidently expect that the youngster will use her visualization skills to think for herself. You guide and support; the child does the doing.

4. *Digital/Analog Skills:* Just as most parents provide play equipment for children to exercise their muscles, there are ways to help children exercise their inherent potential to sequence and generalize. Usually parents initiate those activities that are the easiest for the adults, not necessarily the ones children need. People adept at organizing sequences and quantitative data (digital mode) emphasize those skills when playing with their children. They'll count

things a lot, ask questions requiring details, how many were there, what happened first, then what did you do? They'll emphasize form - sometimes more than meaning. These interactions set the direction for the children's organizing process, the kind of information they think they should notice.

Parents more in tune with analog processes ask different questions, provide different expectations *and their children grow in a different direction.* "What did you like best about it?", "Why do you think they did that?", "Does this remind you of something?" They look for meaning and connections. But this approach needs the counter-balance of the digital process. Without it, children could be hamstrung by their inability to express why and how they arrived at their bottom line conclusions, their inability to sequentially solve life problems. Without the digital component, they'll be left with opinion only, hampered in their communication with the digital majority in our culture.

To help your children be more at ease in both processes, make an intentional effort to expose them to activities and people that call forth these skills. Have puzzles around, encourage hand work, map reading, alphabetizing, counting, telling time, making lists. And also provide fairy tales and other literature, discussions of the themes and what they mean to the children as well as the details of the stories. Ask the children what they think about activities and events. Emphasize the why, the wonder, the unknown as well as the facts. If you are not comfortable in all of these areas, and few of us are - find a friend or teacher who can provide a balance to your preferred mode. This lack of processing balance is one of the primary drawbacks for children who are home-schooled. They get a double-dose of their parents' ways of thinking and seeing the world, and miss the opportunity for developing more balanced skills.

5. *Enhancement*: You may want to consult a professional in behavioral vision, if you live near one. They may be able to work with you so that the visual stress of school work can be reduced, lessening the chances of negative adaptations in your children. Wolff routinely prescribed lenses for all sustained close work, regardless of the person's age. The professional you select may be able to suggest activities or provide direct training that will help your youngster acquire and maintain efficient visual skills.

But with or without professional guidance you can do a great deal to assure that the learning equipment your children brought into this world works for them. You can follow their developmental trail, keep them on the track by offering alternatives, challenges and support that helps them maintain their inherent developmental momentum.

Every child comes with a built-in sense of growth, the potential to reach out, to do. Successful parents watch and help, have faith in and cheer that process.

Kids will, if they can.

If they don't, they probably can't.

They can, when they're guided rather than pushed, pulled or squelched.

When Your Child Has A Problem

Whether your youngster has an identifiable condition like Down Syndrome or cerebral palsy or you're concerned about atypical behavior that hasn't found a name, what you understand about sight, its relation to vision and its influence in your youngster's development can make a critical difference. The behavior tapped by intelligence tests has a visual-movement-language base; that base of learning is fluid, accessible to modification. The behavior labeled ADD or ADHD is characterized by *visual behavioral symptoms:* i.e., poor visual centering, poor visual directions, poor digital/analog balance. The symptoms often can be relieved by the non-drug management of visual learning described here. Contrary to the mechanical model, what's broken often can be fixed. When a child's learning equipment functions less efficiently than it could, there is interference in learning compared to their peers. If this interference continues, it creates the developmental gaps you, your children's teachers or physician see. It's only natural to pay attention to those lags. In fact most parents and teachers find it difficult to move beyond this and stay mostly focused on what the child cannot do. Instead begin to look at what the child CAN do. It is here, where behavior emerges that makes a critical difference in the quality of the child's life. Often the task of dealing with the child's problems means there is little energy left over to see what the youngsters *can* do now, and, crucially, *what they need to learn next.* So, in good stimulus-response fashion, we put braces on children, medicate their in-attention, refer them to special education and spend great energy helping the youngster compensate when our mental model tells us lags can't be fixed. *Just as punishment doesn't teach children what to do to remedy a situation, compensation, mechanical and chemical symptom fixes do not help the youngster learn what's needed to fill in the gap.*

If the case for vision's influence in behavior has been made for you in the previous chapters, then you might want to add these principles to your work with your child. The problems you're struggling with can rest in a different context, amid the factors of *learning* rather than in the midst of *deficits*. One mother asked in complete perplexity, "Did he knock over the lamp because he is cerebral palsied, because he's a boy, because he is hyperactive or because he is 5 years old?" She felt her management techniques would differ depending upon the answer. One suspects punishment could be substituted for management techniques. The teacher of this youngster was able to get her to see that learning to leave lamps standing was something this youngster needed to *learn*, despite his diagnostic labels. Teaching, rather than punishment, became the mother's new focus. Clinical experience based on the ideas presented here has shown that, above all, children are adaptable organisms; they respond to challenges and stresses presented to them. Events can be designed, interactions scripted that challenge and positively stress them so they move toward their next developmental stepping stone. If you have a youngster with a learning problem, you probably agree with one father who said, "I don't want another professional to tell me what my child can't do, I want them to teach him to do it." If you understand your child's learning and visual needs, you can participate in that teaching, and feel secure in the selection and direction of whatever professional help you seek.

Less restricted movement is one principle critical to the development of children with disabilities. If you follow Wolff's tenet of "go toward the norm", you will select physical activities that help your youngster practice whatever would be the next *developmental* movement skill needed. Your child may be 10 years old but needs to practice the six year old task of skipping. Then skip is what you could do together. Give them opportunities to try activities that are slightly advanced from what they can already do; if it's too advanced they will give up and learn little, if it's not a bit of a stretch, no new learning emerges.

The quantity of visual information available to your child and all its ramifications cannot add to children's growth if they *don't look at what they're doing*. Sounds obvious and simple, but observe this behavior in your child. Does he reach with hand only and not eyes? Does he try to figure out how many cookies by looking at you for the clue? Does he talk and look away when tying his shoes requires looking at the laces? How connected are his eyes with the rest of his activity? This vital behavior you can encourage and teach.

Almost all children can learn the next step in their developmental scheme. Too often the focus on disability by traditional therapy and special education obscures the teaching opportunities that make the critical difference, and prophecies become fulfilled.

EDUCATORS

It has reached the level of folklore that some 80% of the information children are expected to learn in schools is visual. Look at the teacher, copy from the board, find your way around the building, do these worksheets, read this chapter, work these problems, take this test. It is also common knowledge that school systems are under great pressure to meet the needs of all children, the able as well as the "at risk", in our rapidly changing culture. One of the modern strategies to meet the needs of students who are not able to cope with traditional education is the use of specialists: speech pathologists who help kids learn to speak more clearly and use English more effectively; psychologists who evaluate the children's intellectual and academic development, who qualify children for special services; counselors who help students plan their academic program, adjust to the school situation and find appropriate help if social and emotional problems emerge. Then there are traditional special education teachers for children who qualify for help outside or inside the regular classroom. Extending the sphere of specialists, some school systems now employ occupational and physical therapists to work with children whose coordination and body knowledge seem to lag behind. Schools offer a lot of services. But isn't it interesting that with the emphasis on specialists and special needs, with 10-40% of our children disconnected to the school's programs, and with 80% of the school's demand being visual, that we don't have specialists in vision?

Until we see that children's learning and school success relate to their visual process it is unlikely that programs or curricula will be designed which enhance their fundamental learning processes. If we particularize the educational process, then we can talk about what it takes for John or Jane to become more efficient learners, to fulfill in academic achievement the promise seen by their parents and kindergarten teachers. After all, *it is always the individual student's interaction with the teacher, curriculum and physical surround that influences his/her success.* The design for the educational system, and the fanciest curriculum comes down finally to one teacher interacting with one child. That one teacher's awareness, one administrator's new point of view can result in changes in what they do and expect from Johnny and Jane, which will help Johnny and Jane change their learning.

Expanded awareness and different viewpoints must be translated into actions to effect change in the students. This section focuses on the actions that can flow once a teacher's or administrator's mental pictures include their students' visual development. Space allows for only suggestions; an exhaustive discussion of visual behavior in education requires its own book. What's offered here is a sampling.

In The Classroom

If you are a teacher and want to enhance your students' visual efficiency be aware of the visual demands of your classroom and the level of the visual development and sophistication of the students you teach. Be aware that their visual/ information processes are not full-blown. They may have sight, but they're building their visual repertoire out of their interaction with you and the tasks and environment you provide.

Reciprocity: As in all human behavior, the child has a reciprocal relationship with you and the tasks of school. You provide tasks, the child attempts them and in so doing exercises his sensory-perceptual equipment and finds out what works and what doesn't. The student adapts to what you present. Depending upon the particular learning organization of a student, those adaptations may foster new learning or they may restrict development.

That's what the student is doing, but what about you, the teacher? Are you affected by the student's response to what you present? Do you see the adaptations taking place? If you are in a reciprocal relationship with the student, you will respond to the student on the basis of what he/she did with your original task, help the student move along the developmental road, not functioning simply as a gate-keeper who hands out grades as tickets: yes, that's it - no, that's not it. Students don't hand in assignments, some teachers hand out detentions, zappers or just quietly enter a zero in their grade book. Some teachers tell the student the assignments are missing, listen to the student's explanation and ask for a specific plan for making it up, and/ or for tracking completed assignments in the future. etc. They do this in order *to teach the student* as well as the social studies. As in a dance, each part of the reciprocal relationship depends upon the response of the other to know what to do next. One educator said it is *the student who becomes the curriculum* when asked to describe this approach in teaching. Particularity, reciprocity. Fundamental principles in fostering visual development.

Visual-Movement Skills

Teachers can also control the classroom tasks so that specific visual-movement skills can be enhanced, or at least not so restricted that learning is impeded. Incidences of nearsightedness among students seems to increase as the demand for near, visual work increases. This is a restrictive adaptation particular students make in order to survive in the classroom. Much can be done to modify those adaptations.

Most teachers expect that the visual-movement foundation of their students is intact and up to the demands of their classroom. Those spatial-movement functions of vision that Harmon describes in Chapter 4 are not usually noted by educators: How the children posture themselves, the light distribution in the room, the helps and hurts in the environment for students to visually center on the teacher, on seat work, on the board. Most educators look at the product the child produces: the quantity and quality of reading, the content and computation in math, the neatness of the handwriting, the quality of the paragraphs, spelling; evidence that content has been mastered; ultimate academic success and independence. Most teachers teach academics. What do you do? I teach 3rd grade; I teach reading; I teach social studies. Awareness of the developing visual process in students can change teachers' identities: I teach 8 year olds how to read; I teach students math. Teaching people how to do something has a different orientation than teaching subject matter. The configuration of the teacher-student-academics triangle changes shape.

Expectations

See the students as capable, as doing the very best they can at the moment, as trying; even the students you are tempted to label 'not motivated' or 'not trying'. Use their errors as guides for future lessons. Try to show them some problem solving strategies (heuristics):

Syllabication:
1. Look at the first vowel letter
2. Name what comes after it (consonant-consonant or consonant-vowel)
3. Match the configuration to the decision pattern: VC/ C or V/ CV.

Students will come to see you as a guide for their own learning and less of a judge of their product. As part of your guidance, help them focus on new behaviors instead of the ones that don't work:

Where are your books?

I forgot them.

We need your books; get them and tell me a plan so you will have them next time.

A detention for non-compliance focuses on what the student didn't do, it is punishment. The rationale for punishment is that it will teach him a lesson, that the student will want to avoid the pain and so will change his behavior. Punishment does not necessarily *teach the student how* to elicit the expected behavior.

Feedback

As a guide, you are part of the student's feedback system. One student told her tutor that she didn't want to be told how to manage her school life, but needed the tutor to be the guard rails while she learned to drive on this road of independent organization. Students need information to know when they are on the track, what it is that they should do again, what they are doing that is off the track. They especially need help to develop plans that will get them back on. One freshman was astonished that her missing assignments actually affected the grade on her card. Because her English teacher sat down with her to average her grades at the mid-term, she could see that if she had handed in all assignments she would have had a C+ instead of the D- she currently had. When she saw what was required to change that D, she was willing to work on a plan to get the work done. Without that feedback, she would give up (as she did in other classes) because her mental picture was that she was only D material, not that what she actually does is what makes the difference. Almost no students want to fail, or set out to do it wrong. What they are about is trying to learn. The particular visual-spatial skills some students need to learn may not be visible to the observer except in the maladaptive behavior they present. Too often what they get in response is a label rather than the lessons they need.

Classroom Management

Look at your classroom from the students' point of view. If you're a primary teacher, be aware that many of your children are visually-spatially unsophisticated. They're just learning how to find where you are in the room, to shift from looking at you and the board to their desks, to using their central vision for finding tiny squiggles on the page. Does the way you've arranged the environment help or hinder their development of those skills? In the attempt at enrichment have you put up so many inviting materials on the walls that they become distractions for the children's peripheral vision? Is it harder than it might be for them to find what they're supposed to see and use?

Spoken words fade away. Whenever possible, have a visible source to reinforce your words: For young children, a daily schedule; a graphic to explain the paper trail you expect; some heuristic drawings to show problem solving strategies in phonics and math. For older students, assignments on the board, assignment schedules for the month, unit or quarter. The students who visualize well may not need these for long, but the visual guides provide a constant for those students who are learning how to keep track of things and time.

Some students listen better when they doodle, or swing their feet or twirl their hair, or tear up the edges of their books. They are inefficient at visual learning and need this support of other modalities. If the demand is to eliminate these adaptive behaviors in the name of paying attention, the student's comprehension may well go down and their resistance will surely go up. Helping them become more efficient visual learners is a more permanent way to solve this problem.

They need to know:
WHERE TO LOOK (visual centering)
WHAT THEY'RE LOOKING AT OR FOR
(visual identification)
WHAT TO DO WITH THE INFORMATION ONCE
THEY'VE FOUND IT (visualization)
They may need specific teaching to apply these skills in academics. Ask questions that will lead them to discover for themselves this construct. What chapter are we on? Where is the section we're discussing? What are the subjects and verbs in those sentences? How will you find them in other sentences? What's the strategy

for finding them? Or if they've been through that; what are you supposed to do now?

Administration

In the design and maintenance of the educational system, whether at the individual school or the system level, the learning needs of students could be factored in. Since so many children of the 90's come to school without mastery of the important visual behaviors on which academic success depends, it may be that the educational system will have to allow children to learn and practice these skills in school. Education reform, the buzzwords of our era, can put visual-learning behavior, as described here, on the agenda along with teachers' competence and salary, structure of the school day and year, and academic outcomes.

Adding the profession of learning therapist or facilitator to the staff may be something schools develop once they decide that those children on the fringes of competence and in special education can actually learn how to learn. From the viewpoint of Wolff and other clinicians who know the results of enhanced visual development, almost all children can make greater than expected strides in closing their learning gap. Many more children than expected can move out of the categories assigned them by their inefficient vision and learning. Educational administrators, at whatever level, can stimulate discussion about these possibilities and tap realities other than cause/effect as models. Chances can be increased that more students will survive academically and because of that, economically in our rapidly changing post-modern world.

SUMMARY: Parents and educators want to positively influence the development and achievement of their children; they create their parenting and educational behaviors from their mental pictures. They can increase their teaching effectiveness by including the principles of visual behavior in their interactions with their children, since these principles address their children's most fundamental learning processes and needs. These principles include reciprocity, perceptual integration, parts/wholes, see more/do more, feedback, particularity and the norm as guide.

CHAPTER 10 WE DO WHAT WE SEE
Vision in business, healing professions, organizations

Implications, Applications, Contemplations

"Man is a visually dominant organism. If he can't see he can't survive without the help of others." If we are involved with people who have sight, we are in touch with the reality of the dominance of vision in their behavior. When your secretary has trouble with spelling, loses your reports, or schedules you for two different appointments at the same time, you live with that person's visual process in action. When your associate soothes an irate customer, asks the pivotal question that makes the next step in problem solving apparent, hands in reports on time, you witness the action part of this individual's visual process.

When colleagues present a new business project, you experience through the medium of language, the quality of their visualization of form, spatial relationships and digital/analog proficiency that underlies their concept and presentation. We even use the term 'vision' when we want to acknowledge the merit and scope of the ideas presented.

The trendy thrusts in our culture, interactive marketing, focus groups, vision statements indicate that as our practices and institutions begin to match our real human needs and behavior, they look more and more like Wolff's description of integrated visual behavior rather than re-makes of the old mechanical model which tradition offers. Welcome to the paradigm revolution!

Professionals in various fields, interested in the application of Wolff's model into their own work, often approached him. Many engaged him in extended conversations, some through bits and pieces over years; others in more intense one-time encounters. As they exchanged realities, they often would discover and relish numbers of junctures where their views merged. What follows are gleanings from such conversations, and some of the implications that can be inferred when the template of visual behavior is placed over the behavior seen by other professionals. Conversations are usually not descriptions or lists of facts; they are exchanges of human interpretations of particular events and experiences. Satisfying conversations raise questions, follow side roads, excite. Satisfying conversations have two or more sides, supporting reactions that contribute to the forward movement for all.

As you dialog with this material, you may find, as other professionals have, that the principles of visual behavior highlight facets of your clients' behavior that may have been in the shadows. Those who have incorporated these principles into their own practice have found, more often than not, their effectiveness increase and their knowledge and expertise expand.

Let's start by making some fundamental connections between traditional therapies and visual behavior. For example, since the professions of *physical and occupational therapy* help people attain greater independence in their movement abilities and vision and movement are two sides of the same coin, it follows that these professionals actually engage their patients' visual process as they stimulate and manipulate the patient's limbs.

Counseling, psychology and speech-language therapies influence behavior in their clients through language; language the clients have attached to their visual-movement experience; language that expresses their visualization of that previous experience and their digital-analog processes; language that hints at the visual-movement base on which it rests.

TIP OF BEHAVIORAL ICEBERG

Susan is the same person who looks in the mirror, knows her own thoughts, sees her physician, goes to physical therapy, talks with her counselor, works at her job. But Susan would be described very differently depending upon the orientation of the expert she consults, including herself. If you put their reports side by side it might sound as if there were many Susans. But with the holographic and cybernetic new-science models, we see that no matter what particular aspect of Susan and her behavior is the focus of specialists, they, like the blind Chinese feeling separate parts of an elephant, *actually see and discuss the same human elephant called Susan.* Varied professional pronouncements do not describe different things, only different aspects of the same thing. This perspective lets us see a possibility that the *whole of Susan could be more nearly described;* that the different aspects of her behavior and her condition could be seen in such a way that we can get closer to identifying *her,* all of her. With that understanding we also could see that if one facet changes, it potentially affects all others.

Part of Wolff's working definition of vision says:

"Vision produces visual space within which its processes can be assessed *to define the person."*[1]

A group of professionals with new-science backgrounds jointly considered the atypical behavior and learning of a young girl. The group included a psychologist, a counselor, behavioral vision experts and educators. It became apparent to them that although their vocabulary differed, they actually were talking about the *same behavioral operation*. Once that unified vision appeared, treatment approaches and priorities were easily designed.

Wolff specialized, devoting his practice to vision and visual problems. In that capacity he consulted with therapists from other disciplines when appropriate. He had the most direct hands-on connection with parents and educators. The implications and applications for parents and educators in the previous chapter rest on actual encounters and therapy approaches tested in the lives of his patients. What follows is an extension of these principles into areas of healing therapies, business, and organizations.

HEALING THERAPIES

Physical, Body Therapies

All of the therapies that deal in movement, muscles and body awareness deal with the visual system as well, since it is through the action system that people learn to see and see to learn. The principles outlined in Chapter 4 of the visual-MOTOR base of the visual process will be most evident in these therapies: Vision as the determiner for the body's response to light; vision as the balancer of the bilateral system in dynamic postures; vision as the guidance system for transport through space. These professions encounter the body warps, the physical manifestation of the visual adaptations. These warps are (1) the asymmetries that occur in all three spatial axes of the body, x (horizontal plane), y (vertical plane) z (rotational plane), (2) restrictions in bilateral, reciprocal movement; (3) mismatches between vision and movement.

These professions; (physical therapy, occupational therapy, massage therapy) see the effects of deprivation and stress played out in sore muscles and inefficient movement. They focus on the capabilities of neuro-muscular systems that cannot tolerate the stress of the activities of daily life either because of accident, illness or functional adaptations.

Traditional science most often taught us that whatever physical problem the patient brings usually is a sign that something is broken or not working right. Treatment often consists of attempts to alleviate the symptoms. If the symptoms cannot be alleviated through surgery, mechanical manipulation, or drugs then compensation is the usual consequence. When diagnostic tests show nothing broken, many patients are told there is nothing to fix, which implies that their pain and reduced function reside somewhere outside their muscular system.

Wolff and the new-science tell us that the body works as an integrated unit, so it follows that the form and direction of the visual adaptations the person has made would be evident in the physical body. The muscle patterns seen result from *the person's total movement-action system,* rather than as isolated problems related only to particular muscles. Think in terms of the x,y,z axes and how the affected muscles and patterns contribute to the person's movement through space, to their dynamic posture when seated at near visual tasks over time, to specific postures and movements in their work. Can you visualize how the asymmetries and stresses and restrictions you observe would look in action? Try to place yourself in the posture of the restrictions of a particular patient. What does that do to your posture and movement? Try to stand, walk or move as your patient does, what can you tell about the direction needed to *re-establish balance and reciprocal movement?* The priorities and directions of your therapy may change when the *patient's behavior and movement become the prescriptors* rather than text-book treatment of particular diagnoses.

Although Thomas Hanna, originator of Somatic Therapy, probably did not know of Harmon's and Wolff's work in vision, his approach to body warps was cut from similar cloth. He described the warps he observed as part of a total movement pattern, resulting from interrupted muscle feedback awareness that he called "sensory amnesia". He probably did not have the advantage of understanding the relationship of vision to posture and movement in the development and alleviation of such warps, but his approach gives a glimpse of new-science view that could be added to traditional treatments. Here's how he described one patient's treatment:

> When James told me his problem (severe low back pain) I did two simple things: I touched him and I looked at him. Palpation - feeling the patient's body - is almost a lost art in the medical world. Why touch patients if you can see inside their bodies with x rays? The reason is because x rays do not show the body's softer tissues, like the muscles. When I touched James's paravertebral muscles, I found that they were not soft, but rigidly contracted, almost like cables. And when I looked at him

from the side, I saw that his lower back was curved into a swayback.[2]

Hanna continued,

> ...The moment we realize that James is a human with a brain, whose functions are however deficient, we know he can determine for himself what functional changes he needs to make. But if we think of James merely as a brainless mechanical doll with a collapsed spinal structure, then we have a desperate medical situation, one that demands a reengineering of the doll's spine - the operation James's doctor could not guarantee. I treated James as a human being who could relearn to sense and control the hypertense muscles of his lower back.[3]

If people can relearn to sense and control their movements and unrestrict habituated patterns, it follows they will need teachers to help them. Teachers, therapists, who understand movement as dynamic patterns, understand that movement emerges from dynamic postures, *warped by visual-movement stress.*

People mold their bodies in relation to their visual-spatial orientation. Harmon described the myopic, nearsighted posture as pulling space in, rounding the torso and shoulders, leading with the chin and the hyperopic, far-sighted posture of extending the chest, pulling shoulders back to cut a swath through space, to be out there. These postures come in as many variations as there are people and certainly illness and injury compound an individual's basic set; but, *people's postural warps reflect a fundamental visual orientation in space.*

MaryAnn, whom you met in Chapter 4, had a stiff neck and muscles spasms in her shoulder. She felt this was a result of visual and physical stress and what Wolff called "critical empathy", when the system can no longer continue in the direction of warp and tries to reach a more balanced state. Traditional medicine had little to offer for the pain and restrictions in movement she experienced except physical therapy which treated only the aching muscle groups. This relieved some of the immediate pain, but did not address the underlying cause: dynamic posture; consequently, the condition was bound to recur. When a non-traditional therapist included MaryAnn's entire body orientation, head to shoulders, shoulders to trunk, limbs to the center of gravity in the therapy plan the condition became manageable and function restored. From this therapist's description of her posture MaryAnn could see that the *direction of adjustment she needed to learn exactly matched the positive visual adaptations* she was re-learning in visual centering and identification: move in, pull space closer, equalize the bilateral balance. The difference was that now she participated actively to change basic patterns instead of feeling like the brainless doll Hanna describes whose symptoms would be worked on, or settling for compensating postures that would alter the quality of her life by reducing her activities.

Healing of the whole person when their symptoms are identified in their skeletal-muscular systems often can be facilitated by attention to visual processes, including consultation with visual behavioral professionals if they are available.

Medicine

From laser surgery, invitro fertilization, to bone marrow transplants medicine has become a marvel. Millions of us who would not have made it a generation ago can attest to the life-saving diagnoses and treatments medicine now offers. The proof is in: *the mechanical, traditional scientific model works wonders*. Especially when you have a specific disease entity or trauma injury, you can feel secure that medicine has help for you.

It is the area of functional problems, where no particular part of the human machine seems broken, that causes frustration for both the physician of tradition and the patient. The non-specific symptoms of headaches, chronic pain, fatigue may get temporary relief, but few enduring cures. The idea that stress alters function has seeped into the mainstream, but it's still rare to hear traditional medicine concur that *function alters structure*. It's even rarer for the patient to hear the implications discussed in the traditional physician's office.

Functional conditions are just that: dis-ease in how something works - in function. *Human beings operate as light-space-gravity bound organisms adapting to their environment in order to move and do*. To understand how they do that means looking at the basic processes involved in functional problems. Since vision plays a fundamental role in human behavior, it would follow that it plays a role in the maladaptions called functional problems.

Tradition speaks through medicine in the language of the scientific model. Whatever will be deemed truth by traditional medicine must come from that model. The pure science of the laboratory makes its conclusions through linear science. *The factors of functional human behavior are non-linear* and require other forms for analysis. Apples and oranges, so we are left with tons of anecdotal data of treatments and therapies from applied, non-linear science and no acceptable procedures for the systematic study of that data or opportunities for dialogue between these two positions. Anecdotal information is unacceptable to the medical profession. Since the scientific model with its emphasis on specific variable controls does not fit the way human behavior works, it is an unacceptable vehicle to demonstrate the determiners of human functions, such as vision, which do not have only one-to-one relationships. Resolving this dilemma will be the challenge of the next century for medicine and alternative therapies. Dr. Bob Arnot, CBS - TV consultant, said it takes three to five years for physicians to change their methods after the publication of verified new information in their fields. It's mind numbing to consider how long it may take for traditional medicine to look at effective new-science practices.

Meanwhile the principles of behavioral vision can be added to the linear, discrete approach of clinical medicine and expand possibilities for particular physicians' clinical practices and their patients. People, whether doctor or patient, are control systems; they seek to act in order to promote and protect their selfhood, in or out of the doctor's office. People act on the world, the world acts on them. Some within the medical community recognize this reciprocal reality. An example is a recent Associated Press article about Dr. Morton Creditor's views on the effects of standard hospital environment on elderly patients. He said:

> For many (elderly patients) hospitalization is followed by an often irreversible decline in functional status and a change in quality and style of life.

He goes on to connect the effects of subdued lighting, high beds, lack of the patient's own clothes, or the presence of orienting calendars and clocks and disorienting hospital routines and bedrest to the elderly patients' tendency toward "complications such as a drop in blood pressure that leads to dizziness and falls, a loss of bone density that results in more breaks and sensory deprivation that may be mistaken for senility." [4]

Dr. Creditor, University of Kansas Medical Center, discovered that *human behavior* including internal physical and mental behavior, *can be drastically affected by individuals' interactions with their environment.* Perhaps these noted elderly are to us what the canary was to coal miners: an early warning, an alert, to the factors that are not life enhancing for any of us.

A pamphlet in one physician's office left no doubt what kind of science he practiced. In an attempt to acknowledge the doctor-patient relationship, the pamphlet listed what the patient could do as part of that relationship. Summarized, the items left the impression that the *patient's role was to trust the doctor, carry out the doctor's prescriptions and advice, and have faith in the doctor's training,*. Nowhere did it say what the doctor would do in this relationship, nor what together they might accomplish.

The bodies and diseases physicians treat in their offices come attached to people. If the principles of reciprocity and integration make sense, they apply here as well. Hans Selye's work on stress and its role in disease has alerted physicians to enlarge their traditional context to include stress factors operating in their patient's lives. Since the visual system functions so integratively, it is an early casualty in stress adaptations; it could become part of the physician's reality.

The physician could add changes in the patient's visual acuity to the history information. Changes in accommodation may be an early warning sign of prolonged stress, particularly if the patient spends a great proportion of time in near-visual activities. Referral to professionals in behavioral vision can help the patient cushion direct visual stress before the adaptations become permanent; and through learning more efficient ways to process information their stress thresholds could be raised. The possibility of visual-body adaptations as factors in non-specific, functional complaints could give the physician another tool, provide possible relief for common complaints of back pain, idiopathic soft muscle pain. The physician's view of the symptom complex could be enlarged. If these conditions are seen as the result of maladaptions of visual-movement patterns, then another therapy direction, toward more positive adaptation in movement/vision, would be possible.

When a physician acknowledges the relationship of vision, movement and learning, options for recommendations expand. Often the pediatrician is the first professional consulted by parents concerned about atypical learning and school behavior in their children. When no physical reasons appear, parents may have difficulty reconciling their literal interpretation of the Dr.'s 'there's nothing wrong' with their child's continuing symptoms of learning problems. It is not uncommon for years to be lost before parental concern breaks through their conditioning and sends them in search of additional help. When we know through standard assessment that a child's sensory thresholds and neuromuscular status are within the norm, that's all we know. *It is not enough information from which to project the quality of their learning and information processing or to make life-determining prognoses.* We cannot know how that youngster uses his/her learning equipment unless we *look at the child's behavior that emerges from his/her particular learning and perceptual organization.* That is best done by professionals with that expertise, just as measles is best identified and treated by those with experience and training in managing that disease.

Medical research to understand how the human body works, how it reacts and interacts with environmental factors more and more includes the human factors, i.e., particular reactions to stress, social connections. The data will not be complete unless information about one of the most fundamental of all human factors, visual behavior is included. Surely visual-movement adaptations produce physical symptoms, surely *visual stresses in growing organisms affect the quality of organization within that and other developing systems.*

Whether or not that interactive, integrated process of human beings and their physiology ultimately can be described depends upon the *visual organization of the researchers.* Their own visual process will determine where they choose to look for answers, what they make of their observations. The hard sciences, particularly physics, now recognize the influence of the observer on the observed. Barbara McClintock said it for all scientific investigators who want to do more than identify parts and treat them one at a time:

> ...one must have the time to look, the patience to "hear what the material has to say to you," the openness to "let it come to you." Above all, one must have a "feeling for the organism."[5]

Counseling - Psychology - Speech Language Pathology

These healing professions work largely through verbal language. The speech pathologist uses speech and language directly as a means to examine and treat speech and language behavior when it negatively affects communication. The psychologist and counselor use speech and language indirectly as the medium to understand their clients' psychic and emotional discomfort and to direct the client toward more fulfilling responses. For professionals in these fields, words are the tools of their trade.

Words come attached to prior experience, that experience registered through their visual-movement systems. Even though these professions know their patients through the exchange of verbal language, *the patient's language describes, in large part, the patients' visual-movement learning.* Even though the patient's treatment hour may be spent talking and listening, the patients present more than ears and mouths; all of the patient sits down in the therapy room. *Whatever total behavior the therapist observes, it emerges from that integrated visual-movement base.* Most therapists and counselors are adept at reading body language; but, few read body language as expressions of the individual's *visual organization* as well as indicators of emotional responses.

Knowledge about the vision and the visual-movement process gives professionals in talking therapies a broader context into which their observations of language and behavior can be placed. Seen through the lens of visual behavior more data about the client can be available. *This information is always and actually present, whether or not therapists see it.* Recognition of this data leads to specific routes in therapy; it may condense the course of treatment.

Psychology, counseling, speech pathology are patient-bound, with less opportunity than the physical therapies to treat the patient as an object. What the client does and tells are the raw materials for these professionals. Their therapist-client relationship is, by its very nature, reciprocal and integrated; but the quality of it depends upon the qualities of verbal language the therapist and client bring to that relationship.

To expand the restrictions imposed by language, try adding observations of visual behavior to your expertise. Here are a few ways to begin.

Standardized Testing

Those professionals who administer standardized tests have the temptation of describing the person through scores, stanines, and percentile ranks. Often life determining prognoses are based on that data. We've all been alerted to the inappropriateness of using I.Q. scores in isolation without support from other testing to describe and predict; but it still happens. Rarely are the tests analyzed to see what fundamental visual-movement processes are tapped by specific tasks and how the individual's visual learning skills influence their scores.

Approaching clients from a visual behavioral point of view gives clinicians tools to describe what they actually see the patient do as well as infer from standardized scores. Individuals, and certainly their behavior, are more than the sum of their scores. Even when the tasks presented are not specifically to test visual-motor behavior, i.e., performance items on intelligence tests, tests of eye-hand coordination, the clients present clues to their visual-movement adaptations. One way to see them, is to *make specific observations about their body posture while they perform tasks:*

Postural Observations

Centering - Identification: Where is the task in relation to the client's center? What is the distance the client maintains from the task? Is that distance constant for all tasks, does it vary? Under what conditions does it vary? It is not unusual for people to move closer to tasks that are difficult or that they do not understand. The Harmon norm (see Chapter 4) for centered near visual tasks is about 13 inches. Consistent distances inside or outside the 13 inches can be considered significant deviations and should be noted.

Dynamic Balance: How does the person align head, neck, trunk, hips with eyes and hands? Note heads that are turned and tilted, rotations of tasks or forms when copying. What asymmetries are noted: head tilts, uneven shoulder heights, body forward or behind hips, leaning trunk to one side, holding up head with one hand for reading or writing tasks. One youngster when reading and looking at pictures, kept both hands resting on her temples, elbows on the table. As she read she slowly slid her fingers to the outside corners of her eyes and applied pressure (an attempt at manual control of her binocular alignment). There is currently no systematic professional training that teaches us to make note of and interpret this kind of idiosyncratic behavior and relate it to visual functions.

Digital/Analog Process

Tasks and the questions asked in a testing situation can be put in the digital/analog framework. That analysis yields information that can be verified either by standardized testing or informal assessment with specific tasks that call upon those skills. *How is the spontaneous or responsive information the client offers organized?* Do they offer mostly opinions and bottom lines, interpretations and reasons(analog); or, do they let you know step-by-step descriptions and explanations which focus on details of events(digital)? Perhaps your own organization predetermines, through your questions, a particular kind of data. Either way, the client's digital/analog organization skills can be verified through analysis of standardized tasks which require these specific visual organizations: visual analogies where relationships have to be identified (analog process) or visual matching of complicated patterns or sequences (digital process). Understanding the client from this perspective adds another dimension to treatment plans. If the goal of therapy is to help the client attain more flexibility and improved skills either in speech-language or in coping and affective response, the patient will reach that goal more easily if he/she has a better balance between digital/analog functions. The client's restrictions will be reduced, their capabilities strengthened.

Verbal Therapy Within Visual Space

Situations you select as therapy because of their language or affective components also have a strong visual-spatial-movement base. The speech therapist who bakes cookies with pre-schoolers in order to learn new vocabulary and practice following verbal directions also *structures the child's visual space, organizes the things within it,* and tells the child what is *important to regard, where to look. All of this visual-spatial experience attaches to the words they learn.* Consequently, the youngsters experience a form of visual therapy as well as speech-language therapy. Probably because this process is so tightly integrated in the therapy experience for both therapist and client, few people see it.

The psychologist who uses play therapy to work on emotional and affective issues, also provides *visual-spatial materials,* stuffed animals, doll houses, human figures, and *sits in particular spatial relation to the child.* The therapist enters into conversation about what is happening: another *structure of the child's visual space.* For some children this is a critical part of their learning and from a behavioral vision point of view plays an important part in their improved functioning. Knowing something about the child's visual status could provide treatment clues in how the visual-spatial components could be *intentionally manipulated* to meet the special visual needs of particular clients. Because vision is dominant in learning, the use of pictorial cues in therapy often facilitates the client's understanding. *The use of stick figures, lines and circles to represent relationships and concepts, flow charts to indicate sequences are a few of the aids that can illustrate and reinforce issues of therapy.*

Speech pathology deals with learning and some aspects of graphic language as well as verbal speech and language. These therapists are trained to understand the concepts of homeostasis and feedback as crucial to their therapeutic skills. It seems logical that their clinical viewpoint could adapt easily to include visual as well as verbal behavior.

Research

Research in psychology and speech-language therapy relies on standard procedures emerging from the scientific method; use of experimental and control groups matched by certain variables. *These variables rarely, if ever, include the visual status of the participants.* It seems an obvious consideration if the experimental conditions require any kind of literal visual behavior: looking at pictures, identifying and classifying visually, etc. Inferences are often made on normal brain function and organization through such tasks *without some consideration of the visual behavioral status of the subjects.* The underlying traditional assumption is that if atypical visual acuity has been compensated to the norm, (a near or farsighted individual has 20/20 corrected sight with glasses) then everything else is equal and any differences in results would not relate to visual organization. *If visual behavior makes any sense, these assumptions might not stand if research studies included this visual viewpoint.*

BUSINESS

The paradigm revolution is alive and well within the business community. Responding to our rapidly changing world order, businesses struggle with adaptations and restructuring; they innovate and create systems of organization that embrace the concepts of new-science: interrelatedness, subjectivity, reciprocity, cybernetic theory, quantum mechanics. Max DePree's *Leadership Is An Art*, and Tom Peters' *Liberation Management* are two recent books that describe how these ideas live in real businesses. More and more the kinds of business organizations that adapt successfully look like models of the visual-movement process.

> Competition is now a "war of movement" in which success depends on anticipation of market trends and quick response to changing customer needs. Successful competitors move quickly in and out of products, markets and sometimes even entire businesses - a process more akin to an interactive video game than to chess. In such an environment, the essence of strategy is *not* the structure of a company's products and markets, but the dynamics of its behavior. [6]

Movement, anticipation, quick response, interactive, dynamic behavior. And we're talking about business? Sounds like visually directed human behavior. These revolutionary concepts in business seem to emerge from a spontaneous, intuitive awareness of how people interact with the world; they tap the same vein of visual behavior Wolff mined even though they do not recognize, necessarily, the role vision plays in these ideas.

Whether managing their employees, satisfying customers, creating products or assessing the bottom line, the concerns of business are the relationships of people. Since the success or failure of a business depends upon people in these various contexts, the ideas of behavioral vision impact business practices as well as therapeutic ones. In fact, *vision* is a concept that emerges frequently in current business philosophy and literature.

> Management and leadership experts say the turmoil at American Express, General Motors, IBM and other companies reflects the failure of big business in recent decades to cultivate visionary leaders for changing times.[7]

These visionary leaders respond to change and chaos in our political and economic environment the same way all people respond: *through their visual-movement-language base of behavior.* Helping people become more efficient visually will help increase the numbers of people who demonstrate these skills of leadership. The successful business leaders of the '90's will know more than traditional business practices and theories. Peters quotes Harry Quadracci, CEO of Quad/Graphics, a company that has made it to the other side of the paradigm shift. Quadracci says, "Our employees look at change and learning as job security." Peters goes on to say that Quadracci's "think small" concept pushes everyone to change "something, anything each day. Just start it, do *something.*"

> He offers a warning: "The message sounds scary. Coddling is out. Lean-and-mean structures, continuous education, self-generated projects, and ambiguity are in. The bad news: Brand-new definitions of careers and new shapes of organizations make the downside - organizations and individuals - onerous for those who don't get it."[8]

Those of us whose visual behavior is the least restricted will be the ones who get it and can do it. Those of us who understand the visual process as integrative and reciprocal can apply these visual principles to the business process and contribute actively in the birth of these new organizations.

One who has done so is Edward Deming whose concept of Total Quality has had wide application. He understood the principles of the cybernetic model, reciprocity, feedback, visualization, centering/identification and developed business practices based on them. Total Quality helps business identify what it is about, what it wants, what it will do based on some knowledge of the market- [the equivalent of centering/identification in the visual process.] It goes on to help business meet those perceived needs through product development- comparable to the visualization and movement phase of visual-movement loop. The Total Quality demand for data that defines whether or not the objectives have been met acts as *visual feedback* to guide further movement.

A management person in one of our largest corporations where Total Quality had been tried said he found Total Quality and hierarchical decision-making incompatible. Hierarchy emerges from the linear, stimulus-response model; Total Quality rests on the cybernetic - feedback loop, non-linear model. Another example of the dissonance created when new scrapes against old.

The new in business requires different structures, different organization patterns which operate more and more like the human visual-movement system. In "Jump In With Both Feet", Tom Peters describes how this works through a study by Kathleen Eisenhardt. She was interested in decision makers in the microcomputer firms and found the "slowpokes took 12 to 18 months to do what the quick set pulled off in 2 to 4."

> ...slow decision makers considered fewer alternatives than their speedy kin. They minutely dissected each possibility while the greased-lightening gang considered a batch of options - all at once.
>
> ...the one-at-a-timers mulled and mulled - and mulled and mulled - often until opportunity passed them by.
>
> ...the fast decision makers thoroughly integrated strategies and tactics. ...Sluggish blokes examined strategic decisions in a vacuum, delaying grubby operational considerations until the "big choices" were made...
>
> "The premium now is on moving fast and keeping pace."[9]

"Moving fast and keeping pace" surely assume knowing where you're going and graphically restate fundamental visual-movement behavior. Vision allows you to pick those targets and tells you whether or not you're getting there, no matter if you're walking to a friend's house or plotting business strategy.

To begin intentional incorporation of the principles of behavioral vision into areas of your business life regardless of its current structure, here are a few things to try:

Mental Set

When faced with problematic issues in your business, think about relationships and their connections rather than reducing situations to cause and effect, stimulus-response, either-or thinking patterns. Allow for inconsistencies and ambiguities as part of the total situation, rather than expend energy trying to eliminate them. Look for the context, the big picture. *Whatever the nature of your issue,* ask yourself where it fits, what does it represent?

Think of the people involved with you as responding and adapting to their environment, rather than as problems or packages you need to re-arrange. Can you see an issue from the other person's point of view? What does the issue look like from there, what do they want, what are they trying to do? Think of how you and your decisions might look to others; they respond and adapt to you and the policies you represent. *You* are what they see.

Visualize your organization, department, and responsibility as if they are doing organisms with the characteristics of visual behavior. In visual behavior terms, the organization:

- Centers/Identifies: selects what it's about;
- Moves toward that identification;
- Has some degree of feedback system to assess whether or not the target is being reached.

Ways To Introduce Visual Principles

If you have decision-making authority that affects other people, consider how the demands of the tasks they do match their capabilities and what you know about their visual behavior. See Chapter 5 and 8 for specific descriptions. *People will be happier and more productive if what they're asked to do fits their particular visual organization.* Often tasks are assigned arbitrarily taking into consideration only the priority of the task *to the organization* and the hierarchical level of the employee, rather than the particular learning abilities of individuals doing the tasks.

Consider the physical demands of the work environment and the kinds of adaptations workers must make to that environment. Often things like desk lamps, chair adjustments, desk placement in relation to windows and open spaces can make a major difference in fatigue levels and comfort in work. If the work is close visual work, encouraging movement and distance breaks can increase the worker's efficiency and reduce their fatigue level. If you have found a behavioral vision professional in your area, referrals for evaluations of an individual's total visual status may be helpful. Lenses to relieve visual stress, to encourage adaptation toward the norm rather than for compensation may also be an option, if the professional has had some experience with using lenses as a training tool as well as for compensation.

Find ways to introduce and maintain some feedback. For the individual worker: a way to track how much they get done in a day, how accurate it was, how close they are to their goal. For the department or your needs: let people know what is expected and how accurate they are in meeting those expectations. This encourages them to independently control their own behavior, rather than just respond to the carrots and sticks advocated by the stimulus-response model, i.e., contests, bonuses.

How do you deal with *error* information? What role do errors have in your organization or job? Often we are so accustomed to error that we build organizational systems to accommodate them and rarely use the information error has for us. Errors act as feedback, alerting us to actions that are not working. Computerese calls them bugs that need to be removed so the system can run as designed. If we look upon errors as signals, we will see that they highlight glitches that indicate areas that can be changed, negatives that can turn into positives, making the difference between giving up and productivity. Errors ignored can lead to continual repetition of faulty actions. When faced with error, use the visual principles of:

Centering: where do you need to look?

Identification: what is it you're really dealing with?

Visualization: what can you do that would apply to this particular situation; what alternatives and consequences do you see?

Try this kind of mental problem solving rather than mechanical adherence to policies or instructions. This kind of visually directed behavior leads to independent problem solving, self-starting performance. The kind of behavior every level of new business says it needs.

Organizations

Not only have we been told by experts that humans are social animals, each of us touches that truth every day of our lives. We live within families, school classes, scouts, sports teams, church groups, professional associations, PTA's, governmental groups, business groups, tour groups, car pools. We rely on friends and family, support groups and professionals to help keep us hail and hearty. Although a prominent American mythic figure, the ideal of the loner actually appeals to us as relative shades of alone-ness, rather than as someone who literally has no connections to others. Some of our groups are formally organized with rules and procedures and have been around for generations: government, churches, large corporations, education institutions. Some are born and die more quickly: ad hoc committees, support groups, citizen action groups.

This time in human history seems to be a period of rapid re-adjustment in our group associations and affiliations. From rearranged nation states to business focus groups, we're experimenting with new ways to be together.

Joseph Campbell, among others, suggested it was that view from space of our fragile 'blue marble' earth that stimulated humanity's quest for new ways to view ourselves and our place in the universe; yet another example of the power of vision to drive human behavior. When we saw the whole thing, we began to look at our place in it differently than when we could see only our own piece of the whole. Aha! The world is not just my house and yard, my neighborhood or even just my state or country or continent. I am part of that blue marble, floating along with it, attached by the invisible thread of gravity. What happens to it, happens to me. When we contemplated that ball of earth floating in the black of space, we could not see the three tiered universe of the here of earth, the up of heaven and the down of hell, ideas inherited from the middle ages and beyond. We saw what we saw; and we have not been the same since. The quest that began with a new view seems, in the 90's, to lead toward greater interest in collaboration and cooperation than at any time in recent history.

Cumbersome, static hierarchies which are authority based and operate from stimulus-response thinking appear on the way out. More democratic, dynamic processes which allow for individual's independent behavior seem trying to be born.

If the 70's and 80's were the Me decades, the 90's seem to be the start of the We era. Family structures, business and politics seem to lead in the experimentation; perhaps because the consequences of their old restrictions impacted so directly on our individual lives and effectiveness. Education, medicine and mainline religious groups seem less eager to embrace new ways of organizing themselves. The consequences of their reluctance are also very apparent.

None of us escapes this paradigm squeeze; few of us are without opinions. Some think the traditional, hierarchical ways were truly the good old days and resist mightily changes that lead us away from there. Some, frustrated by what they see as the inefficiency, rigidity and lack of individual justice and personal opportunity, hope the new ways will liberate more of us. Whatever your group affiliations, you may have already felt the fallout from this cultural crunch.

As groups become more democratic and try to respond to both the needs of their particular members and the demands of the larger society, the more they resemble the visual-movement system. As a group member, whether chief or follower, you may be more comfortable during this time of transition, and you may be better able to contribute to a smoother shift in paradigms if you apply the principles of visual behavior in individuals to your *group's function.*

What follows are some thoughts about the development and functions of organizations to stimulate your observations, questions and conclusions. The ideas have not been tested in the laboratory of actual organizational practice; they emerged from the author's observations through the Eye of Reason of real organizations at work. It is too soon to know the exact fit of the principles of the visual process in particular people and in group process; but the parallels seem obvious: Groups are collections of individuals. It would be illogical to think that the persons who make up the group could bring to the group any system for organizing information and action other than what they have found works in their own lives.

Groups do the same things that individuals do: identify and locate themselves, perform some kind of action, create some kind of result from their action, all dependent upon centering/identification - visualization - action. The credo of visual behavior's hindsight, insight, foresight apply to a group's movement/actions as well as to an individual's.

Visual Principles And Groups

In the new models of group development dictatorship and hierarchical leadership is out; naming, describing, suggesting by all members of the group are in. To put the new model into action, begin by looking at the group's purpose. How was this defined and by whom; how many of the individuals in the group actually agree with it? Using visual principles, a group that allows for and honors the personal development of each member, will have a purpose, goal, mission statement that is clear and owned by all members. The visual analog is centering/identification: This is what the group is looking at; this is the base from which the group plans its action.

In order to walk to the refrigerator to get a snack, I need to know where it is and point myself in that direction *before* I start walking. Think of a group you're in, what is the analogy for the group action? Does it know where it wants to go - or do just a few people make that decision? Does where it wants to go determine the direction of its actions? If not, what does?

As I walk to the refrigerator, I see things along the way that tell me I'm actually headed in the right direction - visual feedback. What is your group's feedback? Does it even know it needs some way of judging whether or not its actions keep it on course? Does it have a course? In hierarchical families, churches, businesses, the individual members may leave it up to one or a few leaders to make all these decisions. This works fine if all the members agree, or have so little freedom they dare not desist. When they don't agree with the group's action, frustration - error signals for some of the individual members arise. Negative feelings and actions to satisfy the frustrations go underground or surface and the group then has a new problem: conflict and the resolution or consequence of it. Sound familiar?

Errors, bugs, glitches. The very information the group needs for accurate guidance is often stifled. If we've been raised to be socially acceptable, we don't want to criticize, to offend, to be the one to say the emperor has no clothes. Most of us find it difficult to introduce this vital information into the group's process, nor, have we learned to accept this kind of information for what it is - information. Too often we respond in personal defensiveness, subverting the group's purpose into interpersonal dynamics. Regardless, the feedback system is faulty and the consequence for this restriction is the same for groups as it is for individuals: Reduced effectiveness, random action, static postures, much action with little forward movement, or no action at all. As with an individual, the group's life will be more stressful, less able to express its potential, using its energy more inefficiently than it might.

People with vision may see all of this. People with vision may be able to visualize plans to help us move more safely and comfortably where the new thrusts in our culture seem to be pushing us: toward greater opportunities for justice and participation for individuals as well as political groups. People with vision may be able to put themselves and their needs within a larger social and organizational context, identifying and naming the frustrations and wants of the group's members. They will literally see more; identifying ways, visualizing plans so cooperation and collaboration can emerge. Can the group's organizational structure make use of their information?

Most of us seek transformation, for ourselves, for our institutions, for our organizations. As Joseph Campbell said, we seek the "experience of being alive". *In transforming experiences we see things differently, we see different things.* We know we are in a different place. For those with sight it is our visual process that allows us to identify and integrate those experiences, to connect with the experience, to see something different. At those moments we live a heightened awareness of the power of vision. Wolff described that power:

> ...I have taught that past experience and anticipation of the future are contained in the specious present and vision supersedes space and time.[10]

If we understand how we move from sight to vision, we can positively influence that process so that our own lives, the lives of those close to us and our corporate, group lives can more nearly reflect our potential, can know the experience of being alive. If we understand how we move from sight to vision, we will be aware of all that our specious present contains the next time we say, "Oh, I see!"

APPENDIX A

Syllabus
by Bruce R. Wolff

s.a. Noel Center Post-Doctoral Course Work 1988-89

Note: Wolff taught a post-graduate course in visual behavior for behavioral optometrists who wished to explore the Wolff model. The course met monthly from 1984-1989. This represents the syllabus for the third year.

Optometry is the discipline of vision. Vision has been understood generally within the "Conventional Wisdom" including most concerned professionals. Clinical experience produced problems that were resistant to solutions with that approach e.g. amblyopia, strabismus, progressive myopia, and chronic complainers.

The beginning of a long series of developments was a different viewpoint of the refractive error, that emmetropia and orthophoria were the norms. (Skeffington) This opened "Pandora's box". More than optics was involved; eventually the eyes of the body became the eyes of the mind. Vision could now be understood as the integrating process above all sensory inputs and the control of all behavior. Seen as such vision is an emergent.

At the present time the most important consideration of that which can facilitate such a different point of view is an understanding of the meaning "paradox". This will place time and space in proper perspective and allow us to approach light and visual space and thence the clinical operations of testing, evaluation, and regimens of care. Traditional care is contained within this.

(see excerpted bibliography at end for suggested reading)

Clinical operations:
   Orientation
   Present- "What brings you in?"
   Past- History
   Future- Expectations
Test battery:
   Operational definitions
   Test forms
   Observing
Evaluation:
   The axis of normality
   The bilateral-binocular base
      movement- direction of movement- form-
      relationship of forms

Regimen:
 Lenses
 Therapy
 Change
  Critical empathy
Maintenance:
 Lenses
 The unknown-chance
Exploring that which needs office centered clinical research:
 Immediate
 Long term
Wilber, Ken, ed.. *Quantum Questions*. New Science Library. Boston: Shambhala Publications.

ABOUT VISION
by Bruce R. Wolff, O.D.

Cincinnati, Ohio 1984
Note: This article appears identically through two publications, one privately in 1984 and one from the s.a. Noel Center, Inc., Lancaster, Ohio in 1987. The Noel Center was incorporated from 1980 - 1989 to conduct research in optometry and education. Wolff originally wrote this as the first chapter of a book he intended to write; he used it as background information for his private, clinical patients.

Chapter I
Notes To Be Read Before The First Examination

The purpose of this pamphlet is to provide information that will make it easier for you to understand the results of the examination and any treatment that may be prescribed. While it is intended primarily for those who are making their first visit others may find it equally useful.

It may be of interest to you to know the sources of referral and reasons for coming other than your own. Referral sources may be from those in education, the medical community, books and other materials written for the general public, and people who either have been patients or know patients. The reasons can be quite varied also: a formal vision screening of some kind, inability to see clearly the chalkboard in school or street signs on the highway when driving, eye discomfort when using a computer, inadequate academic performance problems, a last resort for undefined and so far insoluble problems, and rehabilitation (and occasionally enhancement) of visual abilities that are essential to meet particular visual eligibility requirements.

Whatever the source of referral or the particular reason for coming, two questions asked are outstanding in the frequency of their occurrence:

I.   Is something really wrong?

II. Can anything be done about it?

Close behind in order of frequency are:

III. What do you do in an examination?

IV. What does vision have to do with my kind of problems?

Here are some of the easiest answers to the questions as they are stated above. Questions I and II are taken together for they are interrelated. Abnormal individuals are rare and even rarer still are those in which there is little or no potential for any form of positive treatment. Too often in the process of diagnosing and labeling, abnormals can be "created", particularly by those unfamiliar with current levels of understanding of vision and visual processes. The vast majority are normal persons in difficulty and can be helped to varying degrees depending upon:

1. the evidence in the examination of the available potential.

2. the extent of substitute and compensating behaviors.

3. the value of different but better performance to the individual and those immediately involved.

4. and reasonable adherence to and support of the treatment program described.

The assessment made from the examination data determines what should be done and can be done.

Now Question III? The examination consists of these five parts:

1. The interview
    Here we ask for your reasons for coming and gather pertinent background information.

2. Screening for pathology
    From this we may find pathology that has not been previously recognized (that is, not given in the interview) and is readily observable in a visual examination. For example, the obvious are cataracts and glaucoma; less obvious are indications such as diabetes or hypertension. You will be informed of anything found needing referral.

3. Examining the characteristics of *visual space* and the functions of *centering, identification and binocularity* within it. This is a major part of the examination.

CENTERING is the equivalent of looking to "where it is" in the visual space or the ability to direct the visual system to a volume of visual space, large or small, within which identification is taking place.

IDENTIFICATION is the visual process of seeing "what it is" within the visual space and the continuous recognition and utilization of form and the relationship of forms.

BINOCULARITY is the process that develops two eyed centering and identification within the visual space and resolves similarities and differences simultaneously into unique precepts.

Not exactly easy to understand you say. True, but hang in there, it will begin to clear later. If this is your first encounter with these ideas it is certain that you will have to think about it awhile and perhaps re-read some parts. And, you will have the opportunity to discuss and ask questions about any part of this pamphlet.

4. Integration of the visual with the body postural and movement mechanisms, speech-auditory-language systems and those activities generally regarded as perceptual.

In the previous section we indicated that visual space is developed through experiences. This means "doing and acting" for seeing is a motor system as well as sensory. We see to act not just to see. Thus in the examination we observe the visual-motor, visual-verbal, visual-auditory, and the visual-perceptual and consider the contribution of vision to each of these systems, and the quality of their interaction.

5. Assessment and recommendations

At this time the examination data is presented, translated and compared from in-office performance on the test battery to performance characteristics in the everyday world. These two must be in agreement. One consequence at this point may be a change in the order of problems to be treated due to a new awareness of all that is involved. Treatment alternatives are presented and the consequences of each discussed. Any necessary referrals to other disciplines will be made at this time. All of the results of the examination are recorded and some but not all of the original test data are retained. Those who are responsible for deciding what course of action is to be taken or who are interested in the assessment and recommendations are expected to be present and to have read this pamphlet. Summaries for other professionals will be given by telephone.

You may have recognized that the brief description of the examination given above hints at the answer to Question IV and how vision extends itself into many, many activities.

Vision is a tremendously complex information process that dominates human behavior. The bits of information that can be identified and processed in one glance is enormous and points to one of the reasons vision is dominant. It supplies maximum information in minimum time. It is so much a part of us that it is difficult to stand back and look at it. We reveal how much vision is a part of us by correctly using expressions such as "He is a man of vision", "it looks hot", "let me see if I can remember", "he failed to foresee". Do you "see" the point? Vision is all of these: sight, hindsight, foresight, insight.

When attention is turned to and focused on the term "vision" it is almost invariably associated with and equated to "visual acuity". The most famous measure of average acuity is the Snellen fraction 20/20, often erroneously labeled "20/20 vision". But visual acuity is only a part of the total visual process. There is a profound difference between the many functions of vision and the single function of visual acuity. The understanding of those functions helps clarify how vision can be involved in so many human activities and problems.

The publication in 1949 of *VISION: Its Development in Infant and Child* by Arnold Gesell was a major contribution to the available literature that documented the elaborate nature and importance of vision. More publications have become available for the general public since then, some of which are listed in the bibliography at the end of this chapter, as well as earlier ones. These references are for those who are interested in more detailed and varied information than can be contained in this brief pamphlet. Each contributes something of value and helps to further understanding of vision, when adequately interpreted.

BIBLIOGRAPHY

Bates, William H. *The Cure of Imperfect Sight Without Glasses, Central Fixation Publ.*, New York, 1920.

Huxley, Aldous *The Art of Seeing*, Harper, New York, 1942.

Corbett, Margaret D. *Help Yourself to Better Sight*, Prentice-Hall, New York, 1949.

Gesell, Arnold *VISION: Its Development in Infant and Child*, Hafner Press, New York, 1949.

Kepes, Gyorgy *Language of Vision*, Paul Theobald, Chicago, 1951.

Arnheim, Rudolf *Visual Thinking*, University of California Press, Berkeley and Los Angeles, 1969.

Ames, Louise B.: Gillespie, Clyde; Streff, John W., *Stop School Failure,* Harper and Row, New York, 1972.

Kavner, Richard; Dunsky, Lorraine, *Total Vision*, A. & W., New York, 1978.

Hoopes, Ann & Townsend, *Eye Power*, Knopf, New York, 1979

Lyons, Emily Bradley, *How to Use Your Power of Visualization*, Golden Rule Printing, Willits, California, 1980.

Forrest, Elliott B., *Visual Imagery: An Optometric Approach*, Optometric Extension Program Foundation, Inc. 1981.

Prepared by the Executive Staff of the s.a. NOEL Center, a non-profit institution for teaching and research in vision for education and optometry.

Bruce R. Wolff, O.D.

Sr. Barbara A Jinks, O.P., M.A.

John W. Streff, O.D.

From Sight To Vision
Bruce R. Wolff, O.D.

The Center For Clinical Visual Research
Cincinnati, Ohio

Note: This was the text of a speech given at the Ohio Valley Congress in 1987. The Congresses are part of the Optometric Extension Program's post-graduate study. The Ohio Valley Congress was for optometrists and educators.

Man is a visually dominant organism. If he can't see he can't survive without the help of others. Blindness is a tragedy. Fortunately, the loss of sight by disease is no longer the problem it once was in the past. At the present time serious eye pathology affects a very small percentage of people.

However, the loss of *visual acuity*, the ability to see clearly is a problem to many, many people. The usual solution is to have an eye examination and get a pair of glasses to restore the acuity to its normal state.

Some laymen and a few professionals were concerned about a continuous loss of acuity that frequently occurred, as well as why it happened at all. To consider these changes due to heredity, a favorite explanation, did not make sense. They did not follow the laws of heredity, especially since they occur variously at any time of life, and no specific cause was evident. Another oddity was that some people were more comfortable and performed better with a pair of glasses even though they could "see" very well without them. Since the usual solution was so simple, a pair of glasses (or another pair), and this loss of acuity never resulted in blindness, not much progress was made to find definitive answers to these questions until early in this century.

Foremost among the few professionals who tried was Dr. A. M. Skeffington. A man of acute insight, he had the ability to draw from other disciplines pertinent information that was synthesized into the basis of our present day understanding of vision.

Webster's *Third International Dictionary* defines Vision as "Something seen other than by ordinary sight". One wonders if Webster anticipated the present day knowledge of Vision?

The closest we can come to understanding the difference between sight and vision is a picture taken by an ordinary camera of something with which we have had absolutely no direct experience. We can not identify it but we may read into it and "see" what we imagine it to be.

(Monkeys reared with their eyelids sewn shut have NO sensible reaction to the light input when their lids are released. It is the result of extreme deprivation of experience.)

What we "see" then involves our prior experience. But this is true only if what we have experienced is acquired or "learned", and becomes a kind of hindsight. Vision involves learning and learning involves vision. This interaction of vision and learning produces visual *memory* from which the past can be *visualized* in the present.

Sight is a given for vision. The Vision and learning interaction begins at birth and may continue indefinitely through life.

The next step in understanding vision is that we can learn and remember but not be able to use the information acquired. For instance, a native of the tropics can watch an expert downhill skier finish the giant slalom in record time. He can "know" what he has seen but it would be very risky for him to try to do the same without appropriate experience of "doing" and learning before he tried.

We do not see just to see; we see to act. With our past experience we can project our movements into the future and bring them into the present. You may recognize this as a form of foresight.

Visual learning is enhanced by doing.

Sequencing through a series of movements, either directed or by trial and error we develop "form", a pattern which emerges from the synthesizing or grouping of parts into a whole. Grouping to a criteria is a learning experience. One learns how to move into the future. Grouping which forms a criteria is a creative experience, and a learning one as well.

Which bring us to another step, the relationship of forms. In this process some forms which are recognized as different are also seen in their sameness. It is the analoging process in which similarities, which coexist with the differences, are matched into a new and different form. These new forms do not exist in "sight" but are *visualized* as precepts and concepts.

Sequencing a series of visual-motor movements, is obviously spread through time and the goal is usually anticipated by having been described and/or predetermined. Matching in the analogue process, on the other hand, appears to be spontaneous and instantaneous, seemingly independent of a specific series of observable visual-motor movements and frequently a result neither anticipated nor predetermined.

A true story: "What do you see here- what does that mean?" "*A part of a circle, some slanted lines and some straight lines. Oh, those are letters of the alphabet".* "What do they mean"? *"I don't know".* (At this moment my cat walks into the room, believe it or not!) *"You've got a Siamese ca...THAT spells CAT!"* A perfect example of analoging.

(It is interesting to note that a person born blind can never experience the difference between light and heat. Those who were not born blind but become so later show neuro-physiological evidence of using whatever part of the visual system that remains intact.)

Sequencing and Analoging are Processes within the Visual-Motor System.

SUMMARIZING

The development of vision involves experience and learning. Learning involves doing. Doing involves sequencing parts into wholes and matching different yet similar wholes into analogues. You may call the latter insight.

Vision is an emergent from sight, experience, learning, doing, sequencing, analoging and visualizing. It is an information processing system that has a vast amount of data immediately available for action and meaning.

That emergent contains a function that is unique:

Vision can monitor itself.

From the foregoing description of vision, how it differs from sight, its development, and an overview of its functions, we can understand its enormous importance in human behavior.

Interference in the development and maintenance of vision is accountable to some form of deprivation, or, stressing the system beyond its current capabilities. Under those conditions adaptations made within the system in order to cope are negative in nature, and restrict performance in various ways or another, the most frequent and easiest to recognize being a loss of visual acuity. Other adaptations may not be so easily recognized unless one understands the diffuse extent to which vision affects human behavior. Vision is derived from extent to which vision affects human behavior. Vision is derived from sight, a basic given, but that base can in turn be modified by vision.

Vision is a private world. One can see body language easily and in conversation be able to assess speech and hearing, but how one "sees" is not easily seen.

A competent examiner, schooled in behavioral optometry, can evaluate the status of all the aspects of the visual information processing system, and recommend rehabilitation, maintenance or enhancement as may be desired.

A Short Bibliography for Further Reading and Sources of More Information on Clinical Procedures and Research Data

Gesell, Arnold, M.D. *VISION; Its Development in Infant and Child,* 1949 Paul Hoeber, Inc. New York, NY.

Forrest, Elliott B., O.D. *STRESS and VISION,* 1988 Optometric Extension Program Foundation, Inc. (OEPF) Santa Ana, CA.

OEPF, Inc. 2912 S. Daimler St. Santa Ana, CA 92705

The Center for Clinical Visual Research, 435 Crescent Ave. Cincinnati, OH 45215

Outline of the Development of the Emergent

Intrasystem functions

Centering

Identification

Binocularity

Intersystem functions

Bilateral motor equivalence

Body posture

Speech-Audition

Language

Synthesizing and abstracting on a visual datum

From sight to visualization

The axis of normality

Basic movement patterns

Remedial measures

For omissions due to deprivation during development

For omissions due to partial processing of available data

Negative stressor agents

Enhancement

Extending the ranges of movement

Maintenance

Assuring adequacy to meet changing environmental and physiological conditions

A Window On The Universe
by Bruce R. Wolff, O. D.
Note: This is the text of a speech given at the Ohio Valley OEP Congress in 1988.

Dr. Skeffington was a master of ferreting out and disseminating information, drawn from other disciplines, that was pertinent to our own. His presence is sorely missed.

Recent reading in several of these other areas have given me an insight into the resolution of a particular visual problem that has nagged me for years. The problem was that of integrating into a single or holistic concept that which is known now as well as what is yet to be known about vision. One aspect of the problem was this. Vision in the historical perspective of our discipline was related to the lighted environment or "real" visual space, within which visual acuity was essentially the only criteria, while under the aegis of Skeffington more and more functions of the organism that were considered to be the sole property of other disciplines, such as "minimal brain damage" and "psychological" phenomena were being incorporated into a broader concept of vision. As a result much of the testing and training of those functions subtly ignored the historical perspective, or were being subtly ignored by the historical perspective. One consequence of this was confusion between the other disciplines and ours as to whose turf was being invaded.

Another part of the problem was the inadequacy of the attempt to solve that confusion by the inarticulate assumption that the simple yet however true statements such as "Vision is the dominant process of the human organism" or "Vision is pervasive in human nature" would resolve the controversy. Nor did the articulate demand for hard scientific proof help to resolve matters either.

Horizontal development of various facets of the visual process from either point of view such as refinements in the techniques and observations available when using a retinoscope while adding valuable information within each position did not begin to unify the parts into a whole different than the sum of its parts.

The third question that refused to disappear was a clearer understanding of the function of binocularity and the bilateral eye. It too has had a rather limited attention by all, especially those who have seen "normal" stereopsis with dissociating prisms or the peculiar configurations of "phorias" that are exhibited with dowel rods and dissociating prisms.

In the absence of Dr. Skeffington two friends and a colleague of mine called my attention to three books that are of inestimable value to Optometry. They are:

The Holographic Paradigm and Other Paradoxes
  Ed. Ken Wilber New Science Library 1985
  Snapping
  Conway and Siegelman A Delta Book Dell Pub. 1979
  Chaos Making a New Science
  James Gleick Viking 1987.

I urge you to read them. It is not even remotely possible for me to review them here, only some of the salient points relative to "my problem". Now to consider that problem.

  1) the hard sciences and the soft i.e. physics and
     psychology, have reached the bottom of the barrel. Each
     must now understand the other.

From (*Snapping)*
"simple systems behave in simple ways. Complex behavior implies complex causes". That was the old reductionist program in science, standard linear science. The new: "Simple systems give rise to complex behavior; complex systems give rise to simple behavior". "For the mass of practicing scientists- particle physicists or neurologists or even mathematicians the change did not matter immediately". But "More and more felt the futility of studying parts in isolation from the whole. *For them chaos was the end of the reductionist program in science*".

From ("Chaos")
For those of you who are unfamiliar with some of the above statements "holism", "liberally" defined, is now acceptable. And chaos can have two meanings (directionality in optometric language) randomness without order and randomness with order. Chaos can be ordered-seen-visualized, and it occurs within the bilateral-binocular visual system. In the italicized sentence in the above paragraph chaos does have two meanings. One is that it is a final end ending with randomness. The other is that it is an interim end within which order can be found. This appears to allow for a continuous process which emerges as a satisfactory description of infinite. Consider: an infinite number of Moebius bands that occupy the same space but are never congruent. Or a visual system that can utilize similarities and differences simultaneously to produce an unpredictable. How?

The discovery that order could be derived from chaos was done by the brain of Robert Stetson with the aid of a discarded analog computer. Stetson would be an interesting subject for a visual analysis and would probably prove that order emerges from chaos. Consider: effective performance with or without refractive error.

Of particular interest to optometrists was the discovery of the butterfly effect by Robert Lorenz. This was the observation that one small bit in an enormous number of chaotic bits could produce order out of the chaos. The parallel for optometry is that a continuous sequence of tests producing no discernible syndrome because of consistently high scores can by one low score produce an elegant syndrome by reordering the directionality of some of the preceding "high score" tests. e.g. The best I can think of is "emmetropia".

The essential point in the above (1) is that we are constantly involved with wholes. They may appear to be completely chaotic without any order. Or they may appear to be completely ordered systems that contain flaws e.g. the eye is like a camera. Or again they may appear as more than one ordered system necessary to explain another whole e.g. both wave and particle theory to explain the function of light. A single simple point may bring order to multiple complex array; or a multiple complex array may produce a single simple point. However, in any case the nature of the outcome is not predictable EXCEPT this leads us to:

(2) The Holographic Paradigm. (Chapters by Karl H. Pribram)

None of my colleagues should require a description of a hologram: coherent light split into two beams ("eyes") projecting on an optical storage device ("brain") an image ("vision"-sensory) of chaos obtained from any three dimensional object which can at any time be projected from any piece of that image by a single beam back into space and identical to the original object ("vision"-motor).

Pribram considered the brain to be a hologram "perceiving and participating in a holographic universe. In the explicate or manifest realm of space and time, things and events are indeed separate and discrete. But beneath the surface, as it were, in the implicate or frequency realm, all things and events are spacelessly, timelessly, intrinsically, one and undivided." (Ken Wilber)

"Scientists are, as yet, only barely acquainted with the implicate order which has, however, apparently been explored experientially by mystics, psychics, and others delving into paranormal phenomena." (Pribram)

Thus it is in the implicate order that one may intuit, anticipate and/or predict order.

I have touched upon little of the enormous wealth of ideas in these three books and in no way in the depth in which they have been developed. But from the little this paper contains can we put visual acuity in its proper place, relegate the camera to Kodak's historical museum, cogently relate the plus lens, the phorias et al. to the terrain in visual space that we "see" through "Our Window On The Universe"? We can.

One last thought that shall be labeled "Epilogue".

In the s.a. Noel Center classes I have taught that past experience and anticipation of the future are contained in the specious present and vision supersedes space and time. It would seem that in the implicate domain Dr. Skeffington might still be around. If so I would like to know how you, Skeff, like the scientifically verified fact that memory is not localized anywhere in the brain network because it's in the complex proteins in the brain fluids. Now you know why you always liked red meat. You never lost your memory because you never knew where it was. Lashley didn't either, just where it wasn't.

Macro-dieters, are you beginning to forget where you put the car keys? 30

BRUCE R. WOLFF
435 Crescent Avenue
Cincinnati, Bloom County, Ohio 45215
513-821-3296

In the VBT book the procedures are for the most part, color-coded so they can be matched to the appropriate task. Color coding was originally implemented to assist the non-readers, but also proved helpful for those who read as well.

A series of vertical columns fill the following page. Each one represents a day with the date numerically written at the top. Arrows are drawn from the procedure into the day's column to represent a task to be done. When the task is completed, an "x" or check mark is put on the arrow head recording the completion. This also helps reinforce the process of learning to identify the procedures. Individuals do not have to do the tasks in any particular order, but are encouraged to create their own pattern and order so they become comfortable with what they're doing. The ultimate goal is to be able to organize and move smoothly from one task to another independently — learning to take care of oneself.

ROTATIONS AND FIXATIONS

Rotations and Fixations is a procedure from the CENTERING -identification Binocularity group that deals with basic eye tracking and locating skills. These skills are essential in order to successfully gather information, whether from following the lines of print on a page, or looking from one place to another. *Adequate* comprehension and attention span depend on the *proficiency* of these skills. This is one area where the individual becomes directly involved and acutely aware of the feedback system that is inherent in the visual - motor system and so vital in learning. In the publication *Eye Tracking and Locating Skills* prepared by the executive staff at the s.a. NOEL Center, a non-profit institution for teaching and research in vision for education and optometry, Wolff (project chairman) and his colleagues, emphasized that "motor and sensory functions are synergistic in visual information processing. The motor process is an integral of our perceived experience, and is a contributor to what we see. The visual-motor processes are afferent (conveying impulses toward a nerve center), a feed-forward system as well as efferent, a feed-back system."[1]

NAME:

DATE:														
1 Orientation														
2 Rotations/ Fixations														
3 Stick/Straw														
4 Rotoscope														
5 Prisms near/far														
6 Rope														
7 TET Rock														
8 Loose Lens Rock														
9 Window Rock														
10 VO Rock														
11 Plus Flash														
12 Board Tach														
13 Near Point Tach														
14 Craig Tach														
15 Walking Rail/Prisms														
16 Floor/Prisms														
17 Prisms/Dowels														
18 Prisms/Pegs & Rings														
19 Tracings														
20 XRO Tracings														
21 VO Star														
22 XRO Slides/ Pointers														
23 Pegboard														
24 Prisms/"Blocks"														
25 Fixator														
26 Body Balancing														
27 Balance Board														
28 Board BME Patterns														
29 Deep Wink														
30 Ellipse														
31 Rivalry														
32 Stereo Ranges														
33 Visualization														
34 Visual-Verbal Matching														
35 Visual- Auditory Matching														
Out of Office Assignments														

As part of this visual - motor processing system, Rotations and Fixations teaches the individual what is seemingly a simple task - to direct his visual attention in a spatial environment, to locate, look at and follow a target (1/2 inch silver ball) as it is moved in the near field of view, to locate and look from one target to another (1/2 inch gold ball) and to relate his position to the position of the target within near visual space. The individual will not only learn the skills of tracking and locating but also Accommodation and Convergence/Divergence. Accommodation is the ability to focus, to shift quickly and spontaneously from far to near space and sustain nearpoint focus. Convergence/Divergence is eye-teaming abilities: locating, tracking and sustaining a single target on the Z axis with both eyes simultaneously, from far to near to far space.

Posture

The postural set for Rotations and Fixations was originally a seated position because it is the usual position when doing near centered visual tasks. That posture is still used for the testing sequence but was changed for VBT to create an "at rest" posture for the purpose of eliminating as much internal interference - motor overflow, skews, warps, and asymmetries from postural shifts as possible. It wasn't until years later when my mother, Elaine Wolff, and I began Hatha Yoga with Lilias Folan, that we discovered the posture chosen for this procedure was identical to the yoga posture Sarvasana, or relaxation pose. The individual lies on his back, legs apart, feet flopped out, arms away from the body, palms turned upward, shoulders pushed away from the ears, the head placed comfortably but aligned on the floor with the neck relaxed.

The tracking pattern should eventually become controlled, smooth, with no jerkiness, lags, skips, blinking or peripheral restrictions. The locating skill should eventually be done with ease of movement and no anticipation (jumping prematurely to the next target and not sustaining fixation on the primary target). The accommodation skill is coaxed by easing the tension of the lids, opening them wide allowing as much light in as possible.

Convergence

Once convergence has been learned the two vertical or dissociating prisms can be introduced. These are 4 degrees base up, base down prisms inducing diplopia (doubling). One eye sees the top ball and the other eye sees the bottom ball. The other pair is the reciprocal of the first. Wolff always thought this was such an elegant testing and VBT procedure and, in fact, it is, because "the dissociated condition allows the person to experience what he is aware of from two simultaneous visual inputs in overlapping fields and to compare similarities and differences."[2] *The individual can actually observe and evaluate his own binocular process in action.* Knowing which eye sees which ball, he can compare the similarities and differences of the position of the two targets, their size, color, clarity, solidity, brightness, realness, and amount of vertical space between them. Symmetry and balance in the bilateral-binocular visual-motor system is indicated if the targets remain vertically aligned and are equal in all respects. Any shifts or differences between the targets indicate asymmetry and binocular interferences. The individual now knows when and where the difficulties are and with help and guidance can use this information to bring about the necessary changes.

In VBT the individual learns to work toward balance and symmetry by using both pairs of vertical prisms. It is this reciprocal action between the two that eventually eases everything out and helps bring balance back into the system. The movement patterns used in tracking with the prisms are the same as the occluded. Tracking should eventually be controlled, smooth, with no jerkiness, lags, skips, blinking, or peripheral restrictions. The locating skills should eventually be rhythmic and equivalent. Both eyes should grasp and release the targets simultaneously and evenly.

When the individual becomes proficient in Rotations and Fixations he is well on his way to becoming a more efficient learner with a more balanced and efficient visual - motor system. The relationship between the oculomotor eye movements and the gross motor movements in Board Tach and Body Balancing are one and the same. It's important for the individual to begin to see the relationship between these VBT procedures and how it all "hangs together as a whole."

BODY BALANCING

Body Balancing is from the visual-MOTOR group of the CENTERING - identification category and deals with literally "bringing the body into balance." It is the most versatile procedure available and attends to several important areas: asymmetries within the system, lags and omissions in primary development skills, gross motor skills, stretching, directionality, rhythm, balancing skills, tumbling, visual-motor-verbal matching and atypical orientations in space.

In his "Visual Training Procedures Outline," Wolff said "stretching exercises should be given sufficient attention until the effects of environmental deprivation are minimal."[3] In today's world, too many youngsters lead sedentary lives, sitting in front of the T.V. and computers or just hanging out, and do not get enough exercise and motor activity. Physical and visual flexibility suffer because of this. The postural shifts, skews, and asymmetrical adaptations that Harmon talked about (described in Chapter 4) start to take hold and must be broken loose so balance and flexibility can be reestablished.

Movement is the key to unlocking these embedded patterns. The variety and complexity of movement patterns are enormous. Stretching is so simple and essential that everyone of all ages can do it to restore flexibility and balance. I have been fortunate to have been able to tap into many years of acrobatics, ballet, and Hatha Yoga, all rich in bilateral movement to help me understand more fully movement within the human organism and to help me create routines (movement sequencing) that will bring about the necessary changes within the visual-motor system. Wolff went on to say that concurrently with the stretching exercises, "body balancing routines should begin with the emphasis on visual direction of movement in space and thence the form of this movement."[4] Visual direction in space; right, left, up, down, diagonals, forward, backward, rotations right and left, and forward and backward rotations are learned through movement and the sequencing of movement.

Body Balancing helps teach the individual how to center and posture himself in relation to gravity and everything around him. Stretching can be done on the floor, either sitting or supine, eliminating the complexity of having to stand and deal with gravity. Just like in the Sarvasana posture in Rotations and Fixations, which allows the individual to concentrate fully on the eye movements by being "at rest" physically, being on the floor allows stretching and a multitude of other movement patterns to be practiced as simply as possible. The individual begins to become aware of his own bilaterality this way, learning to define the right side and the left side of his body in relation to his central trunk. Simple basic movements are initially introduced — for example: learning to move his arms and legs independently of each other in all different directions, and matching these movements with the appropriate verbal direction.

The next step is to combine these independent movements into simultaneous bilateral movement. Then the individual can learn to transfer these movements to a standing, stationery posture dealing with gravity, as he learns to balance and center simultaneously. Wolff felt that these body balancing routines should also be practiced with the eyes closed, forcing individuals to visualize what they're doing and where they are — learning to use past movement experiences stored in their memory. Eventually these movements become automatic and they will anticipate and predict the sequencing pattern and execute it with ease. Visualization techniques are new concepts to most people, unaware they can help in school, work and in general learning. Visualizing and executing movement patterns is the first and best way to practice this technique. Eventually they can be transferred to spelling, math, reading, organizational skills and general thinking processes.

With each routine there is always a target in far space for the individual to look at. This helps visual centering and gives a frame of reference to work with. The quality of movement, (thrust-counter-thrust) generated around the individual's Y axis (midline), depends on how balanced and centered the individual is. From a centered and balanced posture the individual has the freedom to move in any direction he chooses - that's why it's so important to break loose any asymmetries within the system.

From these basic movements more complex routines and patterns can be learned which will eventually lead to controlled movement within the individual's three dimensional space. These involve moving forward, backward, laterally, obliquely, rotational and in combinations of these. When learning to move within one's own visual space the individual begins to understand more fully *his/her* role in this total picture. The person becomes even more aware of their own body bilaterality and body scheme than previously. The individual becomes his own frame of reference bound by this bilateral makeup and the Y-axis around which movement, balance and centering are made possible. *Wherever that person stands in space defines that space in relation to where that individual is.* Visualize a person standing in a room, facing a pink wall. The red wall is on his right, the yellow wall to his left, and the blue wall is behind him. If he moves and faces the red wall, his orientation has changed and the red wall is no longer on his right, the blue wall is. Conversely, the environment can change and the individual stays constant. What may have been to his right is now to his left. Or the environment and the person's orientation can change simultaneously — visual space is constantly being defined. This is how the concepts of right, left, up, down, diagonal, forward, backward, closer, further, next to, following, leading, in front of, in back of, are learned. Eventually, the individual projects these concepts into other areas such as form, letters, and figure-ground relationships.

The lags and omissions found in Gesell's primary developmental skills must also be addressed and learned. For some this means going back as far as infant development, to before and after the crawl. This is especially true if someone has experienced a debilitating trauma of some sort. I divide these skills this way because the *crawl is the first time a baby puts all the parts and pieces of the bilateral - binocular visual-motor system together as a whole moving unit with the eyes guiding him through his expanded space.* Included in this developmental progression are the gross motor movements so important for the development of fine motor skills. The individual needs to learn to jump, hop, skip, gallop, and step-hop, to name a few - how to visualize the whole sequence of movement, like a skip, and then be able to slow the sequence down to its basic elements and sustain that pattern as though it were suspended in time and space. From these basic movements the individual needs to be able to create new patterns. From the movement experiences one visualizes how the parts of the patterns can be put together in the future and can predict what the end pattern of action will be. *You may recognize these as the analog and digital skills so important in organizing not only our movements but also our thoughts, words and writings.*

The gross motor movements are bilateral in structure and must be learned as such. For example, both right and left leads are learned in a lateral gallop and hopping on the right is learned as well as hopping on the left. Movements learned forward are also learned in reverse. This can be difficult for those individuals with embedded asymmetries and postural shifts and adaptations. These skills take time to acquire. One must remember how long these adaptations have been in place and constantly reinforced. As visual centering improves, so will balancing and moving. It's important for the individual to know that the speed of movement patterns is important. Excessive speed covers up many omissions and glitches in the pattern. Slowing the movement down and sustaining it allows it to be completed and balanced - it's the same as slowing down and controlling oculomotor eye movements and the drawing action on Board Tach or the walking pattern on the Walking Rail.

Wolff said the form of the movements involves rhythm, which often demands special attention. For example; a skip has a certain upward accent and rhythm to it, as does a lateral gallop. Often youngsters can get the pattern but not the accent or rhythm. They tend to do the opposite, by repeating the pattern with a down accent. Rhythm can be taught by matching the movement with the verbal description. This can control speed as well. For example; in learning to step-hop right and step-hop left, the person says step right and makes the movement at the same time, says balance as he balances, says hop right as he hops right. This is repeated with the left side. With practice this pattern will eventually become automatic. Using a metronome will also help match the movement with the constantly defined sound.

Wolff felt that forward and backward rolls and head and hand stands introduced atypical orientations in space. Many youngsters and adults don't like being upside-down because they lose their visual centering and orientation target temporarily. For that reason tumbling is very scary for many youngsters and adults alike. Their whole frame of reference has changed. Many literally close their eyes when rolling or tend to make the opposite movement when trying to execute the roll or headstand. For example; when trying to roll backwards, instead of staying in a ball or tucked position they open up and start to arch their backs. In a headstand, instead of pointing their toes and stretching their body to the ceiling, they flex their feet and pull their body to the floor, thinking it's the ceiling. *They still operate as though their orientation hasn't changed at all.* They haven't made the connection yet. Through practice they will eventually be able to do this without fear.

Movement is the key to survival. People learn by doing. Parents must realize how important activities involving movement are for their children beginning at birth and continuing throughout their lives. Sports, ballet, gymnastics, martial arts like karate, just to name a few, are opportunities that provide essential visual-motor activity for the child as well as for the adult. This doesn't mean that all children should be on a sports team. It does mean parents should be aware of their child's level and type of motor activity, and if need be, find the variable that works with him to ensure some participation. Remember, learned movement in the early years is extremely important, so it's crucial that the caregivers are careful not to restrict this movement by over-use of cribs, playpens, walkers, swings, jolly-jumpers and strollers. These help foster poor visual-motor skills, and the youngster's dislike of motor activity and the eventual preference of other activities. *The need for visual-motor activity is absolutely necessary to counter-balance the close work stress experienced throughout the day — and this applies to adults in the workplace as well.*

VAN ORDEN DEEP WINK

Van Orden Deep Wink is part of Field Structuring in VBT. Wolff referred to it as "a rather odd procedure" because it deviated from the usual format of all the others. The individual does this one totally on his own, alone, without being prodded or pushed.

Specifically applied, Deep Wink is used for those who do not attend to detail in their overall performance. These individuals have difficulty with size difference of forms reproduced on Board Tach. The individual will reproduce two squares of different sizes as the same size or reproduce two triangles as the same shape even though one is an equilateral triangle and the other a scalene triangle. Wolff said there is generally a poor quality in this individual's awareness of space relationships. His motor movements and orientation to everything in his visual space are hesitant, slow and often disjointed - not quite sure of how everything is organized or fits together.

Generally applied, Deep Wink is used for those individuals who want to improve their distance seeing. They have found that it's really possible to see more clearly than they had before by following this procedure. The individual is required *to go from a posture of total tightening to a posture of total relaxation.*

When I did this procedure an interesting phenomenon repeatedly happened to me which others have also reported. I noticed the letters on the acuity chart appeared to be growing in size and coming closer to me; as if watching a balloon with lettering on it being filled with helium come alive as it continued to grow. The lettering got larger and closer simultaneously. Consequently, this made picking out the letters individually, while looking through the chart at the same time, much easier. The rhythmic cadence also helps by forcing the individual to pick out detail (letters) while looking at and through the whole chart while being aware of his periphery all at the same time.

This technique has proven invaluable years later for myself and others who use an abbreviated version called short Deep Wink. It's particularly helpful under stressful and fatiguing conditions. Most people will squint to see clearly, which gives a quick fix, but in the long run does just the opposite; it restricts the visual field and light input. If this practice were to become habitual over a period of time a negative adaptation would eventually occur. Instead of squinting, Deep Wink can be abbreviated to a mere "tight" blink, followed by widening the eyelids to allow as much volume of space and light in as possible. Many people have already noticed on their own that their *general seeing is much improved if they keep their eyelids open wider than they had before*. This technique can be quite useful for those who need to discriminate quickly and with more detail what's in their visual space.

BOARD TACH

From the centering - IDENTIFICATION category, Board Tach is another versatile training procedure. The individual learns to simultaneously recognize, process and reproduce the information of form, size of form, form placement, and form relationships from visual memory. Everyone, regardless of age begins with the form elements of simple lines and curves and works his way into more complex patterns, which can be as many as four geometric shapes.

Simple but direct instructions are given so there is no misunderstanding of what is expected. The initial postural set is paramount for the success of this procedure. The individual is to stand approximately 5 - 8 feet from the markerboard or chalkboard in a balanced posture, free from motor overflow, feet slightly apart, arms hanging, and looking straight ahead at the board. (S)he is asked to keep their fields wide, use the entire board like a window as though they're looking through and beyond it and not to tunnel in on just one part or area. They are reminded to see the form in relation to the perimeters of the board and to everything else surrounding it. All these factors require a delicate balance that must be sustained until the form is flashed on the board. The flash from the tachistascope, which is projected at the individual's "physiological eye" level when standing, is quite short (approximately 1/100 of a second), and is flashed after the rhythmic signal "ready now". What individuals see and how well they will be able to reproduce it depends on how well they are ready on that signal.

Wolff felt that the preparation of the "postural set" for the task was just as important, if not more so, as the end result of the task itself. In time, individuals will eventually no longer be acutely conscious of posture and how they are seeing, but will assume the postural set automatically and unconsciously. *Wolff always said that one sees more by looking less*. This is also true with the postural set while drawing and reproducing the form on the board. The person stands centered and balanced, and with eyes guiding the hand, reproduces the form directly on the board as best they can. They learn that this centered position is to become their constant frame of reference while drawing. They are then shown the original slide and their reproduction simultaneously to compare the "match" or similarities and differences in the accuracy and quality of their reproduction. Individuals must become aware of their own pattern of similarities and differences that form patterns of performance (too small, too short, too large, incomplete, distorted, etc.) They can then use this information to help precipitate future changes in their performance.

I have already discussed the issue of how the quality of one's drawing and tracing ability are directly related to poor gross motor skills. In Board Tach these skills are addressed and developed through the actual drawing movement, which should be deliberate, controlled and fluent. Good balance and bilaterality are achieved when the asymmetrical balance or rigidity of the embedded dominance on one side and the flexibility on the other side is broken loose by alternating hands each time one draws. This alternation forces the simultaneous crossing of the midline with both the eyes and the hands by using both sides of the body.

I work initially with forms, breaking them down to their elements, beginning with simple lines and curves which become the building blocks for more complex forms and patterns. Dr. Skeffington brought back ideas from Dr. Van Lyons in California, about the use of arrows in various directions and combinations that eventually were incorporated into the procedure. Learning to put these lines together, the youngster begins to understand how to make angles, which can be a very difficult visual concept to reproduce. Once angles have been established, their combinations will ultimately lead to the reproductions of whole single forms. *This form development and reproduction is crucial to learning letters and numbers because they are made from various combinations of lines and curves.* I have added capital and lower case letters and numbers 1-10 for those youngsters who need to learn to reproduce them or need to simply identify them sequentially through visual-verbal matching.

The child begins to be aware of direction of form: right, left, up, down, and diagonals, and the similarities and differences between them. For instance, in the word *bad*, they see the *b* and *d* simultaneously and see that the letters are made of similar elements except that the curved part is in a different position. In reproducing single basic forms such as squares and diamonds, the ability to visualize the whole depends on how well they can visualize the elements that are part of that whole. Visualizing the angle and the reverse of that angle becomes crucial in the reproduction, for example of a diamond. It's made up of a ‹ and the reverse of it ›. It's very easy for someone to get lost in drawing the pieces or segments if they've lost sight of the whole. The end result will be a distorted form.

In the sequence of Board Tach the following sets are introduced: a combination of two complete forms, then superimposed forms, overlapped forms and ultimately 3-4 geometric shapes simultaneously. *As the information in each set is easily absorbed, processed, and reproduced with fairly good consistency of form, size, placement, and relationships, the next set is introduced.*

The versatility of Board Tach is evident when there is a need to tailor it to an individual. The shutter speed can be varied, slowing it to the point of an open shutter. If gross motor skills are extremely poor, actual structuring of the movement can be helpful. If initiating a drawing is beyond the individual's abilities or sophistication, then their literally tracing of the form on the board starts the wheels of learning in motion. If visual fixation or attention is lacking, then their gaze can be structured by holding the head in the direction of the board. If the procedure has been modified, the intent should always be to move toward the norm once there has been success at that particular level.

Another aspect of Board Tach is the use of a digit span. This requires visual-verbal matching and sequencing in time and space. Letters, words and phrases are also used but have more limited application.

With the digit span, the person again stands in a balanced posture with fixation centered, fields wide, and after the "ready now" signal is given, the span is flashed. The person is asked to call back the span in a single digit sequential order. They learn to visualize the sequence so they can repeat it over a period of time into the future. Again, how they prepare for and execute the procedure is of the utmost importance. That preparation takes precedence over the "correctness" of the match. Timing and rhythm are crucial. The person learns to call back the exact number of digits in an even rhythm, whether or not they're sure what they were - even if they have to guess.

Wolff found that the person always saw more than he thought he had. Correctness almost always follows if the procedure is properly followed. The most common error in the call back is scanning and memorizing the span from left to right as if reading. This is more time consuming and inefficient than looking at the span as a whole and visualizing it. Scanning and memorizing the span only works if the span is short. But when the span reaches 5 digits or more, or is scattered in the corners and in the middle, then memorizing proves inefficient. The individual will see the span in bits and pieces and tend to repeat it as such. If a person reads this way, or even sees words as just a sequence of letters and not as a whole, they get stuck trying to figure out the word. They then become word readers. By the time they reach the end of the sentence, they've forgotten the beginning and comprehension is minimal if there's any at all. By the end of the paragraph the person is aware that they need to start from the beginning and reread in order to understand. This process is time consuming, stressful, demoralizing and fatiguing, and definitely inefficient. After working with this procedure for awhile the individual begins to visualize the span so they can call it back in any order asked -reversed, middle numbers only, end numbers only. Eventually they will not be conscious of posture and *how* they're seeing, but will assume the "set" automatically and know from the beginning they will be successful in repeating and matching the sequence.

HARMON WALKING RAIL

The Harmon Walking Rail is from the CENTERING-identification VISUAL-motor-group and addresses *motor adaptability to changes in spatial orientation.* This procedure puts in a nutshell how an individual moves around all day in relation to everything in his visual space. We already know that we move in a three dimensional world and in all different directions and combinations of directions, and that bilateral movement generated around the Y axis depends on an individual's center and balance.

The walking rail is constructed with a center divider for the purpose of providing a constant frame of reference for centering while walking. The yoked prisms are a series of four 15 degree base down, base up, base right, and base left prisms that change the spatial orientation of the individual. The base down prism makes the person feel shorter, as if they're going uphill; the base up makes them feel taller, like he's going downhill, the base right shifts and skews everything to the left; and the base left does the opposite. This procedure is a very controlled one, given the structure of the rail and the prisms, which force the individual to react to what they do. How sensitive the individual is to this procedure and the kind and degree of the visual-motor response produced, depend on the symmetrical balance and centering of their bilateral binocular visual-motor system.

In VBT the individual walks on the rail without the prisms first to feel and experience how he should eventually learn to walk with the prisms on. This becomes the individual's norm. A few specific instructions must be adhered to in order to be successful. The postural set, is again just as important, if not more so, than the end result of walking the rail itself. (1) The individual must organize and center himself first by putting his feet together against the center divider, with arms hanging, and fixation straight ahead; he is then balanced and ready to move. (2) This postural set is repeated at each end of the rail as they get on with the prisms already in place. (3) A straight ahead fixation forces the individuals to relate and move in relation to everything in their visual space.

The most common adaptation is to look at their feet and localize their gaze. This happens because they are not sure yet or confident of what they're seeing or where and how they should move. There are those who want to close their eyes and not have to deal with it at all. By looking down, the person eliminates a lot of information in their visual space. By looking straight ahead they're forced to deal with all this information and, finally, to begin processing it. Dealing with their visual space also forces individuals to visualize what their feet are doing and to anticipate visually where they're going in the future. Even though they *intellectually know* the rail is straight, their actual VISUAL-motor response is usually very literal. *They adapt and move in the direction of the spatial orientation of the prisms*, rather than straight ahead. The integration loop of visual-tactile-movement information being fed in and coming back out is crucial here in order to keep their feet against the center divider. Ultimately this provides the crossfeed of information from the right leg to the left leg; thrust-counter-thrust. One side needs to know what the other side is doing at that moment and what it's about to do. As individuals relate more and more to their environment, they become more confident in what they see and how they adapt their movements to that environment. Soon they discover that the distortions become less severe and eventually almost totally neutralized with everything appearing "normal".

The movement on the rail should be a balanced, centered walk, not too fast and not too slow. The walking motion should be with the heel leading and placed against the divider first, with the rest of the foot following against it. There should be no shuffling or dragging of the feet. Appropriate knee bend should be apparent. There is quite a tendency for many to reverse the walking motion to a toe-heel movement. Getting on and off the rail with the prisms is part of the procedure but may prove intimidating to some who want to stoop down and physically grab the rail in order to get on.

The manifestation of the individual's VISUAL-motor response directly relates to his unique warps, skews, asymmetries and adaptations. The more embedded the patterns are, the more sensitive the individual is to the input of the prisms. The degree of asymmetry of their "center" determines whether the person reacts more to one lateral prism or the other.

It's advantageous to place the rail in the room with a window at one end and a mirror at the other. The window adds more information and space and the mirror coaxes the straight ahead fixation which has a surprise in store for those who are paying attention and looking in it -everything looks "normal"! The mirror not only neutralizes the effect of the prism but also reflects where the person has been as well as where they are going. The individual must learn to deal with all of this information simultaneously.

This procedure is extremely important for the skills needed when driving a car through one's visual space and relating to everything in it. It's equally important for those who participate in sports and need to move through that space and relate to everything in it including the field, court, other players, the ball, hoop, or whatever. General moving around in everyday life requires these skills, as well as for those people who have a fear of heights, get car sick or are sensitive to sudden changes in orientation.

CHEIROSCOPIC TRACING AND VAN ORDEN STAR

The Cheiroscopic Tracing and Van Orden Star are from the CENTERING-identification VISUAL-motor group and deal with binocular integration, centering and bilateral motor equivalence. The indirect tracing is referred to as the eyes-hand coordination abilities and the Van Orden Star as the eyes-hands coordination abilities. These procedures are done on a modified stereoscope called a standing Wolff Cheiroscope with a backlighted vertical drawing surface.

The individual's fine motor skills and the quality of tracing abilities were previously determined in the assessment by the direct eye-hand coordination tracing. In this tracing the outline of a rectangle is placed directly in front of the eye that matches the preferred hand that will trace. The individuals are asked to trace as best they can so their lines are on the black lines of the rectangle. This is repeated with the opposite hand. Both patterns are then compared for similarities and differences. Most people are surprised that their right and left hand tracings are more equally matched and similar than dissimilar. Most people have the preconceived idea that they can't do anything with their non-dominant hand let alone draw a straight line. In VBT they learn that drawing and tracing are two different abilities and the potential to trace well with either hand is readily available for most people to develop. It's our cultural demands that make us eventually chose one hand over the other. Even if there is a physical reason such as cerebral palsy, a stroke or trauma that makes it more difficult to learn to use both hands equally, working toward bilateral motor equivalence is still the direction in which VBT takes them.

A more complex set of forms makes up the pattern of the indirect tracing (eyes-hand coordination), consisting of the same rectangle used on the direct tracing, a centered but overlapped circle, a superimposed smaller square diamond, and a centered superimposed small circle. This combination of forms is processed through *both eyes simultaneously* which is integrated within the visual-motor system and then fed back out again, manifested by the pattern produced while tracing. I often refer to this tracing as the fingerprint of a person's bilateral- binocular visual-motor system. *The indirect tracing represents individuals' unique interpretation of their lighted environment: how they see and organize their visual space and the postural set assumed throughout the procedure.* The individual should be balanced, with both feet slightly apart and aligned properly from the base of his feet to his head, with no motor overflow. This tracing will reflect any shifts, warps, skews, and deviations from this balanced, centered bilateral posture.

In VBT the individual learns the significance of these shifts in his tracings by comparing them to the norm, so he knows what his should look like and what he's working toward. The indirect tracing is different from the direct tracing in that the pattern is *placed in front of the opposite eye of the hand used for tracing.* The ideal or norm is a symmetrical balanced, centered, precisely positioned bilateral pattern traced by each hand respectively as presented here.

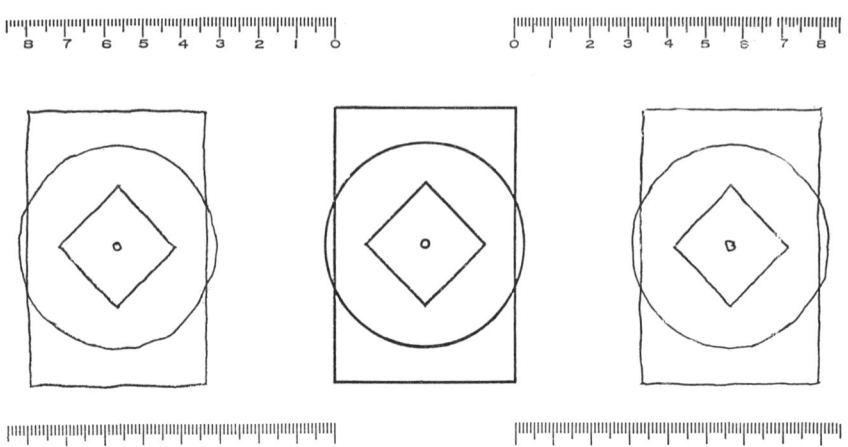

Before tracing, the individual makes sure the pattern appears directly in front of him first and begins tracing the rectangle. The Cheiroscope is set for infinity, so wherever the individual reaches and traces is indicative of where they are focused. Some hit the surface hard because they're looking very close and some reach way beyond the Cheiroscope itself with the arm fully extended because that's where they are looking -too far away. The pencil should be gripped properly and the tracing movement should be controlled, continuous, not too fast and not too slow. The individual is asked to look at the whole pattern at once and trace each form, beginning with the rectangle. When they finish, they look at what they've done to see if their pattern remains exactly on top of the original. They are asked to trace again and this time to visually follow their pencil as they trace the pattern and check again to see if their pattern matches the original. These methods should produce simi-lar results if, when tracing and following his pencil, they don't lose sight of the whole pattern. It's very easy for the beginner to get lost in the parts and pieces of the pattern.

While tracing, the individual should be aware of any movement and disappearance of the lines or pencil, which would indicate suppression. Movement of the forms within the pattern is not necessarily a bad sign. If an embedded shift persists, remember, *movement is the key to change and to restoring the system back to symmetry and balance*. For example, if the right and left tracings are positioned too close together, which reflects a reduction or restriction in the volume of the person's visual space because they are focusing too close, then they must practice looking beyond and through the pattern as if looking to infinity. By trial and error and experimentation the individual will begin to see movement and change; and, in time they will begin to trace the pattern appropriately, spontaneously and automatically. But in order to get to this point, they must understand that they're allowed to experiment and "mess up" the tracing in the process.

For those individuals who experience what is called a crossover pattern, when the end result of the indirect tracing is done as though it were a direct tracing, a different approach must be taken. These individuals attempt to trace the rectangle with their right hand but find the pattern shifts and disappears until their pencil finds the pattern in front of the left eye. They then must place the pencil tip directly in front of the right eye to center and localize their gaze; but, simultaneously they must be aware of the presence or absence of the pattern in the background. Then they are instructed to move the pencil tip directly out to the smallest circle in the center and begin tracing the pattern from the center out. This coaxes the pattern to become more stabilized.

When there is a shift in orientation and the form traced was started at a certain point but finishes in another so the form appears to look open and not closed, it's suggested that the individual start tracing from a different place and/or trace in a different direction.

The *Van Orden Star* records the eyes-hands coordination abilities or the integration of the bilateral motor equivalence with centering and binocular functioning as shown here.

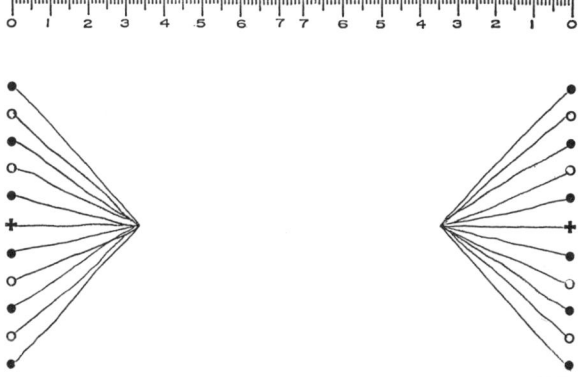

The postural set should again be centered and balanced with feet slightly apart, body aligned and no motor overflow. The individual begins by placing their pencil tips on the plus marks on either side first. Wolff said the "pencils should be held so the fingers are never seen, but are imagined to be very long, and are pointing way out into space."[5] It is stressed that they are to look in the middle of the two plus marks and sustain that center fixation while they simultaneously draw both pencils straight toward each other until the tips *look like they touch*. The individual is reminded not to look from one pencil to the other, but to see both pencils move toward the center at the same time. They do not want to literally feel the pencil tips touch or disappear. Then they place one tip to the top dot of one column and the other tip to the bottom dot of the other column, look in the center and do the same thing. They alternate their pencils up and down until each set is completed. The individual should be aware that when they look in the center between the dots the columns on either side should look like they move closer together. This is the same movement that allows the indirect tracing patterns to move in and out, and the same movement that keeps the ball single while tracking on the Z axis in Rotations and Fixations. When he has completed each set of circles and dots, he is to look at what he has done to see if all the lines meet at one point in the center, which is the ideal pattern desired.

The individual can also try the procedure starting from the center and drawing to the appropriate dots.

The individual evaluates and compares the similarities and differences of their performance with the expected. The lines should all meet at one spot, and not be scattered about, indicating both eyes were sustained on center simultaneously. Asymmetry is indicated if one side has a center that is further or closer and not equally positioned at 3.5 millimeters or one center is open and the other closed prematurely. Tracing pressure should also be equal, as well as the speed of each bilateral motor movement when drawing each set.

It's quite evident that the Cheiroscopic Tracings and the Van Orden Star provide an excellent opportunity for the individual in VBT to work on restructuring and rebalancing the bilateral-binocular visual-motor system. Through them, they become aware of the progression of changes weekly, as all the parts and pieces start coming together "with everything in its place". The tracings and star are usually the last tasks to be incorporated into the VBT routine because of the level of sophistication and the fact that there are many building block procedures preceding it. When the individual compares the tracings and the Van Orden Star from the initial assessment with those at the end of VBT, the differences are quite amazing.

ENDNOTES

CHAPTER 1 INTRODUCTION
1. Wolff, Bruce, "From Sight to Vision", personal publication, Cincinnati, 1988, 1.
2. De Pree, Max, *Leadership Is An Art*, Doubleday, New York, 1989,133.
3. Skeffington, A. M., "Renshaw Revisited: Psychological Optics", *Advanced Therapist*, Volume 34, Number 1, Optometric Extension Program, California, 1.
4. *Ibid.*

CHAPTER 2 NEW SCIENCE
1. Wilber, Ken, *Eye To Eye, A Quest For A New Paradigm*, Shambhala Press, Boston, 1989, 6.
2. *Ibid, 5.*
3. Schaef, Anne Wilson, *Women's Reality*, Harper & Row, San
   Francisco, 1981, 16.
4. Wilber, Ken, *op. cit.*, 13.
5. *Ibid*, 15.
6. *Ibid*, 24.
7. *Ibid*, 24.
8. *Ibid*, 27.
9. Wilber, Ken, "Introduction", *The Holographic Paradigm and Other Paradoxes*, edited by Ken Wilber, New Science Library, Shambhala Press, Boston, 1982, 2.
10. Weber, Renee, "The Enfolding-Unfolding Universe: A Conversation with David Bohm", *Ibid*, 46.
11. Pribram, Karl, "What Is All the Fuss About?", *Ibid*, 34.
12. Gleick, James, *Chaos Theory*, Penguin Publications, New York, 1987, 8.
13. *Ibid*, 8.
14. Glasser, William, *Control Theory*, Harper & Row, New York, 1984, 43.
15. Powers, William, *An Outline of Control Theory*, privately published, 1-2.
16. *Ibid*, 11.
17. Keller, Evelyn Fox, "Glossary", *A Feeling For The Organism*, W.H. Freeman and Co., New York, 1983, 222.
18. Keller, Evelyn Fox, *A Feeling for the Organism*, W. H. Freeman and Co., San Francisco, 1983, 189.

19. *Ibid*, 201.
20. *Ibid*, 204.
21. *Ibid*, 205-206.

CHAPTER 3   PATIENTS: WHO or WHAT?
  1. Keller, Evelyn Fox, *A Feeling For the Organism*, W.H. Freeman and Co., New York, 1983, 198.
  2. *Ibid.*, 103.
  3. *Ibid.*, 207.
  4. Hanna, Thomas, *Somatics*, Addison-Wesley Publishing Company, Inc., New York, 1988.
  5. Hanna, Thomas, "Backing Into The Common Ground", *SOMATICS: Magazine Journal of the Bodily Arts and Sciences*, Somatic Society, Novato, California, 1987.
  6. Edwards, Betty, *Drawing On the Right Side of the Brain*, J. P. Tarcher, Los Angeles, 1979, 48.
  7. *Ibid.*
  8. Berry, Wendell, *What Are People For?*, orig. North Point Press, San Francisco, 1990, currently Farrar, Straus & Giroux, Inc., New York, 201.
  9. Morse, Charles & Ann, *Whobody There?*, St. Mary's College Press, Nashville, 1977.

CHAPTER 4   HOW DID WE GET HERE FROM THERE?
  1. Wolff, Bruce, "About Vision", Cincinnati Center for Visual Research, Cincinnati, 1986, 1.
  2. Harmon, Darell Boyd, *Notes on A Dynamic Theory of Vision*, privately published, Austin, Texas, 1958, 14.
  3. *Ibid.*, 20.
  4. Pappaport, Sheldon, "A Pioneer in Vision and Educational Environments: Salute to Darell Boyd Harmon", *Journal of Learning Disabilities,* Volume 8, No. 5, May, 1975.
  5. "Why Do Children Develop Visual Problems in School?", *Efficient Vision,* Optometric Extension Program, Santa Ana, California, September 1985, 1.
  6. Harmon, Darell Boyd, *op cit.,* 92.
  7. *Ibid.*, 28.
  8. *Ibid.*, 41.

CHAPTER 5   I SAW IT WITH MY OWN EYES
 1. Wolff, Bruce, "Definition of Vision", personal
     communication, Cincinnati, 1988.
 2. Wolff, Bruce , "About Vision", The Center for Clinical
     Visual Research, Cincinnati, 1988, 1.
 3. *Ibid.*
 4. *Ibid.*
 5. *Ibid.*, 2.
 6. Arnheim, Rudolf, *Visual Thinking,* University of California
     Press, Berkeley, 1969, 19.
 7. Wolff, Bruce, "From Sight To Vision", The Center for
     Clinical Visual Research, Cincinnati, 1988, 2.
 8. Wolff, Bruce, "About Vision", Center for Clinical Visual
     Research, Cincinnati, 1988, 2.
 9. Oppenheimer, Jess, "All About Me", *Journal of Learning
     Disabilities,* Vol. 1, No. 1, January, 1968, 66.
10. *Ibid.*
11. Black, Howard and Sandra, *Verbal Classifications*, Book
     C-1, Midwest Publications, Pacific Grove, 1983, 15.
12. Wolff, Bruce, "From Sight To Vision", Center for Clinical
     Visual Research, Cincinnati, 1986.
13. Wolff, Bruce, *op cit.*
14. Wolff, Bruce, personal communication, 1987.

CHAPTER 6   FLAVORS OF OUR BEHAVIORAL CAKES
 1. Glasser, William, *Control Theory*, New York: Harper &
     Row, 1984, 46.
 2. Oppenheimer, Jess, "All About Me", *Journal of Learning
     Disabilities,* Vol. 1 No. 1, Jan. 1968.
 3. Arnheim, Rudolf, *Visual Thinking*, University of California
     Press, Berkeley, 1969.
 4. *Ibid.*, 232.
 5. Keller, Evelyn Fox, *A Feeling for the Organism,* W. H.
     Freeman   and Co., New York, 1983, 102.
 6. Edwards, Betty, *The Artist Within,* Simon & Schuster,
     New York, 1986.
 7. DePree, Max, *Leadership is an Art,* Dell Publishing, New
     York, 1989, 11.
 8. Covey, Stephen, *The Seven Habits of Highly Effective People*,
     Simon & Schuster, 1989, 101.

CHAPTER 7   VISUAL BEHAVIOR TRAINING
1. Wolff, Bruce, "A Window On the Universe", Cincinnati: Center for Clinical Vision Research, 1988, 1.
2. Wolff, Bruce, personal notes, Cincinnati.
3. Wolff, Bruce, "Vision: A Behavioral Optometric Clinician's View", Center for Clinical Visual Research, Cincinnati, 1989, 2.
4. Wolff, Bruce, "Thesis", *Great Lakes Congress*, personal papers, 1985, 1. This was a speech given at the Great Lakes Optometric Extension Program Congress, a professional development program for behavioral optometrists.
5. Wolff, Bruce, "About Vision, Notes To Be Read Before the First Examination", s.a. Noel Center, Inc., Lancaster, 1.
6. Harmon, Darell Boyd, *Vision, Body Mechanics, and Performance*, privately published, Austin, 1958, A-17.
7. Wolff, Bruce, *op. cit.*, 1.
8. Wolff, Bruce, "Vision: A Behavioral Optometric Clinician's View", Center for Clinical Visual Research, Cincinnati, 1989.
9. *Ibid.*, 2-3.
10. Harmon, *op. cit.*
11. *Ibid.*
12. *Ibid,* A-18.
13. Wolff, Bruce, *op. cit.*, 2.
14. Harmon, *op. cit.*, A-23.
15. Wolff, Bruce, personal notes, Cincinnati.
16. Wolff, Bruce, "About Vision", Center for Clinical Visual Research, Cincinnati, 1984, 2.
17. Wolff, Bruce, "From Sight to Vision", Center for Clinical Visual Research, Cincinnati, 1987, 3.
18. Gesell, Arnold, *The First Five Years of Life*, Harper & Row, New York, 1977.
19. Wolff, Bruce, "About Vision", s.a. Noel Center, Inc., Lancaster, Ohio, 1984, 2.

CHAPTER 8   LIVING THE THEORY
1. Covey, Stephen, *The Seven Habits of Highly Effective People,* Simon & Schuster, 1989.

2. Edwards, Betty, *The Artist Within*, Simon & Schuster, New York,1986.
3. *Ibid.*
4. *Ibid.*

CHAPTER 9   HELP THAT HELPS
1. Wolff, Bruce, "From Sight to Vision", Cincinnati Center for Visual Research, 1987, 3.

CHAPTER 10   WE DO WHAT WE SEE
1. Wolff, Bruce, personal notes, Cincinnati, 1986.
2. Hanna, Thomas, *Somatics*, New York: Addison-Wesley Publishing, 1988, 10.
3. *Ibid,* 11.
4. "Hospital Stay Can Make You Sick", New York: Associated Press, February 2, 1993.
5. Keller, Evelyn Fox, *A Feeling For The Organism,* New York: W. H. Freeman and Company, 1983, 198.
6. Peters, Tom, *Liberation Management,* New York: Alfred A. Knopf, 1992.
7. *Ibid,* 8.
8. "Searching for New Leadership", New York: Associated Press, appeared in *Cincinnati Enquirer,* February 3, 1993.
9. Peters, Tom, *op cit.,* 147.
10. Wolff, Bruce, personal notes, Cincinnati, 1987.

APPENDIX B
1. "Eye tracking and locating skills", monograph, s.a. Noel Center, Inc., Lancaster, 1985, 4.
2. Wolff, Bruce, personal notes, Cincinnati.
3. Wolff, Bruce, "Visual Training Procedures Outline", Center for Clinical Visual Research, Cincinnati, 1988, 10.
4. *Ibid.*
5. *Ibid,* 7.

BIBLIOGRAPHY

The resources in this bibliography include seminal works in the development of the Wolff model of visual behavior as well as sources used by the authors in preparation for writing this book. Although from diverse disciplines, each echoes the new, non-linear viewpoint of science. They are included here as touch points on a journey of inquiry which has barely begun.

Ames, Louise Bates; Gillespie, Clyde; Streff, John, *Stop School Failure*, New York: Harper & Row, 1972.

Arnheim, Rudolf, *Visual Thinking*, Berkeley: University of California Press, 1969.

Associated Press, "Hospital Stay Can Make You Sick", New York, February 2, 1993.

Berry, Wendell, *What Are People For?*, originally San Francisco: North Point Press, 1990; currently New York: Farrar, Straus & Giroux, 1994.

Black, Howard; Black, Sandra, *Verbal Classification C-1*, Pacific Grove: Midwest Publications, 1983.

Bohm, David, *Thought As A System*, London: Routledge, 1994.

_____, "The Enfolding-Unfolding Universe: A Conversation with David Bohm", conducted by Renee Weber, *The Holographic Paradigm and Other Paradoxes*, Boston: New Science Library, Shambhala Publications, 1982.

Carse, James P., *Finite and Infinite Games*, New York: Ballentine Books, 1987.

Covey, Stephen, *The 7 Habits of Highly Effective People*, New York: Simon and Schuster, 1989.

Conway, Flo; Siegelman, *Jim Snapping,* New York: Dell Publishing Co., 1978.

DePree, Max, *Leadership Is An Art,* New York: Doubleday, 1989.

Drucker, Peter, *Post-Capitalist Society, New York: HarperCollins, 1993.*

Edwards, Betty, *The Artist Within*, New York: Simon and Schuster, 1982,

_____, *Drawing on the Right Side of the Brain*, Los Angeles: J. P. Tarcher, Inc., 1979.

Forrest, Elliot, *Visual Imagery: An Optometric Approach*, Santa Ana: Optometric Extension Program Foundation, 1981.

_____, *Stress and Vision*, Santa Ana: Optometric Extension Program Foundation, 1988.

Gesell, Arnold, *Vision: Its Development in Infant and Child*, New York: Hafner Press, 1944.

_____, *The First Five Years of Life*, New York: Harper & Row, 1940.

Glasser, William, *Control Theory,* New York: Harper & Row, 1984.

Gleick, James, *Chaos*, New York: Penguin Publications, 1987.

Hanna, Thomas, *Somatics*, New York: Addison-Wesley Publishing Co., 1983.

Harmon, Darell Boyd, *Notes on a Dynamic Theory of Vision,* Austin: privately published, 1958.

_____, "Some Preliminary Observations on the Developmental Problems of 160,000 Elementary School Children", *Medical Women's Journal*, 1942.

_____, "Lighting and Child Development", *Illuminating Engineering*, Vol. 40, No. 4, 1945.

_____, "Light On Growing Children", *Architectural Record*, Vol. 99, No. 2, 1946.

_____, *The Coordinated Classroom*, Grand Rapids: The American Seating Co., 1949 (Revised 1951).

_____, *et al.*; "A preliminary study of the relation of sustained visually-centered activity and certain types of chalkboards"; Coordinated Classroom Papers, No. 1, 1952.

_____, "The School of Tomorow", *Nation's Schools*, Vol. 51, No. 1, 1953.

_____, "Are We Confusing Eyes with Vision?", *Illuminating Engineering*, Vol. 48, No. 4, 1953.

Hoopes, Ann; Hoopes, Townsend; *Eye Power*, New York: Alfred P. Knopf, 1979.

Huxley, Aldous, *The Art of Seeing*, New York: Harpers, 1942.

Fox, Evelyn Keller, *A Feeling for the Organism*, New York: W. H. Freeman, 1983.

Kavner, Richard; Dunsky, Lorraine, *Total Vision,* New York: Addison-Wesley, 1978.

Lyons, Emily Bradley, *How To Use Your Power of Visualization*, Marshall, California: Lyons Visualization Series, 1980.

Morse, Charles; Morse, Ann; *Whobody There?*, Nashville: The Upper Room, 1971.

Optometric Extension Program; "Why Do Children Develop Visual Problems in School?", *Efficient Vision*, Santa Ana: Optometric Extension Program Foundation, September, 1985.

Oppenheimer, Jess; "All About Me", *Journal of Learning Disabilities*, Volume 1, No. 1, January, 1968.

Perkinson, Henry; *Since Socrates, Studies in History of Educational Thought*, New York: Longman Publications, 1980.

Peters, Tom; *Liberation Management*, New York: Alfred A. Knopf, 1992.

Powers, William; *Living Control Systems: Selected Papers*, Gravel Switch, Kentucky: CSG Book Publications, 1989.

_____, *Behavior: The Control of Perception*, Chicago: Aldine, 1973.

_____, "Control Theory: A model of organisms", *System Dynamics Review*, Volume 6, No.1, Winter, 1990, 1.

_____, "Control Theory and Statistical Generalizations", *American Behavioral Scientist*, Volume 34, No. 1, September/October, 1990.

Pribram, Karl H.; "What Is All the Fuss About?", *Holographic Paradigm and Other Paradoxes*, Boston: Shambhala Publications, 1982.

_____, *Languages Of the Brain: Experimental Paradoxes and Principles in Neuropsychology*, New York: Brandon House, Inc., 1981 (fifth printing).

_____, *Brain and Perception: Holonomy and Structure in Figural Processing*, Hillsdale: Lawrence Erlbaum Associates, Publishers, 1991.

Rappaport, Sheldon; "A Pioneer in Vision and Educational Environments: Salute to Darell Boyd Harmon", *Journal of Learning Disabilities*, Volume 8, No. 5, May, 1975.

Schaef, Anne Wilson; *Women's Reality*, San Francisco: Harper & Row, 1981.

Skeffington, A. M.; *OEP Golden Papers and the Best of Skeffington*, Santa Ana: Optometric Extension Program Foundation.

_____, "Learning Lenses in Beginning Reading", Santa Ana: Optometric Extension Program Foundation.

Wilber, Ken; *Eye To Eye, A Quest for a New Paradigm*, Boston: Shambhala Publications, 1989.

_____, editor, *The Holographic Paradigm and Other Paradoxes*, Boston: Shambhala Publications, 1982.

Wolff, Bruce, "About Vision", Lancaster, Ohio: s. a. NOEL Center, Inc., 1984.

_____, "From Sight To Vision", Cincinnati: Center for Clinical Vision Research, 1987.

_____, "Syllabus for Course Work", Cincinnati: Center for Clinical Vision Research, 1987.

_____, "A Window On the Universe", Cincinnati: Center for Clinical Vision Research, 1988.

_____, "Conventional Wisdom", Cincinnati: Center for Clinical Vision Research, 1988.

INDEX

ABOUT THE AUTHOR

Beverly Jones has applied the visual principles presented in *VISUAL BEHAVIOR* in her extensive work with students as educational consultant and speech-language pathologist. Through study with clinicians and scholars whose models of moving, learning, thinking rest on non-linear science, she has found new directions for teaching which show that greater than expected improvement is not necessarily limited by age, diagnosis or developmental level. Her next books will be on the specific application of these new-science principles of learning in teaching and parenting.

Ms. Jones, M.A. in Communication Disorders from Northwestern University, has directed private schools in California and Ohio where these visual principles of learning were integrated into the curriculum for students with special needs. She currently lives and works in the greater Cincinnati, Ohio area where she directs a private, professional practice as educational consultant in the areas of learning, academics and organizational behavior. Her work at Cincinnati Center for Learning says

> We all do the best we can;
> It's not the best we can do.
> Learning makes the difference.

Beverly Jones and Karen Wolff Klaine can be reached through Cincinnati Center for Learning or Wolff Center for Visual Behavior, 9200 Montgomery Road 21B, Cincinnati, Ohio 45242, 513-793-9949.